Life in the
SLIPSTREAM

Life in the
SLIPSTREAM

The Legend of **BOBBY WALTHOUR SR.**

{andrew m. homan}

POTOMAC BOOKS, INC.
WASHINGTON, D.C.

Library of Congress Cataloging-in-Publication Data
Homan, Andrew M., 1964–
 Life in the slipstream : the legend of Bobby Walthour Sr. / Andrew M.
Homan.
    p. cm.
 Includes bibliographical references and index.
 ISBN 978-1-59797-685-5 (hardcover)
 1. Walthour, Bobby, 1878–1949. 2. Cyclists–United States–Biography. 3.
Bicycle racing–United States–History. 4. Bicycle racing–Europe–History.
I. Title.

 GV1051.W35H66 2011
 796.6092–dc22
 [B]

                                                    2010054114

Printed in the United States of America on acid-free paper that meets
the American National Standards Institute Z39-48 Standard.

Potomac Books, Inc.
22841 Quicksilver Drive
Dulles, Virginia 20166

First Edition

10 9 8 7 6 5 4 3 2 1

{for my wife and best friend, shelli}

{contents}

{acknowledgments}

1 owe special thanks to so many people who have assisted and guided me in the last seven years. Anne Homan has gone through the entire process with me tirelessly, from research to translation to editing, and has given careful guidance and perspective as only a mother could. She was my primary source of inspiration. She and my father, Don, have always been there with their love and support.

Andrew Ritchie, a biographer of Major Taylor and a great ambassador for cycling history, minutely scrutinized my manuscript, sharing his wisdom and a great dedication to this project. Buck Peacock has been an incredible resource and has gone out of his way to help recognize the achievements of Walthour well before my research began.

Peter Kupfer helped turn this piece of cycling history into a palatable story. David Herlihy guided me and found volumes of research, including many French periodicals. Renate Franz assisted with all things German and found and translated many magazine articles. Peter Nye was an early source of inspiration, lending his expertise and encouragement. Authors and scholars have shared their knowledge with me, including William Harper, Stephen Goddard, and Jeff Groman. Cheers to Patrick Brady, Tim Grady, Ben Delaney, Brad Roe, and Frankie Andreu for supporting and promoting the Walthour story to the cycling public. Jared Manninen and the folks at Tahoe Writers Works lent helping hands editing early chapters. And thanks to Marianna Monaco for indexing.

I am very glad for microfilm labs at the Fremont (CA) Library, U.C. Berkeley Library, and the University of Georgia Library. As a Society of American Baseball Research member, I was allowed access to ProQuest.

Thanks to Elizabeth Demers and the folks at Potomac Books for recognizing the significance of the Walthour story.

Thanks to Bob and Joan Walthour and Bobby and Kelly Walthour, without whose friendship and support this book would never have been written. Also thanks to the many other Walthour family members I have met and with whom I have communicated, including Charles Walthour, Clyde Walthour, Russell Walthour, Matt Walthour, James and Lorraine Woodley, and Clare Sheaffer. Thank you as well to the family members of other long-forgotten cyclists, especially Russell Leander, Robert Winesett, and Gordon Wright.

I cannot thank my family enough for their love and support: my brother, Ted Homan, and his family; my sister, Becky Davies, and her family; my uncle, James Marshall; and my in-laws, Richard and Nancy Croft, and their family.

And finally, to my wife and soul mate, Shelli, for her unwavering support, encouragement, and endearing love.

{introduction}

Seven years ago, when I started collecting newspaper articles about the history of professional cycling in the United States, my wife, Shelli, and I were graciously welcomed to the home of Bob and Joan Walthour in Carmel, California. At that time, my "collection" was a mass of unorganized material contained in a few three-ring binders. But with my limited research experience and knowledge of the subject, I already knew that the name "Walthour" was a special one in American cycling history.

By the end of the visit, though, I was on to something more. I asked myself two questions: what other American family has crossed four generations with such a high level of sporting success, and why on earth doesn't anyone know about them?

There are four generations of Robert Howe Walthours: Bobby Walthour Sr., born in 1878; Bobby Walthour Jr., born in 1902; Bob Walthour III, born in 1927; and Bobby Walthour IV, born in 1965.

To give an idea of the Walthour legacy, one need only go back to 1983 when Bobby Walthour IV won a California State Greco-Roman Wrestling Championship as a high school junior. Thanks to his championship, Bobby IV got a full scholarship to California Polytechnic State University (Cal Poly), San Luis Obispo. However, as a high school senior, Walthour developed a herniated disc and had to forfeit the scholarship. In 1985, in spite of losing the scholarship, he enrolled at Cal Poly. By the time he was a student there, Walthour had given up wrestling permanently and focused on a sport that had helped him rehabilitate his herniated disc—cycling.

Bobby IV rode his grandfather's (Bobby Jr.'s) Raleigh bicycle, built in the 1930s, in the Bud Light Series Half Ironman in 1983. Although his father, Bob III, had been a great swimmer and was the swimming coach at Carmel High School for more than three decades, Bobby IV gravitated toward cycling and became serious about it. In the spring of 1985, Bobby IV first raced at a track in San Diego. It was obvious to nearly everyone in the sport that Bobby IV was a great talent, and he was immediately placed in the Category 1-Pro division. By the age of 35 he had won a gold medal in the one-kilometer time trial at the U.S. Masters National Championships in Redmond, Washington.

In his early cycling career, Bobby IV's father told him stories of his father and grandfather and how they were great cycling champions many decades earlier. Until then, Bobby IV had been unaware of the detailed history of his family's successes on cycling tracks around the world. Even today, Bobby IV can mention his famous cycling lineage and receive a blank stare from listeners.

Bobby's great-grandfather, Bobby Walthour Sr., had a remarkable career, and it might be argued that he was the Babe Ruth of cyclists. Unfortunately, so much time has passed that few people are still living who knew him. I have had to rely on the many newspaper accounts of his races for detailed information about his life and career. And yet, after the record of his athletic career has been documented, Walthour remains a difficult person to know.

❊

In 2005 Lance Armstrong's successful pursuit of a record seventh consecutive victory in the Tour de France, the world's most prestigious cycling event, catapulted bicycle racing from the sports section to the front page of American newspapers. Armstrong, whose achievement was particularly poignant because of his recovery from cancer, was hailed as a national hero. His success and that of Greg LeMond, who in 1986 became the first American to win the Tour—a feat he repeated twice more after his own recovery from a near-fatal hunting accident—contributed to the surging popularity of cycling, both professional and recreational, in the United States.

But a century ago another American, a young man from Georgia, ruled the cycling world. In his day Bobby Walthour was more dominant in his sport and more famous than either LeMond or Armstrong. During a career that spanned more than twenty years, Walthour collected hundreds of victories and was twice named American and world champion. He was beloved in the United States, particularly in his hometown of Atlanta, and he was also wildly popular in France and in Germany, where he lived for some years. At the peak of his career in 1904, Walthour earned the staggering sum of at least $60,000 ($1,490,000 in today's dollars[1]) in prize money and appearance fees. By comparison Babe Ruth—arguably the most famous American athlete of the twentieth century—earned $80,000 ($1,030,000) in 1930, his highest paid season with the New York Yankees.

❀

The three most common types of bicycle racing in Walthour's day were sprinting, motor-pacing, and six-day racing. Sprints were short, tactical contests that often started at a woefully slow pace and ended in a fury of frame-bending speed. Motor-pacing was a fast, extremely hazardous occupation in which riders followed perilously close to "pacers" on bicycles, and later motorized vehicles, drafting within the protection of their slipstream. Six-day races were grueling, brutal affairs—for spectators and competitors alike. Walthour excelled in all three forms. He started his career as a sprinter and developed into a formidable six-day rider as well, but he achieved his greatest fame as a fearless motor-pacer.

In the 1890s and early 1900s, competitive cycling ranked among the top sports in the United States and was widely popular in Europe and Australia. Thousands of spectators turned out for the events, which were often held in smoke-filled stadiums. The six-day race at Madison Square Garden in New York, considered the most important cycling event of the year in the United States, routinely attracted more than ten thousand spectators (and thousands more were turned away at the gate). Many would leave and then pay to get back in or camp out at the stadium for the entire week, bringing food, blankets, and other provisions.

Professional cycling in Walthour's era was not for the faint of heart. Motor-pacing in particular was notorious for its extreme danger. More than a dozen of his rivals were killed in competition. Walthour himself suffered a long list of injuries—from fractured ribs and separated collarbones to mangled fingers and concussions—any one of which might have ended the career of a less zealous competitor. He won many a race by stoically mounting his bike after getting stitched up and bandaged. In one year alone he was twice given up for dead.

Grantland Rice, a sports reporter for the *Atlanta Journal,* described one of Walthour's many memorable victories in 1903 in his home city:

> It was a dash such as thrills one to the very marrow, one that should live in the history of cycling annals, for track records were smashed to smithereens and the big crowd lifted from its feet in the wildest outburst of enthusiasm that has ever echoed and re-echoed through-out the walls of the coliseum. Not even in the days of old when Roman thousands watched the struggles of life and death in the arena below could there have been more thrilling interest shown.[2]

As a young man, Walthour hardly seemed destined to become a world champion athlete. His father died when he was young, and Walthour and his brothers were forced to fend for themselves. But despite these disadvantages, Bobby Walthour grew up to be one of the greatest cyclists in American history.

{ 1 }

Georgia Peach Blossom

obert Howe Walthour and his identical twin brother, James, were
born on New Year's Day, 1878. *Bicycling World* claimed that the twins
entered the world in New York City.[1] According to his own account,
Walthour was born "just a short bike ride from Savannah [Georgia]."[2] The
boys were the fifth and sixth sons of Sarah Aurelia and William Lowndes
Walthour. "Bobby" had the same blond hair and steely blue eyes as his
Austrian great-great-grandfather, John Casper Waldhauer, who had arrived in Georgia in 1746.[3]

Bobby's grandfather, George Washington Walthour, had been a wealthy
antebellum plantation owner with many slaves. Walthourville, a town in a
flat and swampy region forty miles southwest of Savannah, was named
after his great grandfather, Andrew Walthour.[4]

Bobby's father, William Walthour, became a successful lawyer. About a
year after the South Carolinians fired on Fort Sumter, William left his wife,
Sarah Margaret, and their four young sons at home in Walthourville and
joined the Confederate forces. He became a first lieutenant in Captain
Abiel Winn's company and was later elected captain of Company G, Fifth
Regiment Georgia Cavalry.[5] In August 1864 he received a neck wound at
Murfreesboro, Tennessee. The injury, which left William scarred for life,
came shortly before Sherman's troops captured Atlanta and burned it to
the ground.

The Walthour fortunes, like those of many southern families, took a dramatic turn for the worse during the "War Against Northern Aggression." The Walthour home was apparently one of the last destroyed by General Sherman's troops in their notorious March to the Sea from Atlanta to Savannah. Soon after the war, to make matters worse, the government confiscated the family's vast acreage near Walthourville for back taxes. By the time the twins were born in 1878, the once prominent family had lost its wealth.

In 1868, after twenty years of marriage, William's first wife died. One year later William married his second wife, Sarah Aurelia Papot, in Thomas County, Georgia, near the Florida border. He became a member of his father-in-law's firm, Papot, Shotter, and Company, which built the Vicksburg and Mobile Railroad. In addition to the four sons he had with his first wife, William had six sons with Sarah Aurelia: Samuel, Palmer, Charles Tatnall (C. T.), Russell, and the twins James and Robert Walthour. According to the 1880 U.S. census, the family lived in Liberty County—most likely in Walthourville, with Sarah Aurelia's sister, Carrie E. Parrot.

On December 6, 1890, William Walthour died in Savannah when Bobby was only twelve. William was buried in Laurel Grove Cemetery in Savannah, next to his first wife. Suddenly Bobby's two older brothers, Samuel and Palmer, became the breadwinners of the family. The two brothers had been living together in Savannah; seventeen-year-old Samuel was a horse wagon driver for the South Express Company, and fifteen-year-old Palmer delivered messages. After his father's death Samuel moved to New York City, where he was later joined by his mother, who met a man named William Hall and married him.

Palmer, meanwhile, moved to Atlanta, where he worked as a clerk at S. P. Richards and Son. Other family members followed, and in 1894 Palmer, C. T., Russell, James (Jimmy), and Bobby, along with their Aunt Carrie, were living together at 97 East Georgia Avenue. When Mrs. Walthour was away in New York, Carrie was in Atlanta to help, and Palmer must have served as a father to his younger brothers.

Atlanta city life was a dramatic change for Bobby and Jimmy. In the countryside around Walthourville, they had been free to roam amid the Georgia pines that crowded the flat landscape for miles around. Breaking up the monotony were large grassy clearings with shade provided by majestic oak trees filled with Spanish moss. In spring dogwood trees bloomed, and rhododendrons, hydrangeas, and azaleas filled southern gardens with vibrant colors. In Atlanta, by contrast, the buzzing morning chirps of the Savannah sparrow were replaced by clopping horse hoofs pulling squeaky trolley wagons along the busy and dirty streets.

The bespectacled Palmer, who was blind in one eye and had poor vision in the other, had spent much of his youth at the Pulaski House in Savannah, where he could best learn to cope with his disability. Even with his sight problems, he had an independent and enterprising spirit, and he worked hard to earn a living. Palmer decided to capitalize on the growing popularity of the bicycle. In Atlanta he and his friend Melrose Selkirk started Walthour and Selkirk Company, which delivered messages by bicycle and sold bicycle sundries and supplies. Bobby's lifelong love affair with the bicycle most likely began at Palmer's shop at 62 North Pryor Street. He became immersed in his brother's fledging business, delivering messages and repairing bicycles with his four siblings.

✹

In 1878, the year Bobby Walthour was born, Civil War veteran Albert Pope manufactured the first consumer high-wheel bicycle in the United States. The lofty machines, made at Pope's factory in Boston under the brand name Columbia, cost $90 each ($2,220 in today's dollars). That was a steep price for the average worker, who was lucky to earn thirty cents an hour ($6.66). Pope hired a traveling salesman, George Bidwell, who did high-wheel demonstrations with the Columbia in town squares all over the country.[6] A masterful salesman, Bidwell's performances fascinated prospective clients. At that time the train was the fastest form of travel available, but its route was, of course, restricted to the rails. Although a journey on horseback or in a carriage could be more flexible, horses had to be fed, watered, and rested. Bidwell argued that human-powered locomotion with bicycles offered an economical and practical alternative to trains and horses. The Columbia could travel much faster than a person could walk and used less energy.

The high-wheeled bicycles that Bidwell demonstrated typically had a front wheel of about forty-eight inches in diameter and a trailing wheel of about a third that size. Both wheels had laced spokes and solid rubber tires. One full revolution of the pedals created a single revolution of the larger wheel, similar to the operation of the little red tricycle with which many Americans today grew up. Theoretically the larger the front wheel, the faster a cyclist could go.

Bicycling in Great Britain was a few years ahead of the United States. High-wheel cyclists began racing one another in English town squares around 1870, and they also competed against trotting horses at local race tracks. Speeds of twenty miles per hour could be reached over short distances. There were many accounts in the press of high-wheel cyclists in Britain traveling distances of one hundred miles and more.

However, the high-wheel was a dangerous contraption that required riders who were athletic enough to mount and dismount them. In his book, *Bicycle: The History,* David Herlihy describes the difficulty: "The bicyclist could thus run alongside the vehicle, place the left foot on the step, and then pull the rest of the body up for a final leap onto the saddle. After landing, the rider had to catch the spinning pedals with the feet and quickly gain control of the moving machine."[7]

By 1887, when Bobby Walthour was nine years old, Albert Pope's firm was competing against several American bicycle manufacturers in addition to those from Europe. In 1886 Pope had visited a number of British companies that were producing the "safety," a new type of bicycle with a diamond frame that was driven by a chain. The safety was much lower to the ground and had two wheels of the same size. Pope was not overly impressed. He predicted that the new style of bicycle would suffer a quick demise, and he and other American bicycle manufacturers remained committed to the high-wheel. Yet by 1890 Pope finally switched course, stopped production of the high-wheel, and manufactured his new Columbia safety bicycle exclusively.[8]

As the high-wheel became obsolete, safety bicycles opened doors for many more people—young and old, male and female—to own and ride a bicycle. The basic design of the safety closely resembles today's bicycles. The safety did not require the perfect balance of riding a unicycle, as the high-wheel did, and it could be ridden much faster.

At about the same time that the safety bicycle was gaining popularity, John Dunlop, a Scotsman who lived in Belfast, invented the pneumatic tire. Dunlop stumbled on the concept while trying to make a tricycle more comfortable for his son.[9] His pneumatic tire was far superior to the solid rubber tire previously used, because it was lighter and provided a cushioned ride. In 1891 Frenchman Edouard Michelin further advanced Dunlop's idea with the detachable tire. Other technical advances, such as a chain with interlocking aluminum and steel links, came quickly and continually reduced the bicycle's weight. In racing circles, wooden rims replaced the heavier steel rims, thus reducing weight even further.

In 1895 the typical safety bicycle weighed twenty-seven pounds, and a brand new Columbia could be purchased for $100 ($2,640). In addition annual model changes created a large secondhand market. That year one million Americans joined the bicycle craze that was sweeping the globe.[10] Bobby and his brothers were among those who discovered the simple pleasure and independence the new bicycle provided.

No doubt the Walthour brothers—and particularly the industrious Palmer—first saw men aloft the precarious high-wheel in Savannah while their father worked for the railroad. By the time the family moved to Atlanta in the early 1890s, the cycling industry's transition to the safety was complete. The high-wheel bicycle was outmoded. With Palmer's experience as a messenger in Savannah, he understood the advantages a bicycle could bring to the trade.

✳

Harry Silverman, a well-known and wealthy tobacco store owner and sports gambler in Atlanta, probably first encountered Bobby and his twin brother when the boys delivered packages to his residence or business. Silverman apparently saw something in Bobby that impressed him, because he soon offered the boy a job delivering messages.

No doubt it was an enticing offer for Bobby, who probably did not earn much money working for his brother. Silverman grew to trust Walthour and took him under his wing. Navigating through rough and seedy neighborhoods to secret cockfighting establishments with large wads of cash tucked in his pockets, Walthour developed the skills that served him

well in the future—quick thinking and fast riding. Whether during a melt-
ing hot day or a torrential downpour at night, Walthour had to carefully
weave a path through the helter-skelter city traffic, avoiding people and
animals. The impressionable young man also made many trips to Piedmont Park, home of Atlanta's horse racing track, to place bets for Silverman. Walthour was generously rewarded for his speed and daring. Bobby
never forgot the heart-thumping lessons he learned racing through the
streets of Atlanta, nor did he ever forget Silverman's generosity. The two
remained friends for decades.

According to Andrew Ritchie, bicycle racing had become increasingly
organized in the United States, and "national championships were held
over short distances on the track [and] longer distances were covered
on the challenging roads of the time."[11] Colleges such as Harvard and
Yale began fielding cycling teams. Spectators paid race organizers to see
the races, especially at the finish line. Based on how much an organizer
thought he could clear, he enticed riders with money simply to show up
for a race and offered big purses if they won. Riders also were paid to race
with certain brands of frames, wheels, tires, and components.

By 1894 hundreds of cyclists had joined the professional ranks in pursuit of fame and fortune. The purse for winning a race could be hundreds
or sometimes thousands of dollars. The American leading the charge to
professional cycling and big money was Arthur Zimmerman of New Jersey.
Zimmerman, six feet tall with a lanky but muscular build, initially rode a
high wheel, but by 1891 he had switched to the safety. Zimmerman reportedly made $40,000 ($1,030,000) in 1894,[12] thus creating America's first
international superstar athlete.

Walthour's name began appearing in the Atlanta press as "Bob Walthour" in 1895 with other young local amateur cyclists, including Kendall
Speer, Hugh Caperton, Cleveland Bolles, John Chapman, George Quinn,
Bert Repine, and Ned Chalfant. Each rider showed promise. Young Walthour aspired to outdo professional riders like Zimmerman, but for the
most part he had to settle for impromptu speed and distance races with
his fellow bicycle messengers in Atlanta.

Walthour rode a fixed-gear safety, which did not include brakes. To
slow down, he had to work against the inertia of the forward-moving ped-

als or simply hop off and run alongside the still moving bicycle. Financed by the earnings from his job or by Silverman, Walthour could afford to ride a gleaming new Sterling racing bicycle. Other than its wooden rims and lack of a gooseneck (the handlebars were connected just above the steering tube), the bicycle, down to its toe clips, was remarkably similar to the track bikes popular in the 1980s.

Walthour competed in several official and unofficial races in and around Atlanta as an amateur in 1895. He also raced in Louisville and Chattanooga, where he won one race and finished second in another. His time for five miles was 14 minutes 20 seconds—not bad considering he was pedaling over hills and dirt with a fixed-gear bike. In August of that year, Walthour and Kendall Speer raced side by side going nowhere very fast on a stationary machine at the fireman's benefit in Atlanta, and in September he returned to Chattanooga and finished second in another five-mile road race.

At the Atlanta Fair in December, Walthour won a gold medal worth $25 ($660) by taking second in the one-mile state championship. He also took second in the half-mile, winning a diamond pin.[13] This brief racing experience gave the seventeen-year-old a taste of the recognition and riches that were to come.

{2}

Bobby and Blanche

Walthour's bike messenger job took him through a wide range of neighborhoods, from the downtown Atlanta business district, to squalid slums, to the neatly manicured residential precincts. During one of his deliveries for Harry Silverman, a pretty and trim thirteen-year-old girl with golden hair answered his knock at the door. Blanche Cooledge took the package, and the messenger boy went back to work. Walthour delivered more packages to this address, and each time he stayed a little longer.[1] Blanche was taken in by his charm and shyness, but when their conversation turned to cycling, it was soon clear that he was no longer shy.

During their tentative courtship thousands of excited spectators in Atlanta lined up to witness the start of the second annual Piggott Road Race on April 26, 1895. An amateur race, it started and finished on the corner of Peachtree and Forest streets. A detachment of police was on hand to control the crowd, and a brass band gave the event a festive atmosphere. A white canvas tent pitched on a neighboring lawn furnished shelter to the riders before the 4 p.m. start. Some of the prizes were highly unusual by today's standards—a box of cigars, bottles of beer, and a Smith & Wesson pearl-handled revolver. The coveted prize for the winner, however, was a new lightweight Victor racing bicycle provided by the Piggott Cycling Company.

The race was handicapped so that the favored riders known as "scratch-men" started last. For this race, the scratch riders were Hugh Caperton and George Quinn. Kendall Speer and Walthour also had handicaps: they started one minute ahead of Caperton and Quinn. Before the start, Caperton, Quinn, and Speer made arrangements to pace each other and leave Walthour in the dust. Each rider was supposed to take a turn at the front, to equalize the pace-making burden. But the group of three conspirators broke up when two realized that Quinn refused to do his share of the pacing and instead tried to save himself for the sprint finish.

The ten-mile course went uphill, downhill, and through plenty of mud. It was an out-and-back course, and from the thousands lined up along Peachtree Street came a cry, "Here he comes!" Police cleared a path for the finish, and a lone rider could be made out; it was Charles Langford, who had been given a two-minute handicap. He received a roaring ovation. Langford won the race and the Victor bicycle and finished with the best time of 33 minutes 37 seconds. Hugh Caperton earned second best with 33 minutes 57 seconds, and young Walthour came in sixth with a time of 34 minutes 57 seconds. Walthour's ride was perhaps the most remarkable because he had dismounted twice to fix a loose pedal. For his efforts, Walthour won a bicycle saddle and a medal.[2]

In June 1895 seventeen-year-old Walthour told Blanche he would be racing in another amateur road race, and she promised to be at the finish line. As he crossed the finish line in first place, their eyes met, and she waved enthusiastically, jumping for joy. Her equally excited younger sister, Nona, was there with her. Walthour was making a name for himself, and Blanche rarely missed a race. She became his most devoted fan. She developed a habit of hiding her eyes while he raced. She could not bear the thought of him crashing and hurting himself. Walthour was the established hero among the bicycle messenger crowd; some of them thought he should be more serious about his racing and not be sidetracked by a girl, but he ignored their advice.[3]

As the 1896 Piggott Road Race approached, Walthour spent more time training and less time carrying out his messenger duties. But his energetic courtship of Blanche Cooledge continued. Blanche and he took leisurely afternoon bike rides on Brookwood Road. Blanche had delicate features with high arching eyebrows over blue eyes that looked fondly at her Romeo. She was of average height, five inches shorter than Walthour and with an attractive figure. Her vivacity complemented his quiet and determined personality. Love was in the air.

The April 28 race was scheduled to start and finish on the corner of Peachtree and Fourteenth streets. H.J. Piggott was the official starter. The course consisted of four circuits—out to Joe Thompson's property and back—making it a ten-mile race. The winner would receive a Norwood bicycle from the Piggott Cycling Company. With quite a name now for himself in the cycling community, Walthour started from scratch, along-side his training partner, Cleveland Bolles. Other handicapped riders started minutes ahead. By the end of the first circuit Walthour and Bolles had caught all the handicapped riders and taken the lead. With Bolles up front and Walthour on his wheel, Bolles slipped and went down, taking Walthour with him. The cyclists untangled themselves and Walthour took the lead. He didn't come in first place, but he did earn the best time of 35 minutes 55 seconds, with Bolles two seconds behind.[4] The clerk of the course was Gus Castle, whose job was to ensure all the riders stuck to the rules. Castle was about ten years older than Walthour and became his first trainer.[5] Like many of his contemporaries, Castle used Zimmerman's 1894 book, *Points for Cyclists with Training*, to guide Walthour.

Walthour at eighteen was a sturdy 5 feet 10 inches and 155 pounds. His athletic build suited him for both short and long distance races, perfect for the rough and tumble world of professional cycling. Walthour's frigid blue eyes could stare down opponents, but for the most part he had an easygoing nature and enjoyed sharing humorous anecdotes with friends and family.

In 1906 an older and wiser Walthour recalled receiving his first bad review in the press on May 9, 1896. He had entered seven men's races at an event in Columbus, Georgia. He won all of them. The next morning the local newspaper printed the headline—"Walthour Greedy."[6] "I was more than proud of winning those races," said Walthour. "I took the medals I had won and pinned them on my coat and felt mighty big about it. That time has passed; I would not wear them now."[7]

A week after this so-called greedy triumph in Columbus, Walthour returned home to Atlanta. Early in May, he jumped on his bicycle to ride to a friend's house. The fork broke, and he was thrown to the ground and knocked unconscious. Coming around quickly, he was helped home by a kind stranger. A doctor was summoned; he found no broken bones but plenty of bruises. Luckily, Walthour escaped serious injury.[8]

Blanche was shocked when she saw Bobby's scrapes and bruises. His full recovery was slow, and she was unhappy when he persisted in his daily training under Castle's supervision. Six weeks after his first serious cycling injury, he started his first professional race, on June 22, 1896. He remembered this event in a later 1906 interview:

> I decided to turn professional and I went over to Montgomery to take part in a professional race held there. George Quinn, a professional from Boston, had three riders with him. He was paying them a salary and grabbing the prize money for himself. He saw me and asked what I was doing. I told him that I had turned professional. He laughed at me and told me, 'You had better get back home quick.' Well, we started out in the first race. It was a mile heat and I was as green as grass and strong as the devil. I jumped into the lead on the dirt track and took the first quarter in the lead. Then I took the second quarter and was still ahead of the bunch. When I got to the third quarter I commenced to wonder where the rest of the fellows were and I turned to look at them. By George, they had all drawn together in a bunch a short distance behind me and were preparing to start a great dash so as to go by me in a hurry, and leave me completely out of it. I was lucky that I saw them. I "dug" and not one of the guys passed me, not only that, but I won the other two races also, and Quinn was just about as sore as he could be. He went out in front of the [grandstand] and said that I could not ride and did not know how to, and a lot of other things.[9]

Two weeks later, Walthour was back in Columbus with fellow Atlanta rider John Chapman. Before a large crowd and a military band, Bobby won all three races he entered: the open mile, the two-mile handicap, and the five-mile handicap. For his victories he received a silver medal, a new bicycle suit, and a new set of tailor-made clothes. In the two-mile race he established a southern record of 4 minutes 27 seconds.[10]

The next day, Walthour crossed the finish line of the Georgia State Championship race in first place, mere inches in front of Chapman. But his triumph was short-lived. Fred F. Dudley, the defending champion, claimed Walthour had fouled him. Although it was not clear on how he was fouled, the judges agreed, and Dudley retained his title. Undaunted, Walthour took the first-prize gold medal in the ten-mile handicap and first prize in the open two-mile, winning a pair of Wright and Morgan tires. A sketch printed in the *Atlanta Constitution* showed Walthour with his hands on his hips and a serious look on his face, in a racing suit with a star on his chest.[11]

✳

On August 11, 1897, perhaps inspired by the song "Daisy Bell," written by Henry Dacre five years earlier, nineteen-year-old Bobby Walthour and fifteen-year-old Blanche Cooledge rode out from Atlanta to Decatur on a tandem "bicycle built for two" and were married without the knowledge of their parents. Walthour called on his bride at the Cooledge house on Lloyd Street, on the pretext that he and Blanche were to see the trapeze artists perform at Exhibition Park. A friend of Walthour's who rode on the amateur circuit, Zenus Fields, took up his watch at Palmer's shop on South Pryor Street and waited for the happy couple to pass by. Fields spotted them and raced ahead to the corner of Pryor and Auburn avenues, where he had a tandem waiting. The trio cycled to Edgewood Avenue and then on to Decatur. Once they arrived in Decatur, Fields was put to work to find a minister, while the two lovebirds rode leisurely circles around the town square.[12]

Zenus Fields found Rev. Dr. McClesky, pastor of the First Methodist Church, who was willing to perform the ceremony. They rode up to the courthouse, surprising a few farmers playing checkers, and went straight into the ordinary's office. "I want a marriage license," stated Walthour with his bride, rosy and radiant from the ride. With paperwork completed, they made a happy dash for the tandem, and off they went toward Rev. McClesky's with Fields in the lead. The blonde pair was quickly married at

McClesky's home. As the wedding party passed the courthouse again on the way back to Atlanta, a farmer said, "Hit's er runerway b' gosh."[13]

Blanche's family members had a history of eloping. Her sister and other members of the family had done the same. Blanche thought it wise not to break tradition. When they told Mr. and Mrs. F. H. Cooledge the news, all was forgiven and the two were taken into her parents' house.

The newlyweds wasted little time honeymooning; Walthour returned almost immediately to his training and racing. The newlywed couple welcomed their first child, a girl they named Viva, in 1898.

It was a joyful time in the young couple's lives. While Blanche was home with little Viva, Bobby was making relatively good money as a new professional and was trying to earn a name for himself.

{ 3 }

Prince of Atlanta

the first professional bike race Walthour ever witnessed was at Piedmont Park in Atlanta in May 1894. Until then the Piedmont track had been used strictly for horse racing. Groundskeepers labored to roll a smooth dirt surface for the well-known professional cyclists, who included John S. Johnson (Minneapolis), Eddie Bald (Buffalo), and Jack Prince, at that time a thirty-three-year-old in the twilight of his athletic career. With twelve hundred other spectators, Walthour was there that warm afternoon with his brothers and his bike messenger friends cheering on as Bald beat Johnson in the main event. To cap off the evening of thrills, Jack Prince surprised everyone by racing against and beating Atlanta's fastest trotting horse in a mile race. Walthour's first glimpse of cycling superstardom in his hometown had a profound influence on the sixteen-year-old.[1]

Born in Coventry, England, in 1859, Jonathan "Jack" Shillington Prince had been a natural athlete. At the age of sixteen, he had established himself as one of the best cricket bowlers in the country. Injured in a game, Prince's mangled hand forced his retirement from that game.[2] He transferred quickly to bicycling, and although it took Prince six months to learn to ride the high-wheel bicycle well, he eventually turned professional. As early as 1881 he was in Boston competing on high-wheelers against some of the best in the world—Thomas Eck, Albert Schock, and later on, Arthur Zimmerman.

Prince's distinctly British accent delivered in a deep and sonorous voice surprised and amused those around him on the race tracks. He was a self-made man and a natural promoter. He made friends quickly, but his sharp tongue set him back more than once. He was not afraid to let a little fib or even a big whopper get in the way of a good story or a business venture. Like Harry Silverman, Prince was a mentor to Walthour, but one the youngster was not afraid to disagree with when it came down to business.

Two years after Walthour had seen Prince race against the horse in Atlanta, he and John Chapman packed food, water, spare parts, and tools and rode the two hundred miles from Atlanta to Nashville. Their goal was to meet Jack Prince, who by then had become a successful bicycle race promoter and track builder. The impressionable youths were dumbstruck. Prince took them to the middle of the track at his newly constructed coliseum and pronounced that Walthour would be the next American champion and that Chapman would be a great rider too. Chapman did indeed have a successful career in racing but left his mark most significantly as a race promoter. In Walthour's case, though, Prince's prophecy was ultimately fulfilled.[3]

Early in 1897 Prince negotiated with several southern cities (including Memphis, Nashville, Chattanooga, Montgomery, and Atlanta) for a new racing circuit that he hoped would attract professional cyclists to come south for the mild spring weather. Prince talked Walthour up in the press: "You may talk about fast men and all that," he told the *Atlanta Constitution*, "but I predict that your Atlanta kid, Bob Walthour, will be on the top match for that championship. I would be willing to bet that with good, fast pace setting, Bob could make the mile on one of our tracks in one minute and fifty seconds. Why, Bob licked Arthur Gardiner, one of the fastest men in the country in New Orleans, and ran within six inches of Jay Eaton, the champion indoor rider of the world. "[4]

Walthour had raced in New Orleans shortly after his nineteenth birthday. Many years later, Walthour recalled this race in the Big Easy and especially his encounter with Nell McHenry, the official award presenter at the Tulane Theater: "Well, it was about the first time I was ever in a theatre in my life and I thought she was the best-looking woman I had ever seen. . . . I was sitting kinder far back and I couldn't see the paint and stuff on her face. I didn't know she was painted up, but I thought it was natural. Well, when I saw how pretty she looked—to me—I began thinking up a good speech and before my time came I had a crackerjack." McHenry called out Walthour's name, and the proud youngster nervously started for the stage to accept his award in front of the big crowd. McHenry took his hand and hoisted the 155-pound professional cyclist up on stage. Either McHenry was a cross-dresser or an incredibly strong woman. Suddenly Walthour was inches away, staring straight into McHenry's painted-on face, nonplussed. A silent and uncomfortable moment passed before McHenry handed him his award for having beaten Arthur Gardiner.[5]

Prince hoped that if a southerner like Walthour could do well on his circuit, the crowds would come out in droves. Up to this point no southern professional cyclist stood out in the national racing scene. Prince envisioned the 1897 southern circuit hosting professional racing beginning in April. Prince and Albert Mott, the newly elected chairman of the Racing Board of the League of American Wheelmen (L.A.W.), agreed to have the national circuit chasers, who primarily raced up north, dip south for a brief period. With a $40,000 budget from the L.A.W. ($1,070,000 in today's dollars), a good amount of prize money was available for a southern circuit.

To become the 1897 southern circuit champion, Walthour faced tough competition. But he was determined, especially as Prince had touted him so highly. Among the elite cyclists with whom Prince expected to sign deals were John "The Terrible Swede" Lawson (Chicago), Con Baker (Columbus, Ohio), Earl Kiser (Dayton, Ohio), Jay Eaton (Elizabeth, New Jersey), Floyd MacFarland (San Jose), and brothers Nat and Tom Butler (Boston).[6]

Early in April Earl Kiser, who had captured the championship of Europe the prior year, was ready for Walthour at the opening of the southern circuit in Memphis. Kiser champed at the bit and expected to dominate the field, but as the *Atlanta Constitution* reported, "In the fifth lap Walthour took to the bank and spurted by the other riders down the south stretch. Kiser was after him as soon as he shot by, but Walthour tenaciously held on to his advantage. Kiser and the Atlantian fought it out alone; the finish was so close that the judge finally called it a dead heat. Kiser just nipped Walthour as he was on the tape."[7] The race not only boosted Walthour's confidence but gained him favorable publicity.

Nonstop traveling was required to become a circuit champion, and the tireless Walthour went on to race in Chattanooga. From there almost forty riders boarded a train for Atlanta. Walthour headed home in third place in the standings behind Al Weinig and H.R. Steenson. He had earned $107 ($2,860) in just ten days, a sizeable sum for the young cyclist when the median household income was than $500 a year.[8]

Jack Prince, who liked nothing better than being the center of attention, spoke enthusiastically about the success of the southern circuit. Reporters peppered him with questions about the various tracks and riders. Prince predicted that more people would turn out for the races in Atlanta than in any other city.

As it turned out, Prince's prediction came true. More than four thousand people streamed into the updated Piedmont Coliseum in Atlanta. The bowl-shaped track was brightly lit with electric lights, and the well-dressed crowd, with men sporting bowler hats and women in the latest fashions, took their seats to music played by the band of the Fifth Regiment. Many spectators noticed how steeply banked and dangerous the track was, as the riders warmed up in their brightly colored sweaters and tights. In a blatant ploy to make money, the indefatigable Prince announced through a megaphone in his booming British-accented voice: "Everybody must have a program. Each rider has a number on his back and to pick them out you must have a program."[9]

After several heats the crowd became aware of some kind of a disturbance. Police ran through a gateway to the dressing rooms where, according to the *Atlanta Constitution*, "a highly interesting scrap between Al Newhouse of Buffalo and John Chapman" was taking place. Newhouse thought he had been fouled by Chapman, and the two got into a shouting match. Newhouse rushed at Chapman. More than a dozen attendants were needed to pull the two young sweaty, dirty, and bloodied men apart, but neither was seriously hurt.[10]

The loudest ovation of the day was saved for the local kid. Walthour won the fifth heat in the one-mile event, open to all contestants, finishing ahead of his own brother Russell. In the finish of the one mile Walthour and Jay Eaton nearly locked handlebars at over twenty-five miles per hour, but both lost to a streaking Al Weinig, the leader of the southern circuit with winnings of $210 ($5,600).

Unfortunately the southern circuit became plagued by financial problems, and racing was suspended in late May 1897. The lumber for the tracks Prince designed for the southern circuit was purchased on credit. Although Prince lost money, he had accomplished more than most had given him credit for. He had introduced the first organized bicycle circuit racing in prominent southern cities. And the hard lessons Prince learned ultimately helped him. He knew more about how to market his ideas. He now understood that improved coordination and communication with cities, venues, and cyclists was essential. Ultimately, however, the southern circuit failed because the audiences were not large enough to support the cash prizes.

Prince accused Jay Eaton, who eventually earned the most money that year, of conspiring to break up the southern circuit. Although Prince did not reveal the details of these charges, he may have had good reason for them because years later, Eaton was exposed as a disreputable character and a cheat. Among the promoters in the United States, there was fierce competition to bring in the fastest riders to generate the most money. Prince commented to the *Constitution,* "The racing [news]papers of the north, of course, fight racing in the south because they do not want to see the cracks come south. It means money and sport to keep them in the north and if the southern circuit had been a success they would have been down here. The circuit is not dead, but simply suspended, and with the experience I have had this year I will make it a grand success next year."[11]

❊

Walthour was fifth in earnings tables with $230 ($6,140) when the southern circuit was suspended. In June he headed north and raced in Michigan, Wisconsin, and Illinois, earning good money. In Detroit he rode his personal best paced mile—1 minute 52 seconds. In Racine, Wisconsin, he beat Chicagoan Johnny Nelson in the first heat of the professional open mile. Tom Cooper, a cycling sprinter with a national reputation, won the final heat, and Walthour finished a respectable second.[12]

Walthour arrived back in Atlanta from the 1897 northern circuit tour early in July. He was happy to rest and heal up before the national meet in Philadelphia. Only his family and Gus Castle knew that he had been in seven accidents up north, fighting his way through crowded fields. In one race, forty-six riders were on the track, and he had been compelled to skirt dangerously along the track's perimeter. In his first eight races, he had won three firsts, one second, and one third. He told the *Atlanta Journal* that there was not a friendly feeling up north, and the racing was highly competitive.[13]

The day after Walthour's return to Atlanta, Jack Prince, eager to profit from the young professional's tremendous appeal in his hometown, talked him into a local match race against Bert Repine. Large wagers were made on Walthour, and a purse of $50 was set for the best of three heats.

The first heat was one mile, each cyclist paced by a tandem bicycle. Walthour hung on to the tandem until the fifth lap, and the race became a fight for the finish. The crowd cheered wildly, and with perfect timing the brass band added to the excitement by playing "Dixie." At the tape, both riders nearly lost control of their bicycles, and Repine won by inches. The second heat was supposed to be run over three miles, but by mistake it was put on the program as two miles. Prince pulled the two pacing tandems out and rang the bell lap indicating a half-lap to go, but the riders had only ridden one and a half miles. The surprised cyclists shifted to sprint mode, and Repine crossed the tape first by three inches. An objection was raised as to whether it was a two-mile contest or a three-mile contest. Ever the gentleman, Repine told the judges he had signed for a three-mile race and offered to race the second heat over. The crowd stood up waiting for a decision.

A loud mix of cheers and jeers fell over the stadium when it was announced that the race would be run again. On the last lap of the repeated heat, the two riders were even, and Walthour broke away. As they went around the last turn, Walthour's rear tire tore off its rim, and he went down hard into a post. He was not seriously injured but added to his collection of bruises.[14]

Two weeks later Walthour had nearly recovered from his injuries, and a large and boisterous crowd again assembled early in the day to watch him race. When Bert Repine, the southern champion from Nashville, and Walthour, the clear Atlanta favorite, came out on the track, rooters yelled out, "Go at him Bert!" and "Do him one Bobby!" Repine won the first one-mile heat by half a bicycle length, but Walthour put things on even terms by winning the second heat, a three-mile race. Prince announced a fifteen-minute rest before the final and deciding five-mile heat, and the young riders readied themselves. Late in the fourth mile, the last pacing tandem came off the track, and the sprint for the southern championship began. The two cyclists reached speeds that seemed impossible. Side by side they strained every muscle down the backstretch, with Repine on the outside. Into the final turn, Walthour took a slight lead, and the noise from the fans shook the coliseum. On the finish stretch, he seemed to lose ground but crossed the tape three inches ahead of Repine. Hats were thrown in the air, umbrellas raised, and the band was drowned out. When Walthour came around and dismounted, frenzied fans rushed the track and carried him around on their shoulders.[15]

Walthour was the new darling of the South in July 1897. Prince was the center of attention. It was a match made in heaven.

{ 4 }

Bipartite Bicycling

t he League of American Wheelman was formed in 1880 by Albert Pope. At that time the L.A.W. limited itself to defending the rights of all cyclists, improving paved roads, and allowing cyclists access to roads previously denied. By the time Walthour turned professional in 1896, the L.A.W. had grown and controlled the national racing circuit. By 1898 a wave of discontent among professional cyclists rippled through the organization. Many argued that the L.A.W. management was greedy and received the lion's share of profits while the riders who were risking life and limb were short-changed.

In March 1898 professional cyclist Jay Eaton was named manager of Atlanta's Piedmont Coliseum track. The move was probably designed to avoid a full rebellion by the disgruntled riders. Eaton planned to go to Louisville, where all the big names were training, and entice the riders to race at Piedmont.[1]

Eaton induced George Kraemer from Chicago to go against Walthour in a match race. The two had raced twice before. Walthour had beaten him at Madison Square Garden, but Kraemer had achieved revenge at the Fountain Ferry track in Louisville. Kraemer had raced in Europe the previous season where he scored many victories. Eaton suggested to Kraemer that the $500 purse ($13,300 in today's dollars) be divided and the winner awarded the larger portion. But Kraemer would have none of it; he insisted on winner take all.

The Fifth Regiment Band struck up lively patriotic numbers—the American public was in a fighting mood over Cuba. Weeks earlier on February 15, the battleship USS *Maine* blew up in Havana's harbor, killing 262 American officers and men. Harry Silverman, the man who had employed Walthour as a bike messenger, vowed to leave his prosperous business to volunteer for the fight.[2]

The match race between Kraemer and Walthour was the featured event of Atlanta's first big professional bicycle race of 1898. In spite of cold and rainy conditions, crowds filtered in until the coliseum was packed. The sheer novelty of sport was a great factor in attracting crowds; four years would pass before Atlanta's first organized professional baseball team, the Atlanta Crackers, would play at Piedmont Park.

In the first heat Walthour shot past Kraemer ten feet before the tape. In the second heat Walthour won with ease, eliminating the need for a third heat. Manager Eaton's first meet was a big success thanks to the hometown kid.[3]

On June 29, 1898, Arthur Gardiner, whom Walthour had beaten in New Orleans the year before, led the standings in the L.A.W.'s prestigious national sprint title with fifty points. Tom Cooper from Detroit was second with twenty-three, Eddie Bald had sixteen, and Major Taylor, the young African American rider from Indianapolis, was fourth with ten.[4] Although Walthour didn't have a single point to his name, he was making good money.

Three months later the standings had changed significantly. Eddie Bald led with 153 points by a slim margin over Major Taylor with 127, and Floyd MacFarland was third with 112.5 points.

About that same time in early September, more than sixty racing men from all over the country converged on the Trenton House Hotel in New Jersey for a conference to voice grievances against the L.A.W. racing board and its leader, Albert Mott. Mott was there to appease the crowd of professional cyclists, but he was laughed at by the riders, who had grown cynical from his failed promises to improve their financial position and other conditions for the riders and trainers. Points leader Bald was elected chairman of the event. Attendees drew up a petition of independence declaring the formation of a new organization and signed by most riders at the Trenton House:

> We, the undersigned, professional bicycle riders and trainers of America, band ourselves together for mutual protection and the furthering of our interests, agreeing to ride under the rules of any organization which may be formed in the future and meeting with out approval. In our opinion such a body should be formed of tracks, clubs, race promoting associations, and professional racing men. We insist that as one of the provisions in such a body that local option be embodied, and that in any part of the country, where the local option permits, there shall be racing on any day of the week.[5]

By the end of the conference, a rebel professional organization was formed called the American Racing Cyclists Union (A.R.C.U.).

The primary concern of the minority who did not sign, including Major Taylor and Tom and Nat Butler, was the petition's last sentence, which brought up the issue of Sunday racing. Walthour generally did not support Sunday racing, yet he did sign on with the rebel union represented by the National Cycling Association (N.C.A.). Although exactly when he did so—whether at Trenton or later—is unclear.

On September 29 Bald issued a proclamation about the cause of the revolt, stating that professional riders had been dissatisfied with the L.A.W. for a long time and that in many ways the organization impeded the sport's development. L.A.W.'s racing body had forced riders to compete for small purses when larger ones were available. Bald said, "The method of deciding a champion this year is far from satisfactory to us, but we will contest three big score championships in order to finish the season of '98 as originally planned."[6]

The contentious battle between riders and L.A.W. management continued throughout 1898 and into the following year. Although Walthour was not an outspoken critic of the L.A.W., the organization suspended him indefinitely along with many other rebel riders for competing in "unsanctioned" races. The L.A.W. demanded the riders pay sizable fines to be reinstated.[7]

Eddie Bald wrote an article that appeared in the *Decatur Daily Review* and other publications, which summed up many riders' views: "There is only one way in which the question of control of professional bicycle racing can be settled and that is for the L.A.W. to get out and allow the N.C.A. [National Cycling Association] to run matters properly instead of the former trying to retain command of the field and putting affairs into a far worse muddle than it did last year."[8]

In February 1899 the L.A.W. held its National Assembly in Providence, Rhode Island. The question on everyone's mind was whether the L.A.W. should continue its control over racing. A clear answer emerged with an overwhelming majority vote in favor of the L.A.W. to continue its control.[9]

The World Cycling Championships were held in Montreal in August 1899, but the timing was unfortunate because of the political climate within the professional and amateur racing communities. Shortly before the World Championships, cyclers still didn't know whether members of the "outlaw" N.C.A. movement would be able to participate. Although Amos G. Batchelder, president of the rebel N.C.A., traveled to Montreal to lobby on behalf of the new organization and was allowed to make a statement to the International Cycling Association, the resulting decision made for a lukewarm competition. Not only were big-name American professionals such as Eddie Bald, Earl Kiser, Floyd MacFarland, Jay Eaton, Frank Kramer, and Bobby Walthour excluded from riding, but many great European riders thought the championships not worth their effort to travel across the Atlantic.

While the World Championship races took place in Canada, Walthour raced at "outlaw" tracks such as New York's Berkeley Oval, Philadelphia's Woodside Park track, and Newark's Vailsburg quarter-mile board track. The L.A.W. faithful rode primarily at Boston's Charles River track.

At Vailsburg on August 13, Walthour won the second heat of the Good Will Half Mile Open, which put him in the final against five other riders, including Eaton and MacFarland. The final was a sprint from the start with riders constantly changing positions. At the bell lap Walthour and Eaton were in the back. Eaton came out wide with Walthour tucked in behind, and both passed the other riders on the outside. Eaton held on to win before the five thousand screaming fans, and though he took second, the race earned Walthour more national recognition.[10]

By early 1900 cycling politics had calmed down. The N.C.A. mapped out a circuit for 1900 that sprinters and paced riders were to follow to earn points for the national championships in both categories. Prior to this sprinters and paced riders were not separated but lumped into one all-around cycling category.

The L.A.W. subsequently divorced itself from racing and went about its original business of advocacy for bicyclists' rights. Newly elected New York governor Theodore Roosevelt set an example to cycling citizens by promptly renewing his L.A.W. membership.[11] The vast majority of professional riders in the United States had established themselves safely in the American Cyclists' Racing Union.

The few riders who had not yet joined the union applied for reinstatement to race, most notably Major Taylor. There was talk of a lifetime ban for Taylor because factions of N.C.A. riders were opposed to his skin color.[12] Taylor was reinstated but only after paying a fine.

In the end most of the professional riders got what they wanted: their independence from the L.A.W., an organization out of touch with racing. The National Cycling Association remained in place for years thereafter.

{ 5 }

In the Slipstream

for decades the Tour de France has been the grandest and most beautiful bicycle race in the world. In every stage of the three-week race, except for the time trials, a team leader from among the nine riders on each team is identified. This leader is protected on the road by the other riders on the team, who draft for him as much as possible along the entire route of the Tour so that he can conserve his energy for the moments that really matter.

The riders at the front of the peloton (the main group of riders) take the brunt of the wind—especially in the face of a strong head wind— while the riders behind, who are still in close contact to the group, have an easier time of it. The peloton has the potential to move very fast since many different riders switch off and share the pacing work at the front. A breakaway occurs when a single rider or a small group of riders attempts to surge ahead of the peloton to win a stage. Winning a stage at the Tour de France can make a rider's career.

Breakaway attempts in the Tour de France are often unsuccessful. Managers of the teams know when to force the pace of the peloton to catch the breakaway before the finish line. Typically, the responsibility of catching these breakaways falls to the team with the leading rider in the general classification so that he doesn't lose any of his overall time. Lance Armstrong's team, for example, when he won the race from 1999–2005, always had to force the pace of the peloton to chase down breakaways, with Lance right behind being drafted by his teammates.

Today, in individual time trial stages of the Tour, all riders wear specially engineered helmets and skin suits and ride bikes with frames and wheels aerodynamically designed to slice through the wind because they are not being drafted by anyone. Withstanding the rigors of wind and air resistance, the best time trial riders in the world can maintain twenty-five to thirty miles per hour for about an hour.

Greg Lemond is famous for his experiments with time trialing technology and wind tunnel tests in the 1980s. On the Champs-Elysées in Paris in the final stage of the 1989 Tour de France, Lemond wore a wind-cheating helmet and was able to crouch like a downhill skier using his extended "aero" handlebars. But Frenchman Laurent Fignon and his managers had calculated that their fifty-five-second lead would be impossible for Lemond to make up. Lemond was in second place on the general classification, and Fignon planned to win, no matter what wind-cheating equipment the American had.

In a show of bravado Fignon opted to ride without an aerodynamic helmet, allowing his ponytail to flap wastefully in the breeze. In addition he rode a bike with traditional time trial "cow-horn" handlebars.

With the entire race on the line, Lemond rode the time trial of his life, made up the deficit plus eight seconds, and won the closest Tour de France in history. Seconds before reaching the finish line, Fignon knew he had lost. The bespectacled Frenchman in the yellow skin suit tumbled off his white bike seconds after crossing the finish and lay on his back in disbelief. The press instantly engulfed every inch of space around him and shoved microphones in his face, asking how he could have lost the Tour by eight seconds—to an American. Meanwhile the Lemond contingent celebrated wildly.

❋

Pacing has long been an important element in bicycle racing. The basic principle of bicycle pacing is that a rider behind another rider, or behind a moving object, will use less energy going at the same speed than the rider or object in front. This is the same principle race car drivers use to draft behind one another, and it is also why ducks or geese fly in a V formation. In a slipstream, the airstream creates reduced air pressure and forward suction directly behind a rapidly moving vehicle.

One of the most astounding cycling feats occurred at the Bonneville Salt Flats in Utah on July 20, 1985, when John Howard set a world record traveling 152.2 miles per hour on a bicycle.[1] Howard received some help from a 650-horsepower vehicle designed with a Plexiglas fairing that sheltered him within its draft. To generate the speed required, Howard used a specially designed bicycle with a long, stretched-out frame that enhanced stability at high speeds. The sleek machine had two chain ring systems that equated to a 280-tooth front sprocket. A single rotation of the pedals propelled the bike nearly half a football field.

Nearly ninety years before Howard's record, on August 27, 1896, professional cyclist E. E. Anderson in his St. Louis hometown performed a death-defying stunt. Anderson rode a bicycle for one mile, paced by a steam locomotive. Hundreds of people found seats on the bluffs near Union Station, where Anderson was expected to finish. Engine No. 7, one of the fastest locomotives in the country, was able to reach sixty miles per hour in less than a half-mile. At 3:50 p.m. after two test runs, Anderson gave the signal to his trainer William Buckner, who was seated in the cab next to the engineer, to begin the test. Anderson rode on wooden planks carefully laid between the rails. For protection he wore long black gloves and a pair of smoked glasses. At the starting point of the measured mile the train was traveling fifty miles per hour and Anderson hung on with ease. But as the train gained speed, he dropped back 12 feet. Fearing for his life, Anderson used every fiber of muscle and pedaled his way out of the heavy turbulence and back into the protection of the train's slipstream.

When the whistle blew announcing that the measured mile had been completed, the timer was astonished to see that Anderson had traveled at nearly sixty miles per hour. He rode a mile in 1 minute 3 seconds. The bike weighed 19 pounds, and he used a 92-inch gear.[2] There was a celebration at the back of the train when Anderson announced that although he was happy with the results, he had wanted to do the mile in under a minute. The bicycle withstood the ride well, except for the glue holding the tires to the wooden rims. When Buckner carried the bicycle back to Anderson's quarters, the melted glue dripped to the ground.[3]

Anderson never attempted to break this record again. But three years later, in 1899, professional cyclist Charles Murphy of Brooklyn was determined to beat Anderson's time. Murphy's track in Maywood, Long Island, was ready for the attempt on June 18. Its exact length of two miles and 962 feet would allow Murphy a half-mile to get to speed and more than a half-mile to slow down. Joseph Cummings, the superintendent of bridges and buildings of the Long Island Railroad Company, had worked with a sixty-man crew to fit joists between the rails. They placed 16-foot long smooth surfaced planks on the joists; five planks were needed between each rail, and they were carefully selected.[4]

On June 22 twenty-nine-year-old Murphy rode a test run on a Columbia bicycle with a 112-inch gear. The ride went practically without a hitch. Murphy's test run was ridden in 65 seconds. Many newspapermen were aboard the train, and the *Davenport Daily Republican* (Iowa) reported on the finish of the test run: "As Murphy straightened up and tried to decrease his speed, which was no easy matter at the rate that he was traveling, and the engine drew away from him, his wheel swayed from side to side and all his strength was needed to control it. The swaying was caused by the suction from beneath the train and Murphy said it was the most trying part of the ride. He had a hard time getting his machine under control and did not succeed in stopping before the end of the board track was reached."[5]

Murphy realized his predicament, and since he had already slowed down considerably, he was able to jump off his bicycle and land on his feet unhurt.[6] "There was no strain," Murphy said, "except on the eyes. My eyes got crossed toward the last from keeping them fixed on the white board. So far as physical exertion went, I have felt it more on a home trainer."[7]

News of Murphy's 65-second test run and his impending try on June 30 to ride a mile in under a minute was reported across the United States. Walthour, who was racing in New York at the time, was among the thousands who lined the abandoned stretch of Long Island railway to see if Murphy would succeed, fail, or even die.

At 2 p.m., the locomotive performed a test run without Murphy to allow officials, timers, newspapermen, and railroad men aboard to familiarize themselves with different flags and precautions. Then the officials announced that they were ready.[8]

The tall, lean 154-pound rider with a thick handlebar mustache and black hair parted down the middle grabbed his light blue enameled bicycle updated with a 120-inch gear. Murphy wedged his leather bicycle shoes tightly into his toe clips.[9] He wore a light blue jersey emblazoned with the initials "K.C.W." for Kings County Wheelmen, and black racing tights.[10] The signal was given to start and he nodded to his wife and children.

At first Murphy followed with ease, but the train sped away quicker than he expected and he dropped back. Those in the rear platform with the best view thought he had lost his nerve. But he looked up and smiled and shouted to Hal Fullerton, the Long Island Railroad Company's official agent that he was fine. He caught up again to the train. Engineer Sam Booth pulled the throttle wide open and Engine No. 74 reached sixty miles per hour at the start of the measured mile, which was indicated by a flag. Murphy kept close to the rubber buffer rail that separated his front wheel from the train. But inch by inch he lost ground. As the gap to the back of the train widened people on the viewing platform craned their necks for a better look. A whirlwind of dust caught Murphy squarely in the face and practically blinded him. As he pedaled frantically his face wrinkled in agony. Those on the train thought it was all over. Murphy's head rolled from side to side as he made one last-ditch superhuman effort. His bicycle wobbled dangerously close from one side of the rails to another, and with the enormous effort he succeeded in regaining the lost ground.

The train passed the mile flag and began reducing its speed, but Murphy didn't slow down with the train. His front wheel crashed into the rubber buffer. Superintendent Cummings and Fullerton were on the train platform closest to Murphy waiting for just such an emergency. They grabbed Murphy under his arms and hung onto him. They pulled him up, bicycle and all, with legs still thrashing, to the safety of the platform inside. Murphy sank to the floor, semi-conscious. For several spectators, the scene was too much and they had to lie down on the floor of the railroad car.[11]

When he had fully regained consciousness, Murphy exclaimed, "I just decided myself that I could make it and I rode into that train deliberately and caught hold of them before they knew what I was doing. . . . It seems to me the hand of God saved me from certain death, for I saw death at the finish of the ride."[12]

Five official timers confirmed that Murphy had completed a measured mile in 57.8 seconds. From that moment on, he was known as Charles "Mile-A-Minute" Murphy. He was offered $5,000 ($133,000 in current dollars) to try again, but apparently the money wasn't enough.[13] Years later Murphy became one of New York City's first motorcycle policemen.

Walthour's final year as a sprinter was in 1900. Unfortunately for Walthour and many sprinters, 1900 was also Frank Kramer's first year as a professional cyclist. Kramer was a big, chisel-chinned kid from New Jersey with a finishing kick any sprinter would die for. He made his professional debut on May 6, 1900, at the open-air Vailsburg track in Newark, New Jersey. Walthour, Kramer, and two other sprinters made it to the finals of the inaugural Half Mile Open.

On the bell lap Walthour was in perfect position in second place—tucked in just behind the leader. Kramer was in last place and benefited from the other three riders' drafts, including Walthour's. On the last turn the three leading riders swung wide up the steep banking at a blazing speed. Kramer churned his pedals and passed all three riders on the inside. Kramer won his first-ever professional race. And Walthour came in last.

In 1895, the year before Walthour turned professional, Arthur Zimmerman had created a sensation by riding a mile in 1 minute 57¼ seconds (more than thirty miles per hour) paced by a quadrulet.[14] A "quad" was a two-wheeled bicycle much like a tandem but with a frame stretched to fit four seats and four sets of pedals. Quads with four strong riders could sustain speeds above thirty miles per hour much longer than a single rider could. They were specifically designed to pace one rider. Even larger human-powered machines were made, and there was talk of a "quindecuplet," which would carry fifteen riders. These were serious ideas, not fantasies. But eventually competitors understood that these "multicycle" machines were too cumbersome, and the most effective and practical human-powered machines for pacing were triplets, quads, and quints. The eventual evolution of pacing machines, however, was toward motor-powered machines, driven at first by steam, then electricity, and eventually gasoline. These were the machines that Walthour would race behind.

Before motor-pacing emerged, human-powered multicycles supplied pace to the riders, who were known as "stayers" because of the need to stick like leeches to the rear wheel of the pacing machine. If he dropped, the cyclist was finished. Multicycles were like steam locomotives—slow to start, but once the team of four or five riders on the multicycle gained momentum, nothing was faster on a bicycle track.

Any rider who could stay behind a multicycle at top speed was in demand, and nobody was better than Jimmy Michael. Welshman Michael was barely five feet tall and was known in this politically incorrect era as Jimmy "The Welsh Midget" Michael. Walthour first met Michael in October 1897 when the cycling national circuit came to Atlanta.

Although Prince's southern circuit had failed, the profit potential of Atlanta, the Gate City of the South, was clear. The much-anticipated national circuit came south with its two special train cars, "Iolanthe" and "Pickwick," which carried many professional cyclists from city to city in style and included managers, trainers, cooks, and porters. The baggage car was laden with bicycles and pacing multicycles of different sizes including triplets, quads, and quints. The ten-seater Orient, the biggest multicycle ever put together at the time, came south with them, but it was too long to be used on the Atlanta track's steep banking.

A special curiosity on the national circuit was Joe "Baby" Grimes, who tipped the scales at 540 pounds and was said to be the largest man ever to straddle a bicycle. Baby's job was to ride a Cleveland bicycle, thus displaying its ability to withstand the punishment his enormous weight inflicted on its welds. The traveling professional athletes and Grimes arrived in Atlanta on October 27.[15]

Walthour knew the track better than anyone, and he was able to welcome nationally known riders to his hometown, including Tom Cooper, Earl Kiser, John Johnson, Floyd MacFarland, and Nat Butler. Jimmy Michael, perhaps the most revered and well-known cyclist in the world after Arthur Zimmerman, was also there. Michael always seemed to have a toothpick in his mouth and rode effortlessly with an erect posture on a tiny bicycle with a monster 108-inch gear. Michael joined the forty or so other professional cyclists, in their brightly colored racing suits, in training at the track.

The next day a brass band led the riders in a morning parade. Each cyclist was in a carriage, and banners advertised his name and the brand of the bicycle he rode. The parade started at Marietta Street and wound its way through the principal points of the city.

Cycling fans in Atlanta had the opportunity to see twenty races over two nights of competition. On the first night, Walthour won the first heat of the open mile and the first heat of the semi-final but did not place in the final, which was won by Eddie Bald, who was the favorite of the ladies. According to the *Atlanta Constitution*, every time good-looking Eddie came out on the track, women shuddered to imagine that he might crash and "mar his beauty."[16]

Jimmy Michael did not participate in races against other riders. He came to Atlanta only to ride a time trial, an attempt to cover twenty miles in forty minutes, which he had done previously on an outdoor track. His mile record for a paced mile was 1 minute 36 seconds, which was a record on American soil.

Not much detailed information was reported about Walthour's daily training routine early in his career. But the *Constitution* followed Michael's workout one day and gave a rare insight to a world-class rider's training techniques. Walthour probably followed a similar regimen:

[Michael] gets up in the morning at 6:30 a.m. and the first thing he does is to take a light exercise with a pair of five-pound dumb bells. He does just enough of this to get up a light glow and then he is ready for his liniment bath that his trainer gives him every morning. This done he goes for a walk of one hour, but does not take it fast. He is back from his walk in time for an 8 a.m. breakfast. All of his meals consist of the most substantial food and he must know what everything is that he eats. A short rest after breakfast and then he goes for a brisk walk of fifteen to twenty miles. At 11 a.m. he walks from the Aragon hotel where he is stopping, to the coliseum and is ready for his work on the track. He rides twenty miles on the track and then, after a good rub down, he walks back to the hotel. He dines at 1 p.m. and in a short while he takes a ride on the road for any distance that suits him. This ride varies from forty to fifty miles and he ends up at the coliseum, where he goes on the track again for a practice of ten or fifteen miles. His ride over, he puts on the boxing gloves with his trainer for more exercise and then he gets another good rub down. A walk back to the hotel and he is ready for supper at 6:30 p.m. At 7 p.m. one would naturally think that he would be ready for bed, but his work is not done. At seven he puts on his heavy sweaters and goes for a fast walk that lasts until 9 p.m. How much ground he covers in those hours is not known, but he goes at a good pace and it takes a fine walker to keep up with him. As soon as he gets back to the hotel he goes to bed and while his trainer is rubbing him down he goes to sleep.[17]

On November 8, Michael and Eddie Bald gave exhibition rides at Atlanta's coliseum. Bald broke Zimmerman's one-mile track record by several seconds with a final of 1 minute 52⅗ seconds. Michael failed to make twenty miles in forty minutes but came close. Until the eighth mile he was on pace, but his multicycle pacemaker teams could not go fast enough. Michael cried out for more speed, but all in vain. His last mile was the fastest and he passed his pacemakers, finishing it in 1 minute 55⅖ seconds. His time for the entire distance was 40 minutes 37⅖ seconds—nearly thirty miles per hour.[18]

Just as drafting is crucial in today's Tour de France and other races, it was equally as important a hundred years ago. For Walthour, the slipstream was his bread and butter.

{6}

Six Daze

One of the most popular and colorful events on the annual cycling calendar in the 1890s was the six-day race at Madison Square Garden in New York. It was held during the first or second week of December and lasted for 142 consecutive hours—just two hours short of exactly six days, so that it would neither start nor finish on a Sunday. The rider who rode the greatest distance in those days was declared the winner. The carnival-like event was the Super Bowl of cycling.

As many as ten thousand spectators would jam into the Garden to watch the riders endure almost unimaginable physical and mental pain as they circled the sharply banked pine track, hour after hour, day after day. The "grind," as it was called, began just past midnight on Monday morning and continued nonstop until 10 p.m. Saturday night. The crowd was as raucous as any Alp d'Huez mountain climb in today's Tour de France— but the Garden spectators didn't need to wait two days, as they do in today's road race, just to see the riders climb for half an hour.

In 1897 Walthour received an invitation to compete in the preliminary events at the six-day at Madison Square Garden. The invitation was proof of his success in his second season as a professional. In December Walthour and his wife, Blanche, packed their bags and headed north. The couple was about to embark on a huge adventure—their introduction to the most commercially successful international bicycle race in the world in the nation's grandest city.

Jack Prince promised to manage and train Walthour for the exhibition races that preceded the main event, but negotiations with Prince stalled, and the two could not agree on terms. So in place of Prince, he hired his twin brother Jimmy as his handler and manager. "I am riding now better than I ever did in my life," Walthour told the *Constitution* before he left, "and you may expect to hear from me in some of the open events. What I want most is to race with Bald or Eaton, and I will try to get it. I know that I am going up to win, and am full of confidence."[1] A crowd of well-wishers came to the train depot in Atlanta to see the Walthours off to New York. Traveling with them was Charles Miller from Chicago, who had been training in the South and was heading for New York as well to participate.

For the preliminary events thousands of fans lined up early on Saturday morning, December 4, shivering outside Madison Square Garden amid the snow and slush. Men and women fought and pushed for position. When the doors finally opened, the big building quickly filled with more than ten thousand cycling-mad New Yorkers. The *World*, a New York newspaper, reported:

> The first rider who appeared on the track, which had not been completed more than an hour or two earlier, was greeted with a roar of applause, and from then on to the finish of the meet, announcer Fred Burns might as well have talked to the men working on the turret of a monitor. His voice is noted for its clearness and carrying powers, but no one could hear it in the bewildering, deafening thunder of cheering.[2]

The Walthours probably stayed in New York with either his newly remarried mother, Mrs. William Hall, or with his brother Samuel. Although the usual size of the board track at the Garden was ten laps to the mile, the 1897 edition was slightly bigger: nine laps to the mile and eighteen feet wide. It was still considerably smaller than the track to which Walthour was accustomed. He took second in the fifth heat of the open mile, failing to reach the final, which was won by Jay Eaton. It was a disappointing debut for Walthour in the largest and most important competition he had ever entered. But it was the first time Bobby's name appeared in the pages of New York newspapers.

Charles Miller, the twenty-three-year-old grocery clerk from Chicago who had accompanied the Walthours on the train from Atlanta, won the main event, conquering 2,093 miles. Miller, a chunky 5-foot-6, 160-pound man with dark brown eyes, was hailed a champion. When he dismounted his bike, he could walk only with difficulty and soon sunk helplessly into a chair while an American flag was dropped into his lap. "Miller! Miller! Miller!" shouted the crowd, unaware that he could barely even wave the flag. Miller had beaten thirty-seven contestants from around the world and had ridden farther than second-place finisher Joseph Rice from Wilkes-Barre, Pennsylvania. For his victory Miller received $1,500 ($40,000 in today's dollars) in cash.[3]

The riders in the six-day race burned a huge number of calories and became haggard during the race. According to his race diary Miller ate "3½ pounds of rice, ½ pound of barley, 1 pound of oatmeal, 4 ounces of beef extract, 60 pints of kumis, 1 orange, 4 dozen apples, 3 pounds of grapes, 6 eggs, 3 quarts of barley broth, 4 quarts of coffee and 9 quarts of milk.[4]

A few days before the following year's race at the Garden, Board of Health president Michael C. Murphy threatened to call on District Attorney Gardiner to prosecute the managers of six-day bicycle races because of the physical ordeal to which the riders were subjected. "I think it is a beastly exhibition, and one that no white man should look upon," Murphy stated. "The suffering of the men as described in the last race was so inhuman that I feel that the authorities ought to step in and prevent it. You cannot call it an exhibition of this kind of sport, when men become crazy on the track."[5] Dr. E. S. Potter retorted that he had examined Miller after the previous year's race and found him in perfect health. Despite Murphy's threats, the six-day race took place as planned.

Thus, in 1898 on the Saturday before the main event, Walthour once again headed north with an invitation to sprint and paced exhibition races. The new track measured ten laps to the mile. Ten thousand noisy New Yorkers packed the building and enjoyed peanuts, popcorn, candy, lemonade, and other refreshments. In the arena below, the track was thick with tobacco smoke, and a brass band played in the center. Walthour fared better than the year before, taking second to Nat Butler in the final heat of the open mile.[6]

Eddie Bald, looking dapper in a frock coat, silk hat, and suede gloves, proudly marked the new era of the A.R.C.U. by firing a pistol to start the six-day race proper. Thirty-one riders from eight countries, including Charles Miller, John "The Terrible Swede" Lawson, Charles Turville from Philadelphia, and Irishman Teddy Hale (the 1896 winner) set off to compete for $3,500 ($93,400) in prize money. Why Walthour did not ride in the six-day race remains a matter of speculation. In those days sprinters were in a different category than long-distance men, and common opinion may have been that a sprinter could not do as well.

After five days racing, Miller had his second consecutive victory well within his grasp, and preparations for the wedding ceremony with his fiancée, Genevieve Hanson, in front of thousands at the Garden were under way. Eddie Bald was the best man, Arthur Gardiner gave away the bride, and Alderman Wentz of Brooklyn performed the ceremony.

Patrick T. Powers, the manager of the race, tried to induce the riders to suspend it for a half hour, but Frank Waller, who was in second place, thirty miles behind Miller, refused. Gardiner, in full dress with a top hat, escorted Miss Hanson down one of the upper aisles to a specially decorated enclosure near the finish line. The pretty Miss Hanson wore a dark, tasteful wedding dress, while the square-jawed Miller waited in the enclosure, calm and collected in his sweaty racing uniform, with bare legs and arms, having already completed 136 hours of racing.

With Waller and other riders continuing the race, Wentz, standing on the edge of the track, began to speak: "Ladies and gentleman, I have been asked to unite Charles W. Miller and Miss Genevieve Hanson, both of Chicago, in marriage. I wish your close attention while the ceremony is being performed, and have been requested by the management to be as expeditious as possible, as Mr. Miller is anxious to return to the track to finish his grand ride."[7]

In riding more than 2,190 miles in six days, Miller received $1,500 for the victory and $200 ($5,340) for breaking his own previous record.

❋

A few months later in January 1899, while Walthour was in New Orleans, preparations were being made for a six-day race at Mechanics Pavilion in San Francisco, which turned out to be the last continuous, individual six-day event held in the United States. The races were notorious for their brutality, and they attracted many rowdy and unsavory fans, some of whose primary objective was to witness the suffering. The February San Francisco contest was perhaps the straw that broke the camel's back: three months later, New York governor Theodore Roosevelt signed the Collins Bill, limiting the length of endurance contests. The piece of legislation stated that no one individual was allowed to ride more than twelve hours in any given day.[8] Although the law applied only to New York State, it soon became the accepted principle throughout the world.

Many of the leading six-day riders, some coming west immediately after the New York race, were at Mechanic's Pavilion in San Francisco, including newlywed Charlie Miller, Irishman Teddy Hale, Louis Gimm from Pittsburg, Burns Pierce of Canada, John "The Terrible Swede" Lawson, and Walthour's friend John Chapman from Atlanta. Miller didn't leave the track until the eighty-first hour of the race, by which time he held a 14-mile lead and had ridden 1,416 miles and 7 laps. Gimm, second to Miller, seized his opportunity and gained miles on Miller.

Eventually Gimm succumbed to fatigue and was forced to rest as well. Leaving the track, he entered his tent and during a brief rest, was apparently drugged. Who drugged him, with what drug, and by what method, remained a matter of rumor, speculation, and intrigue. Some people thought his trainer, Eddie Leonart, was responsible, and others thought some prankster had slipped something secretly into his drink. Gimm spent four months in San Francisco's St. Luke's Hospital but eventually made a full recovery.[9] On February 19, only two months since his New York victory, Charles Miller won the San Francisco race by riding 2,193 miles.[10]

Before the Collins Bill the six-day race at the Garden was always one man against another; only a rider who could endure the rigors of riding six days with minimal sleep could win. The combination of the six-day race and the new restriction left promoters scratching their heads until Patrick

Powers and James Kennedy conceived a brilliant idea. Instead of one-man teams, the great event would have two-man teams.[11] So 1899 was the first year in which the race would have teams of two. And this time, rather than inviting distance specialists only, Powers and Kennedy included sprinters.

Walthour and Jay Eaton were invited and signed up as partners for the event. In October the pair went to Jacksonville to train. In the warm Florida weather, Eaton and Walthour worked out on the track and on the roads in and around Jacksonville. On the track, they practiced "pick-ups" in which a rider ready for rest would signal his partner. The fresh rider would hurry to the track with his cycle and match his teammate's speed. Coming up behind, the new rider tucked in behind the exhausted rider, then came around on the inside and received a friendly shove in the back or pull on the arm from his partner—this was called being "sling-shotted" ahead.

Walthour and Eaton practiced this new art over and over until it was perfected. Walthour told the *Atlanta Journal*: "The new style six-day race will be a great improvement over the manner in which they were formerly run and little or no damage will be done to the riders. Faster times will be made, probably 3,000 miles in the six days and the sport will be much more exciting than before."[12]

Walthour and Eaton arrived in New York as one of the nineteen teams and named their team The Indoor Kings. The great bicycle carnival opened on Saturday, December 2, again under the American Cycle Racing Association. Just shy of his twenty-second birthday, Walthour entered individually in two of the preliminary events: the one-mile open and the one-mile handicap. He won the second heat of the one-mile open but failed to make the final. In the handicap race, he was an also-ran. But he had hopes about a big payday in the main event. In the early hours of Monday morning, thousands arrived at the Garden to see the riders start their long journey around the ten-lap track. Perhaps because of the new law, the arena was not sold out as usual. In past years fans expected brutality, misery, filth, and profanity, but the passage of the Collins Bill may well have dissuaded some rougher spectators from attending the newly tamed sport. Beer was five cents, soft drinks ten cents, and whiskey fifteen cents. The familiar tobacco smoke hung in the air amid the bright electric lights and music from the band, creating a festive atmosphere. Champion boxer James J. Jeffries fired the pistol, sending nineteen riders off, including Walthour. He was not used to so many riders on such a small track, pushing and battling for positions. Before the race was two hours old, Walthour, Frenchman Jean Chevalier, A. J. Peltier of New York, Philadelphian Charles Turville, and Austin B. Stone from Denver met with an accident. Each rider had cuts and bruises, but Chevalier suffered the worst of it with a badly cut head.[13] Four teams quit the race early Monday morning because the pace was too fast.

Most teams adopted the system of riding 2 hours at a stretch, but Walthour and Eaton traded every hour. After 24 hours, Eaton replaced Walthour and caused great excitement by sprinting away from the pack. Eaton succeeded in gaining a full lap and put The Indoor Kings in the lead a lap ahead of The Flying Dutchmen team of Charles Miller and Frank Waller and The Favorites team of Burns Pierce and Louis Gimm. The mileage for the leaders at 2 a.m. on Tuesday was 540 miles and 2 laps.[14]

Eaton and Walthour kept their lead for sixteen hours when another accident for Walthour's team occurred. Frenchman Albert Champion, who had participated in exhibition races but not the six-day race, rode up onto the track to stretch his legs. Champion was much fresher than the pack, and Miller's partner Frank Waller rode up to him, showing the Frenchman that he could hold the quicker pace. The field made a mad dash for Waller and caught him. Waller shrugged his shoulders, sat up, and suddenly slowed down. Eaton plowed into the back of Waller's bicycle. Before Eaton could mount a fresh bicycle, he and Walthour lost four laps. The referee decided the mix-up was not Eaton's fault and gave back three laps to the Walthour-Eaton team. Waller, who by all accounts caused the accident, made a protest and said he would take the case to the courts.

An hour and a half after the incident, Walthour and Eaton had a mix-up of their own and were off the track at the same time—they lost five laps. An hour later at 8:30 p.m., Eaton announced his intention to drop out because of stomach problems. The plucky Walthour was allowed to continue individually but could only ride twelve hours in a day.[15]

After 3 days, 8 teams remained, led by the team of Charles Miller and Frank Waller. Inspired by the presence of his wife, Walthour battled for the $500 individual rider prize money.[16]

Each day, attendance picked up. Some people left the Garden and paid to get back in, and others stayed for the duration. While dozing soundly in his box seat, a spectator named Thomas Martin fell forward to the floor under the track and broke his jaw. Martin's injury caused quite a commotion in the Garden; he was rushed to Bellevue Hospital.[17]

Charles Miller and Frank Waller won the race by riding 2,733 miles and split $1,000 for first place. Waller earned an extra $200 for his third place individual score. Otto Maya and Archie McEachern split $700 second team money, and Louis Gimm and Burns Pierce split the $400 third.

Walthour received first prize for the best individual effort of 1,402 miles, winning $500—the biggest payday of his young life.[18] When the race was finally over, most of the riders, trainers, and managers went to the Turkish baths, followed by a well-deserved sleep at their hotel rooms. Race manager Powers arrived at the Bartholdi Hotel, bringing large bags filled with double eagle twenty-dollar gold pieces.[19]

The next day, the winning riders were introduced one by one to the crowd and received their winnings. Walthour was there with his partner, Jay Eaton. Standing on the podium he looked gaunt but otherwise healthy. The day after, he, Blanche, and little Viva boarded a train for Atlanta, rich beyond their dreams.

{ 7 }

Gentlemen, Start Your Engines

Like many other people attending, the first time Walthour saw a motorized bicycle was at the 1898 six-day race at Madison Square Garden. Henri Fournier had arrived from France with a newly designed tandem bicycle with a gasoline engine mounted on the frame between the two riders. The "motorcycle" was equipped with pedals for the riders (presumably to start its forward motion) and a variety of drive-chains attached to the engine. Supposedly, it could go at a mile a minute, although on a cycling track it recorded no faster than forty-five miles per hour. Even so, this motor tandem was able to go faster than anything except a train. When Fournier started his engine, the crowd howled with delight and surprise; most of them, including Walthour, had never even heard of such a contraption.

One of the featured events before the six-day was Eddie McDuffie riding an exhibition mile, paced by Fournier's new machine. McDuffie followed close behind Fournier's motorcycle through the steeply banked turns. Helped by the slipstream of the motorcycle, McDuffie rode the mile in two minutes nine seconds.[1]

After the six-day main event had started, Fournier brought out his tandem motorcycle each night to pace another "stayer" or paced rider in a one-mile time trial. McDuffie and Fournier had introduced a sensational new aspect of the sport. He paced Arthur Gardiner one night and Harry

Elkes on another. But the riders' wives didn't think it was safe to have exhibition races during the six-day race. It took every ounce of energy and concentration for their husbands simply to keep awake while riding. A four-hundred-pound gasoline-powered pacing machine circling the small track among the riders definitely increased chances of an accident occurring. The big crowd shared a hearty laugh when, on one occasion, the noisy motorcycle pulled away from under its two riders and Fournier ran to catch it.[2] Fortunately no one was hurt.

In the United States and abroad, there was a lot of discussion in cycling circles of the speed possibilities of motor-pacing. Fournier, pacing with his "infernal machine," was a popular attraction at many subsequent races in which Walthour competed. In Europe, the old style of human pacing with multicycles was becoming passé. In Paris in May 1899, a large crowd was thrilled at the big outdoor 666-meter Parc des Princes track when 4 bicyclists were paced by electric tandems. The winner made the 50 kilometers in 57 minutes at a speed of more than 30 miles per hour.[3]

❋

As the 1899 racing season was winding down in late September, Walthour was in eighth place in the national sprint points and had earned $778 ($18,700 in current dollars). But motor-pacing expert Harry Elkes had earned nearly twice as much as any other cyclist, having earned $4,340 ($116,000), and Elkes's prize money was an obvious enticement to sprinters to switch to paced racing.[4]

By October Walthour was home in Atlanta, preparing for the Georgia State Fair races on a six-lap dirt track that was under the management of Eli Winesett. Winesett had plans for many of the best riders to come south, including brothers John and Iver Lawson, John Chapman, Jay Eaton, and Charles Miller. Motor-pacing, a special feature not seen in Atlanta before, was advertised as the main attraction of the cycle race meetings. John Lawson shipped his motorcycle from Salt Lake City, and F. Ed Spooner, secretary of the A.R.C.U., informed Winesett by telegram that he would bring three more gas-powered pacing machines from Nashville.[5]

Bobby Walthour and Eli Winesett gave Gus Castle $500 ($13,300) to arrange the purchase of an Orient tandem motorcycle manufactured in

Waltham, Massachusetts. Walthour and Winesett's motorcycle was the first to reach Georgia. The machine, ordered from Henry Thornton of the Orient factory, was the same make and model that paced Major Taylor to a mile in 1 minute 22 seconds and Eddie McDuffie to 5 miles in 7 minutes 38 seconds. Both times were new world records behind pace.[6] "I will name the new motor pacing machine after the great sea-fighter," said Walthour, referring to Admiral George Dewey. "I am going to call it Dewey and I expect to carry it to New York in December for the racing carnival."[7]

When the Dewey arrived in Atlanta, Walthour and several well-known riders and trainers crammed into the Southern Express Company's office to feast their eyes on the newfangled machine. Christmas had come early. They opened the crates and saw the new motorcycle gleaming with red enamel paint. The spokes were as thick as pencils, the black metal tubing was broader than that of a bicycle, and the tandem came equipped with seven sprocket wheels, four chains, and "cans and motors attached to the frame."[8] Nobody knew what parts went where, especially Walthour, but it certainly was impressive. Between the assemblers and the manufacturer, telegraphs went back and forth from Atlanta to Waltham until the Dewey was ready. It was cleared to go only the day before the scheduled race against Charles Miller on October 19. A dozen men stood gawking at the new prize; when the engine finally ignited, the men were overjoyed.

Walthour and Miller had an impromptu training race in the gathering darkness paced by the noisy machines. Neither human being nor animal had ever heard such a sound in Atlanta. Only an occasional thunderclap could be heard above the terrific racket. Exhilarated by the noise and speed, the riders paid no attention to the falling rain. Walthour caught Miller and his pacer and sprinted past, and fans at the side of the track yelled themselves hoarse. An excited Walthour declared that he wanted to enter into the motor-paced ranks.[9]

At the race itself, Eli Winesett announced Miller and Walthour to the crowd, and they both received enthusiastic ovations. When the starter's gun cracked, a Mexican band began to play, although the music was heard only with difficulty over the roar of the motorcycles. The crowd was excited to see and hear the sputtering gasoline machines. No one was ahead until the last few miles when Miller, slightly behind, began gaining on Walthour. Something was wrong with Walthour's pacing machine, and with three laps left Miller was within twenty yards of catching him. Walthour realized he had no chance to win following the failing motorcycle, and so he broke away on his own. Miller was slow to react. He had not expected Walthour to leave his protective draft and to start his sprint with a half mile still to go. If Miller kept behind his pace, he would lose the race, and so Miller started his sprint too. Walthour tired; Miller caught and passed him by inches at the finish. Though the hometown kid didn't win, spectators agreed that it was the best and most exciting race the South ever had.[10] Atlanta was in love with motorcycles.

The following day, thousands of fans returned, anxious to see Walthour and Jay Eaton race behind the motors for another fifteen-mile race. Walthour's tandem was ridden by Frank Waller and W. F. Stafford, and after the third mile, though nothing was wrong with the motor this time, Walthour sprinted past his motorcycle as he had done the previous night. This time he broke away too early. Eaton urged his motor tandem on, and they gradually caught the unprotected rider. For Walthour the race was lost, yet he fought gamely on to within a half lap. Blanche and little Viva were in the stands near the finish line and cheered wildly with the rest of the crowd. Whether Walthour won or lost, he put up his best fighting effort.[11]

On October 22, the motor-paced races took place at the half-mile dirt track at Exhibition Park in Atlanta, which was rolled and scraped as smooth as marble, the way it had been when Jack Prince raced his bicycle against a trotting horse five years earlier. Even though Walthour did not race that day, six thousand people made a rush for the track. "I never in my life saw anything with the real drawing power of these motor machines," said Georgia Fair Secretary Martin. "Every man, woman and child in the ground made a run for the half-mile track when their choo-chooing was heard."[12]

Walthour hoped to take revenge on Eaton in Birmingham, Alabama. The pacing tandems left the track after the sixth lap, and the two fought it out alone for the last quarter mile. Walthour's sprint beat Eaton by a mere eight inches. Walthour also won in Jacksonville, Florida, beating Eaton on November 12 at the cement three-lap Panama track. He rode the first 5 miles at 9 minutes 6 seconds, 2 seconds ahead of Eaton. Then he rode the next 5 miles in a scorching 8 minutes 7 seconds, more than 35 miles per hour. He finished the total 15 miles in 26 minutes 49⅗ seconds and set track records behind pace for 5, 10, and 15 miles.[13]

The pacing motorcycles brought a new element of danger to cycling, a sport that was already dangerous enough. Before Fournier's motorcycle in July 1897, in his second year as a professional, Walthour had been training inside the Piedmont coliseum with several local riders to avoid the heat in Atlanta. During the workout Walthour and an amateur rider, Brooks Kline, entered into a speed contest, lapping the track at thirty miles per hour, each paced by two strong men on tandems. On the last lap the tandems pulled off to one side. Walthour began to sprint for the finish, and Kline went with him. As they rode up and around the last banking before the home stretch, Walthour's inside pedal struck the track, and he nearly lost control of his bicycle. Right behind Kline rammed into Walthour's rear wheel and flew over his handlebars off the track toward a window above the banking.[14]

Kline's right arm and head crashed through the glass, and his body was suspended from the window for several seconds before he fell in a heap to the floor. Riders rushed to his aid, fearing that he had been killed. They carried Kline to the dressing room to wait for a Grady Hospital ambulance. The timer, Mr. Thompson, recalled, "We did everything possible for Kline until the physicians arrived, but we were afraid that he was going to bleed to death. I never saw a man bleed like he did, before in my life."[15] Kline survived his injuries, but it was a scene Walthour did not easily forget.

By 1900 human-powered multicycles had been replaced by the gasoline-powered motorcycles. Their added power, as well as the growing experience of professionals like Walthour, made the game faster and more dangerous. By the beginning of the 1900 season, tracks all over the United States opened by including the high-speed excitement of motorpacing.

The outdoor track at Waltham, Massachusetts, opened May 30, and Jimmy Michael was there. He warmed up the Waltham audience with a five-mile exhibition behind a motor tandem, and the ten thousand fans stood and cheered for him. The main attraction was a twenty-mile race with four riders, each behind his own newfangled motor tandem. The crowd stood up as the riders readied themselves. Toeing the line were Albert Champion (France), Archie McEachern (Toronto), Everett Ryan (a local cyclist from Waltham), and William Stinson (Cambridge, Massachusetts). Pacing Stinson's tandem were Harry Miles of Lynn, Massachusetts, and William Stafford from Cambridgeport, Massachusetts.

Shortly after the first mile, Stinson made a bid for the front by sprinting after his tandem on the backstretch. When he reached the turn, Stinson's speed took him up to the top of the banking. At that moment witnesses claimed that Champion looked around, causing him to touch wheels with the rear tire of his own pacing tandem. Champion was sent flying. Luckily he rolled safely from the top of the track to the grass on the inside.

At the time when Champion fell, the motorcycles were crowded nearly side by side. Miles, who was steering Stinson's tandem in an attempt to avoid running over Champion, went up the embankment toward a picket fence surrounding the outer edge of the track. Miles did not realize a telegraph pole was directly in his path. He crashed into the pole and dropped to the ground while his fellow tandem rider Stafford was catapulted into the air. Stafford's head and shoulders were driven through a picket fence. From the crowd, hundreds rushed to the scene and gently pulled Stafford and Miles from the wreckage. Blood gushed from the ears and mouths of both riders. Miles died at the scene and Stafford a few hours later. Several people in the crowd near the telegraph pole were injured, one with two broken hips and others with broken legs.[16]

Miles was to have been married on June 13, and his young fiancée, May Nolan, was in the crowd. Stafford had paced Walthour in the South seven months before the tragedy and had crashed on a tandem in that race, after he had correctly predicted that someday he would be killed pacing.[17]

In spite of the unfolding calamity, the race did not stop. McEachern and Ryan forged ahead after Champion was pitched off, and Stinson continued without pace. At fifteen miles, McEachern was a lap ahead of Ryan, his nearest competitor, and finished the twenty miles in thirty-five minutes forty-two seconds.[18]

The Waltham track was perhaps the first in the world to have motor-paced fatalities and quite possibly the first motorcycle fatalities in the United States. A few days later, with Miles's and Stafford's blood hardly washed from the track surface, riders were again racing at the Waltham track. Promoters, track owners, and professional riders felt obligated to supply the excitement the public craved, and they were not about to let a few fatalities hold them up.

{ 8 }

Twentieth Century Fox

In spite of his stated ambition to pursue motor-pacing even after the Waltham tragedies, Bobby Walthour devoted his 1900 professional season to sprinting. Like most sprinting professionals, he joined the N.C.A.'s circuit to earn the most money and accumulate points toward the national sprint championship title. Walthour raced on the best tracks in the country, which were primarily in the northeast. Although his season was successful, he did not garner the respect he probably deserved. The *New York Times* spelled his name many different ways that summer, including "Waltham," "Walthouse," and "Walthauer." He raced against the best cyclists in the United States including Tom Cooper, Orlando Stevens, Floyd MacFarland, Jay Eaton, Frank Kramer, and Major Taylor.[1] By early September Walthour had won more than $700 ($18,400 in today's dollars) on the circuit.[2]

In 1900 Frank Kramer and Major Taylor battled for the coveted U.S. professional sprint title. On August 19 Taylor led his rival Kramer twelve points to ten while Walthour lingered in a tie for sixth place with two points he picked up in New Haven, Connecticut.

Marshall "Major" Taylor was eleven months younger than Walthour. Five feet eight inches tall, Taylor was shorter than most of the other sprinters. But his superb athleticism and impeccable bike handling skills made him one of the fastest in the game. Taylor, a black man, had muscled his way into the sport against intense racist opposition. His early success paved the way for other professional black cyclists of the era including R. A. Brooks, Woody Hedspeth, and Melvin Dove.

By 1900 Taylor was much sought after, and a persuasive European promoter offered him $10,000 ($264,000) in guaranteed appearance fees plus prize money to go to Paris. In the United States, Taylor was subjected to routine, blatant racism, and he hoped things would be different in Europe. But if he raced overseas, promoters would require him to race on Sunday. Taylor was a religious man and strictly opposed to Sunday racing. And since Taylor was able to negotiate with the A.R.C.U. to race on N.C.A. tracks for 1900, he chose to stay home and fight for the U.S. championship. Major Taylor made history that year, beating out his white rival, Frank Kramer, for the U.S. national title.

❀

With the 1900 season over in the fall, some of the best professional riders shifted gears in preparation for the six-day endurance race at Madison Square Garden. Walthour's season wasn't particularly noteworthy. Even so, Charles Miller, the champion six-day rider at the Garden for three years running (twice individually and once with Frank Waller in the first two-man event), was impressed with him. Miller handpicked Walthour as his six-day partner for the December race. With Walthour's sprinting ability and Miller's winning record at the Garden and his famed endurance, the pair was a favorite. Other top teams included paced star Harry Elkes and Floyd MacFarland, who had recently arrived from racing in France; Canadian team Burns Pierce of Nova Scotia and Archie McEachern of Toronto; and French team Caesar Simar and Jean Gougoltz.

The ten-lap Garden track was constructed with higher and steeper banking than in previous years. The young spectators in the galleries swarmed the building at early hours while the 65th Regiment Band played up-tempo numbers. In the arena below, dozens of trainers in sweaters and golf caps argued over spots for the best location for their teams at the side of the track. As the arena began to fill with tobacco smoke, visibility became more and more difficult for those above to see the track down below.

As the *New York Times* reported, "Far up in the lofty gallery on the Fourth Avenue side of the hall a dozen demonstratively enthusiastic boys stirred up spasms of interest in the progress of preparation at irregular intervals by that peculiar cheering in imitation of the approved style of the college yell, their efforts never failing to impress the remainder of the crowd with the belief that something of the moment was on. 'We're here for the week,' screamed one of the lads, and the ostentatious display of packages of food and the arrangement of benches for sleeping purposes appeared to confirm his announcement."[3]

Walthour had never been in the spotlight like this—on the favored team in the most celebrated bike race in the United States, if not the world. Shortly before midnight on Sunday, December 9, the seventeen brightly dressed riders assembled on the 27th Street side of the track. One by one, teams were introduced to the crowd of six thousand, and each team rode a lap of honor. Walthour and Miller circled the track carrying Old Glory before the band played the national anthem.

From the crack of the starter's pistol, Walthour, MacFarland, and Simar rode off their nervous energy and set a blistering pace to start the long grind. Miraculously the three gained a lap on the field after just ten minutes. Walthour had put his team in the lead, and Miller came out in relief of his partner. But rather than keeping a strong steady gait, Miller struggled to keep up with the pack. Walthour was forced to come back in. At the side of the track Miller was doubled over with stomach pain.

Hours went by before Miller came out to replace Walthour. Almost immediately, Miller was in trouble and lost the lap Walthour had worked so hard to gain. Then he lost another. Before the race was seven hours old, Miller was forced to quit. Walthour became a fan favorite by single-handedly putting his team into the lead, but that year the race managers at the Garden had decided not to allow riders to race individually if their partners became sick or injured. So, unfortunately, Walthour was out.[4]

The race to ride the farthest in the 144-hour contest continued on with all its zaniness. In the mornings when he was not riding, Frank Waller dressed in a business suit, smoked cigars at the side of track, and drank whiskey and Bass Ale. Another rider, Jean Fischer, appeared on the race track wearing a gigantic black wig. When he was not riding, Fischer also helped Pons, a well-known champion wrestler, finish off a bottle of champagne at the side of the track. Jimmy Michael, with newly crowned American Sprint Champion Major Taylor, dazzled the crowd with exhibition rides behind motor-pace.

Taylor also took the role of spectator and sauntered around, perhaps happy that he did not have to subject himself to the tortures he once endured on the Garden's track. Taylor's first race as a professional had been the 1896 six-day race at the Garden.[5] He declined to give his expert opinion on a probable winner, but he told a *New York Times* reporter, "It's a fearfully hot pace but all the men are in very good condition, and, having passed the second day, they all appear fit to continue to the end."[6]

A crowd of 15,000 cycle-crazed fans watched as the team of Harry Elkes and Floyd MacFarland won the race. The pair missed the mark set the year before by Charles Miller and Frank Waller, but they rode an impressive 2,628 miles and 7 laps, each of them covering more than 200 miles per day. They shared the purse of $1,500 ($39,500). After the race MacFarland said, "Never again for me. They said I would quit. Well I didn't. I suffered a lot and I don't want any more of it. I will be satisfied with short-distance races and handicaps in the future. We won the race because Elkes was my partner."[7]

❁

Within weeks after the six-day ended, Boston hosted its own six-day race. This inaugural race at Park Square Garden was a celebration for the new century, ushering in 1901 and was called the Twentieth Century Race. Walthour was one of nineteen riders to compete in an impressive field that included Jean Gougoltz, Archie McEachern, Louis Gimm, Will Stinson, and Frank Waller.

Madison Square Garden hosted the traditional six-day race of 144 straight hours, but Boston's event had different rules. To avoid any cyclist staying in the saddle more than 12 hours in a day—and thereby breaking the law enacted by the Collins Bill—the 19 starters were to race individually 10 hours per day. From 1 p.m. to 6 p.m. they were to ride, take an hour break, and then ride another 5 hours from 7 p.m. until midnight.[8]

The race started on Monday, December 31. About half an hour before each five-hour round ended, riders picked up the pace considerably. Riders in front looked over their shoulders, and those at the rear craned their necks to make sure nobody would break away from the front. In the last minutes, they rose out of their saddles and struggled mightily for the finish. But unless a precious lap had been gained during the five hours, a win did not mean much. Walthour kept mental notes as to who had a good top-end speed and who was the fittest of the bunch.

The next five-hour round of the first day ended as the New Year and the new century began. The early afternoon crowd grew from 3,000 people to an overflowing 10,000 cycle-mad fans, rivaling New York with its craziness and the thick haze of tobacco smoke. Fifteen minutes before the clock struck midnight, the biggest New Year's Eve party in Boston celebrated wildly as the big pack of riders whirled on at high speed. The crowd counted down from 60 seconds and then 10, 9, 8, and Walthour summoned a power within him, electrified by the cheering, and went into the lead like a man possessed. The noise shook the building to its foundations and the atmosphere escalated into an implausible frenzy. Walthour crossed the finish in first place, a wheel ahead of the local boy Will Stinson and Frenchman Jean Gougoltz. But since he had not succeeded in lapping anyone, Walthour was tied for first place with 8 others at 210 miles and 3 laps. He still had a long way to go for overall victory. Walthour crossed the finish on January 1; it was his twenty-third birthday.

The pace slowed considerably the second evening, and Walthour remained tied for first place with six other riders at three hundred miles and six laps. On the third night he decided to take matters into his own hands. He sprinted powerfully down the backstretch and quickly put sixty yards between himself and the field. The crowd rose to its feet, and the other riders chased after him like dogs on a foxhunt, led by Archie McEachern. After two laps, Walthour was reeled in, and everyone slowed down to catch their breath.

Just as the crowd was about to be lulled to sleep by the monotonous pace of the pack, they were surprised by the revving motor of Harry Elkes's big German-made pacing tandem. As the riders continued around the inside of the track in the form of a time out, Elkes caught up to his gas-guzzling machine and rode an exhibition mile so close behind his motorcycle that it looked like he was being pulled along. Elkes covered the mile in one minute forty-two seconds, thrilling the crowd with his breathtaking speed.

On the fourth night, McEachern, who wore the Canadian Union Jack around his waist, had his flag come undone and almost caught in his chain. He made several unsuccessful attempts to tie it back around his waist while riding but gave up when the pace livened up. Eventually, McEachern managed to put the flag around his neck and tied a knot with the aid of his teeth.

On the fifth day, the riders continued their slow pace. They knew that if one rider attempted to break away to steal a lap, the pace would heat up considerably. The most drama occurred when Frenchman Albert Champion arrived on the scene and rode behind his roaring motorcycle while wearing a white silk racing suit. Champion had broken his arm in a recent track accident, and it had not been set correctly, but ignoring the injury, the daredevil went around and around, shooting up and down the bank at a terrific speed. He rode one mile in one minute thirty-seven seconds, beating Elkes's time by five seconds and averaging almost forty miles per hour on the tiny track.[9] The riders cheered Champion during the brief time out and were grateful for the rest.

Ten thousand people packed the arena for the sixth and final day. In preparation for the final five-hour stretch, most riders dressed in clean racing uniforms. Jean Fischer wore a pair of purple tights under white tights with black socks coming halfway to his knees. Karl Kaser was dressed in a European racing suit of maroon, gold, and black. The man from Toronto, Archie McEachern, wore a red, white, and blue suit with his Union Jack, this time carefully tied around his waist.

The riders took off and continued at a steady pace. The stadium was filled to capacity with no seats available; a continuous stream of people circulated in the standing-room-only area down on the floor called the pen from where action on the track was almost impossible to see. Hinting that something would happen soon, Walthour quickly exchanged his "plugging" bicycle for one better suited for a specialized sprinting with dropped handlebars, a raised seat, and a larger gear.

With an hour to go until the finish, Babcock and Muller, the eighth and ninth place riders, were called off the track and given a nice round of applause. The seven remaining cyclists gained a little more space to fight it out. All but Fischer and Kaser had changed to their sprinting bikes, and around and around the wooden oval they all went, strung out in a long line of leg-churning rivals going up and down the steep embankment.

After 60 hours of racing, the 7 riders tied for first place had traveled 1,098 miles. The race halted momentarily in preparation for the final 1-mile sprint that would determine the first through seventh placings.

All ten thousand men women and children were on their feet at the gun. Kaser took the lead, with McEachern second, Walthour third, Stinson fourth, McLean fifth, Downey sixth, and Fischer last. Kaser kept the lead until three laps from the finish, when Fischer came around the field on the inside. The riders engaged in a desperate high-speed fight for position before McEachern swung out and passed Fischer. Walthour stayed right on the Canadian's rear wheel. The packed throng became a surging mass of waving arms amid the chaotic noise. McEachern and Walthour tore around the track, closely followed by Stinson and the rest of the bunch. The riders rose out of their saddles, pushing their bikes violently from side to side. Walthour turned loose a fury of speed, and despite the strongest efforts from McEachern, he passed the Canadian in a dramatic surge of speed and won. Stinson, entering the home stretch, also passed McEachern so that the two Americans won first and second money, while the Canadian came in third. Hugh McLean came next with Fischer on his rear wheel. The last half mile was timed at one minute three seconds— nearly thirty miles per hour.

The next day Walthour was $750 ($19,800) richer and eager to reach Atlanta to see his wife and their new baby daughter, Nona. He made more money in six days than during the entire season up to that point. He also made headline news across the United States—and this time his name was not misspelled. For his great effort he was crowned as the individual sixty-hour champion of six-day racing. In his southern drawl, he told the *Boston Daily Globe* that he figured out how to win by sprinting at the end of each five-hour session. Like a wily poker player, he had learned to outfox his opponents, searching for their strengths and weaknesses.[10]

{ 9 }

Cold Start, Big Money

With his victory in the Twentieth Century six-day race in Boston, Walthour had established himself among the elite riders of the United States. Several trainers and managers were interested in shaping his future. Walthour could not say no.

One man he hired was Tom Eck, a Canadian who had trained some of the best cyclists in America: John Johnson of Minneapolis, for example, as well as Jimmy Michael, the "Welsh Midget." Four years earlier Michael was the reigning world and French paced champion. Eck had convinced him to leave Europe and compete in the United States. Eck had been an exceptional athlete himself. Growing up in Prince Albert, he attracted notice as a cricket player, a lacrosse star, and an accomplished ice skater. When Eck was 17, he ran a quarter mile in 52.4 seconds, a remarkable time even today. His professional athletic career began as a jockey, and he later drove harness horses. After that Eck became involved in high-wheeled cycling and competed against the best professionals, including Jack Prince. In 1886 he became the first cyclist to ride 100 miles in under 6 hours.[1]

By the time Walthour began training with him in 1901, Eck was forty-three and well past his athletic prime, a frail-looking man with a droopy white mustache. He wore a straw boater that covered his white hair. Yet

Eck was younger than he looked, and he fooled people with his seemingly unusual vigor.

Walthour went south to train with Eck at Panama Park, a three-lap-to-the-mile cement track in Jacksonville, Florida. There he met a number of other stars who were working with him, including Harry Elkes—the pencil-thin American motor-paced title holder—and Jimmy Michael.

In Florida Walthour also was represented by Al Smith and Dave Coburn, two little-known managers. Smith paid the bills and arranged Walthour's 1901 season schedule. But Coburn, like Eck, was under the impression *he* was to train Walthour, and suddenly there were too many cooks in the Florida kitchen. Was it a simple misunderstanding? Was there a nudge-nudge, wink-wink promise that had gone astray? Regardless of the reason, Walthour summarily dumped both Smith and Coburn. As a result, he was called up before the N.C.A. Board of Control to explain why he had broken his supposed contract with the two. But the N.C.A. ruled in Walthour's favor and allowed him to train and be managed under the exclusive guidance of Tom Eck.[2]

"Camp Eck" hummed and buzzed like a baseball team in spring training; success could only come from a willingness to prepare. Eck supervised closely, making sure that kinks were worked out and legs were limbered. When the cyclists' muscles grew sore, they received massages; when the riders crashed, they were properly bandaged. Eck tested different bicycles and equipment and ensured that tire pressure was consistent, carburetors were adjusted, and gas tanks were filled. He kept his three star pupils busy walking, running, shadowboxing, and eating well. He also made sure they spent a proper amount of time sleeping.

And there was also, of course, the riding. Distance rides to the countryside, lung-burning sprints on the track, and everything in between. Walthour, Michael, and Elkes practiced behind the big, coughing gasoline-powered motor tandems in the warm Florida sunshine. Eck wanted them fit enough to ride forty miles in an hour, which was no easy task. Danger lurked in their workouts, and the riders had to trust the men controlling the machines moving inches in front of them. Without that bond a rider could easily lose his nerve. If the narrow front tire of the bike touched the rear tire of the motorcycle tandem, the rider could be sent flying and land on the unforgiving hot cement—an experience not unlike jumping out of a car at forty miles per hour.

When the riders were not busy training, they were mapping out schedules and negotiating with track promoters for potentially handsome paydays. Train tickets had to be purchased, hotel accommodations booked, and bicycle and motorcycle equipment shipped. Communication was sent off and received by letter, cable, and telephone.

Frank Caldwell, a professional rider from Hartford, Connecticut, trained briefly with Eck and the others in Jacksonville. In a letter to his friend Archie McEachern, the Canadian who lost to Walthour at the Boston six-day race, Caldwell predicted that Walthour would do well on April 19, Patriot's Day—the season opener at Charles River track in Boston. McEachern wrote a letter of his own to the *Boston Globe* and scoffed at Walthour's predicament of having too many managers. Like many riders of the day, McEachern preferred to manage his own affairs without the benefit of high-priced coaching.[3]

Eck, Elkes, and Walthour traveled from Florida to Boston by boat. On the trip north, Elkes and Walthour entertained themselves with a two-foot-long Okeetee corn snake. Growing up in Georgia, Walthour probably had seen many of these beautifully colored orange reptiles with their deep red blotches, each blotch surrounded by a distinct black border. Like a pair of school kids taking their revenge, the two riders tortured Eck with their adopted pet, as he had tortured them with his impossible workouts.

In Boston everyone helped carry heavy trunks down off the boat. The mechanics hastily unpacked wrenches and other tools and adjusted the bicycles to rider specifications. Eager helpers wheeled the big motor tandems down the ramp in preparation for the afternoon workout.

Hundreds of curious people came out to watch Walthour, Elkes, and William Stinson practice at the Charles River track. Stinson, a local professional motor-pacer who was entered in the April 19 race with Walthour, was a dark-haired, bulky man who had braved the Boston cold all winter and spring, preferring to workout on the icy banks of the Charles River track. Although he was to race Walthour in a few days, Stinson was eager to show his mettle. A rivalry began to develop between the two. But Eck preferred to wait until the official race on Patriot's Day and disappointed the local railbirds by pulling Walthour and his pacing tandem off the track.[4]

Seven thousand fans turned out at Charles River to watch the much-anticipated twenty-five-mile race behind the tandem motors. Walthour, Stinson, and Johnny Nelson from Chicago—who was even shorter than the diminutive Jimmy Michael—took their places at the starting line. The six motorcycle pacers lined up the three tandems side by side one hundred feet or so behind the riders and revved up their four-horsepower, air-cooled motors. When the starting gun was fired, Walthour, Stinson, and Nelson began rolling with a shove from their handlers. They pedaled their big fixed-geared bikes slowly at first, steadily increasing speed. The motorcyclists quickly caught up to the cyclists and rolled up alongside them, each tandem matching the speed of its racer. Then at just the right moment, the cyclists tucked into the slipstream behind the big machines. After three-quarters of a lap, the motorcycles were traveling at nearly full speed of forty miles per hour, with the three bicycles hard on their rear tires. The crowd stood up in unison as the noisy cavalcade roared by the grandstand.

Walthour, the odds-on favorite, was riding comfortably a few inches behind the pace of his tandem team. But as the laps were reeled off, his gloveless hands turned purplish-red from the frigid winds, then his feet, then his face. By the tenth mile his whole body had turned into a rigid mass of shivering gooseflesh instead of a warm and fluid leg-pumping machine. Walthour watched helplessly as Stinson lapped him. Nelson, who had trained in the warm California sun that spring but was used to the Chicago cold, lapped him as well. The southerner could not wait for the inauspicious start to his 1901 season to end so he could return to the warmth of the locker room.

❉

Fortunately for Walthour, the season turned brighter—and warmer. He scored a series of impressive victories—including one over Frank Kramer, the nation's best short-distance rider, in a sprint.

As a result of these successes, Walthour was offered the chance to race against Nat Butler and Jimmy Moran, considered two of the best motor-paced riders in the country at the time. The race was an hour long behind tandems at the open-air stadium in Revere, an eight-lap-to-the-mile track a few miles northeast of the Charles River. Walthour would be facing a pair of hometown favorites: Butler's hometown was Boston, and Moran, nicknamed "The Milkman" because of the milk business he started with his brothers, grew up in nearby Chelsea.

On race day, June 17, the grandstands around the new wooden Revere track were packed to overflowing. Walthour's motorcycle tandem included Zenus Fields, who had been the best man at his wedding and who was up front steering, and big Eli Winesett, who sat in the rear and could lean way back and give Walthour plenty of draft protection. Walthour drew the pole position on the inside, with Butler in the middle and Moran on the outside. Walthour took the lead quickly and accelerated to 40 miles per hour. As the bulky mass of motor tandems, bicycles, and men circled the track, the structural integrity of the 220-yard oval was put to the test. Its designer claimed that the track, with its 40-degree banking, could be circled safely at a speed of 45 miles an hour.[5] But how could he account for the massive force of weight going round his track? Perhaps the track designer was in attendance, praying that it did not give way under the stresses. Every time the big machines thundered past the grandstands, belching exhaust fumes, the spectators felt the vibrations ripple through the strained structure.

Butler ran into early mechanical problems and was lapped repeatedly. After ten miles, the race had turned into a two-man contest between Walthour and Moran. Walthour held a narrow lead after fifteen miles, but by the twenty-mile mark he had opened up what appeared to be an insurmountable three-lap lead over Moran. Fortune intervened for Moran when a tire on Fields and Winesett's tandem went flat. Walthour's pacers continued for several miles on a dangerous and bumpy ride as Moran shortened the gap on Walthour. In a show of good sportsmanship, Butler's spare motor tandem was summoned and picked up Walthour and paced him the rest of the way. Even with this piece of good luck, more trouble was on the way. Walthour's front tire punctured near the end of the race. Yet like his mates on the tandem, he continued riding. For the last mile he was barely able to keep his wobbling mount upright, but he managed to hold off a hard-charging Moran to win by a mere one hundred yards. Walthour averaged almost thirty-seven miles per hour—a new Revere track record.[6] Moran's desperate effort to take an early lead may have doomed him. As the *Boston Daily Globe* put it, "The milkman was all in and the pace he thought would kill off Walthour had killed himself."

A week later the big three-lap-to-the-mile Manhattan Beach track opened the racing season in New York. Sultry summer weather sent people flocking to the beach, and many found their way to the race track. More than six thousand were in attendance to see the seven riders, each paced by his own motor tandem. The twenty-five-mile race was announced as the most dramatic motor-paced competition ever to be seen on American soil, and certainly the noisiest too. The seven starters were Walthour, Archie McEachern, Frank Caldwell, Nat Butler, Jimmy Michael, Burns Pierce, and Freddie Hoyt.

As the cyclists raced around the sharply banked wooden track, tucked in behind their roaring motor tandems, the fans rose in unison and cheered at critical moments. Strong winds blew sand from the nearby beach across the track and pelted the riders in the face. By the second mile with a cool wind howling down the backstretch, Walthour took the lead, followed by Michael in second and McEachern in third. Michael and Walthour steadily left the rest of the field behind. Michael attempted to pass Walthour several times but failed, and the frustration began to show on his face and body. Every time he moved in close to Walthour, the crowd rose to its feet. The little man from Wales finally managed to overtake his American rival in the nineteenth mile. Walthour countered with several unsuccessful charges in an effort to retake the lead. Finally, in mile twenty-two, he sliced straight into the wind and passed Michael. He hung on to win, and the crowd erupted in a wild celebration.[7]

Walthour left Manhattan Beach $600 richer ($15,600 in today's dollars)—more money than the average American worker earned in an entire year. After his disastrous start at Charles River on April 19, in less than three months Walthour had earned a remarkable $5,300 ($138,000)—more than any other American cyclist. Johnny Nelson was second with $4,465 ($116,000), and Will Stinson was third with $4,450 (also around $116,000). Walthour's winnings came from both sprint races and motor-paced races, while Nelson and Stinson rode exclusively behind the motors. Nelson stood in first in the standings among the motor-pacers for the American motor-paced championship with fifty-six points and was well poised to defend his previous year's title. Stinson was second with forty-seven, and Walthour was third with forty. The points awarded by the N.C.A. were based on the number of first place wins, second places, and third places. The importance of the races—and thus the amount of points at individual races—was predetermined by officials at the N.C.A. Board of Control.[8]

The next big event on the cycling calendar was the Golden Wheel six-day race at the Charles River cement track that was scheduled for Monday, July 1. Walthour was entered, along with Jimmy Moran, Johnny Nelson, Frenchman Albert Champion, and Will Stinson. Each night, the riders were to follow motor-tandem pace for two hours. On the first night, Walthour was leading the field at forty-two miles when he unceremoniously pulled off the track and quit. Walthour claimed he could not handle the longer distances. But, as it turned out, he had an ulterior motive. He wanted to race at Manhattan Beach the following Saturday, where he had the opportunity to win $1,000 ($260,000). If he had continued with the Golden Wheel six-day, there would have been a conflict. A. G. Batchelder, the chairman of the N.C.A. Board of Control, did not take kindly to the deception. He telephoned Walthour and suspended him for one week, thus preventing him from racing at Manhattan Beach and possibly cashing in on another big payday.[9]

Walthour's scheduling shenanigans may have been his own idea, but Eck may have pushed him. In either case, twice in five months Walthour had drawn trouble with the N.C.A. and had been publicly rebuked. Evidently, something was not going well between Walthour and his white-haired coach. The two severed their relationship in August.

{10}

At the Edge of the Garden

a t the dawn of the twentieth century, professional bicycle racing in America was more popular than ever—thanks in large part to the high-speed excitement of motor-pacing. The most profitable tracks in the country at the time were Manhattan Beach in New York, Charles River in Boston, and Vailsburg in Newark, New Jersey. Other tracks in Baltimore; Washington, D.C.; Springfield; Providence; Buffalo; Philadelphia; Hartford; and Salt Lake City also played host to races that routinely attracted thousands of spectators. The New York six-day race held in December 1900 was one of the most successful bicycle races in the history of Madison Square Garden. That event, won by the team of Floyd MacFarland and Harry Elkes, attracted more than sixty thousand spectators and receipts totaling $40,000 (currently around $1,050,000), according to race manager James Kennedy.[1]

After MacFarland's dramatic victory at the Garden, Patrick T. Powers, president of the Eastern Baseball League, saw an opportunity to cash in on cycling's extraordinary popularity. Powers, a rotund, balding, round-faced man, offered $1,000 ($26,000) to anyone in the world who could beat MacFarland, the lanky cyclist from San Jose, in a motor-paced race of any distance between ten and twenty-five miles. The obvious choice for MacFarland's opponent was Johnny Nelson, who was leading the fiercely fought battle for motor-paced champion in 1901. The two men agreed to square off in a fifteen-mile race on June 24, 1901, at Madison Square Garden.

The Garden usually promoted only one cycling event a year—the big six-day race in December—but Powers persuaded the Garden's management not only to host the additional event but also to build a new 10-lap-to-the-mile track. The new track was the same small size within the Garden's available footprint—only 176 yards long—but it had unusually steep banks that were designed to sustain speeds of 40 miles per hour or more. In the days leading up to the event, MacFarland and Nelson tested the limits of the new track, both with and without pace from the big motor tandems. On race day the capacity crowd pouring into the Garden could smell the burned oil and exhaust from the training rides. Fans excitedly pointed to the tire marks high up the banking made by the motorcycles during their training runs.

Even before the race began, the atmosphere inside the Garden was electric. There was a palpable sense that something would go wrong. As MacFarland and Nelson and their tandems climbed up and plunged down the banking, the spectators sat on the edge of their seats waiting.

Rounding into the fourth lap of the thirteenth mile, MacFarland's 400-pound tandem slipped out from under its riders and hit the track with a deep thud. Shards of pine splinters flew high in the air, and twisted metal parts scattered. Grooves were cut into the wood as the motorcycle careened down the embankment. The tandem riders, with their heavy boots and thick sweaters, spun safely away from the wreckage. But Mac-Farland was so close to the machine he had no time to react. He went headlong into the unforgiving mechanical mess. His left cheekbone was crushed, and his upper lip was split open. He lay unconscious next to the smoking debris. Nelson was close behind MacFarland at the time of the accident, and he followed into the mess and fell, narrowly avoiding Mac-Farland. Track attendants rushed to aid the unconscious rider; Nelson was able to get up and continue. While holding a handkerchief to his bleeding face, Nelson managed three more laps before he was declared the winner by default because MacFarland could not continue.[2]

Both MacFarland and Nelson survived the incident, but it served as a dramatic reminder to them and to other motor-pacers about the dangers of their sport. But accidents were not the only risk. A doctor attending to the cyclists at Manhattan Beach warned motor-paced riders of "bicycle heart," claiming that riders would literally drop dead if they were permitted to compete in too many heart-pounding races. Harry Elkes noted the doctor's advice in his interview with the *Boston Daily Globe*: "A man following the pace game should not race more than once a week and it would be better if he rode only every fortnight. This trying to race every day and travel between times is a killing proposition. I thought I was dying in Saturday's race at the beach. I did not know where I was, and the puffing of the motors had put my brain in such a condition that I wanted to scream with the pain in my head that I never before experienced. The doctor warned me against starting."[3]

On August 17 Walthour competed in an hour-long race—a showdown against Elkes at Manhattan Beach. This time Elkes did not bring a note from his doctor. The race was the first in a series of three for a purse of $3,000 ($78,100). Walthour took the early lead, but Elkes passed him after the first mile. Three times Walthour came close to regaining the lead, and each time the crowd of four thousand stood up and cheered the popular rider from Atlanta. On the fourth attempt a determined Walthour, his legs churning like pistons and his eyes riveted on his pacing motorcycle's rear tire, finally shot past the New Yorker. Fans burst into wild applause. After the pass Walthour kept up a killing pace that Elkes could not match, and the southerner won by a half mile.[4]

The following week Walthour was matched with Johnny Nelson in a fifteen-mile race behind the tandems at Madison Square Garden. Nelson returned to the scene of his accident two months earlier. The spot where he and MacFarland had crashed had been meticulously repaired, leaving no trace of the violent collision, but mental images of the wreck apparently lingered in his mind. Except for the peaceful droning of Nelson's tires riding the bowl during training, the track was eerily quiet.

Thousands packed the Garden to watch the race between Walthour and Nelson, but the contest became predictable. Walthour outclassed Nelson from start to finish, lapping his rival no less than 14 times. Each of Nelson's 2 motor tandems broke down, but the mechanical problems were not all that stymied him. With memories of the frightful accident with MacFarland still fresh in his mind, Nelson timidly followed pace on the tightly cornered 10-lap track. Walthour, meanwhile, displayed no fear whatsoever and set a track record of 24 minutes 19⅗ seconds.[5]

Johnny Nelson, still leading the motor-paced ranks, was determined to prove he could come out of his Madison Square Garden setback. On September 4 he met Welshman Jimmy Michael in a fifteen-mile match race at the Garden. Just over three miles into the contest, as they tore around the tiny ten-lap track at more than thirty-five miles per hour, Nelson's front tire suddenly blew, and the Chicagoan was thrown violently onto the track. Michael's hulking tandem was close behind, and his pacemakers had nowhere to go but right over Nelson. Michael managed to escape the wreck by riding high up the track. Nelson's left leg tangled in the tandem's chain sprocket, and his calf was cut clear to the bone. Nelson sat up holding his leg, wailing for help. A policeman named Beckman was the first to arrive on the scene; he managed to extricate Nelson's bloody leg from the oily chain and tie a tourniquet above the gash. Two doctors from the stands rushed down to help Beckman until an ambulance arrived and took Nelson to Bellevue Hospital.

The *New York Times* reported, "Nelson had been afraid to race behind motor tandems on the steep Garden track ever since the accident to Floyd MacFarland, and his manager F. Ed Spooner had made several attempts to have single motors substituted. It was announced by the management of the track after the accident that only single motors would be used in future."[6] Tandems were much bigger, more powerful, and ungainly compared to the smaller, single-seat motorcycles. The Garden was much better suited to smaller motorcycles, but fans and promoters wanted speed, danger, and fear. And they got them.

Despite the horrific accident, the show went on. The next night, with Nelson's blood barely dried and cleaned up from the Garden track, thousands turned out to watch Elkes and Walthour compete in a fifteen-mile match race. The smaller and safer single-seated motorcycles were substituted to pace the riders, but Elkes was clearly tentative and "seemed afraid to keep up with his pace," according to the *New York Times*. Elkes crashed during the race, but he was already so far behind that the accident had little bearing on Walthour's lopsided victory.[7]

Two days later Nelson's leg was amputated at the thigh. Doctors had desperately tried to save the leg, but gangrene had set in, and they were concerned the young cyclist would not even live through the operation. Two days later Johnny Nelson died at Bellevue Hospital. He was twenty-three years old.

Scores of associates and fellow professional riders, including Floyd MacFarland, Tom Cooper, and Iver Lawson, attended Nelson's funeral on September 11 at Evergreen Cemetery in Brooklyn. Johnny's younger brothers, Emil and Joe, and his trainer, O. L. Pickard, were the chief mourners, and George Leander was a pallbearer. A grieving Will Stinson summed up well the feelings of his fellow riders:

> When I received the first information that Johnny's leg would have to be amputated, I was shocked inexpressively. I really could not conceive that any rider in our game would meet with such a horrible accident, although we are racing all the time amidst great danger and we look on accidents as minor affairs. But to think that he will never race again, or never see him again seems to me to be a dream. I liked Nelson as well as any boy I ever raced against, and it was with a feeling of sorrow that I read the news that he was dead.[8]

Nelson's death was reported in newspapers around the country. The *Washington Post* published an editorial lamenting the perilous nature of his sport: "Cycle racing is a great sport, but it has been developed in the last few years to the point where it is accompanied with too much danger. Anyone who likes his sport with a little excitement in it can find nothing equal to cycle racing. By the side of it, football appears a game fit for juveniles only."[9]

❋

After a long season pursuing the American motor-paced championship, which was ultimately won by Elkes, Walthour went home to Atlanta to rest and prepare for the six-day race at Madison Square Garden. He signed up for the race with Archie McEachern as his partner—the same man who had poked fun at Walthour for having two managers—and the two planned to train together in Baltimore.[10]

Nelson's manager, F. Ed Spooner, came to Atlanta, and many speculated he was vying to become Walthour's new manager. The *Atlanta Constitution* reported on a rare roundtable discussion between Walthour, Spooner,
Gus Castle, and Zenus Fields, Walthour's tandem steersman. Fields was
recovering from a scalp wound he had received on the wooden boards of
the Garden. The conversation turned to the dangers of the sport. "The
decision to use motor tandems no more as pace [at Madison Square Gar-
den] was made after I lost my boy, Johnny Nelson, by an accident," Spooner said. "Johnny was loved by everyone and recognized by all as the most
popular of the pace followers. The management in New York dared not
risk other riders' necks on the small track after that terrible affair in which
Johnny lost his life. I foresaw that accident at the time Walthour raced
Nelson on August 26." Walthour paused before responding to Spooner's
comment: "I realized the risk, of course," he began, "but a man will risk
a great deal where there is good money in sight, for it is the money that
keeps the roof over our head and the bread in the mouths of the wife
and little ones at home. I would never have ridden the Garden track after
Johnny's accident except back of singles. I loved Johnny as did everyone
else who knew him."[11]

Weeks later and closing in on the six-day race at Madison Square Garden, Walthour received a telegram informing him that McEachern had
set a record by riding 26 unpaced miles in one hour on the Baltimore
track. The big 185-pound Canadian was clearly in great form and training
hard under the guidance of Frank Caldwell. Walthour knew he had better get serious about the Garden race. He turned his growing backyard
chicken ranch, with a full layout of incubators, over to one of his brothers—probably Jimmy—and summoned his brother Russell from his home
in Birmingham, Alabama, to help relieve the tedium of the long training
rides around Atlanta.[12]

Twice daily Bobby and Russell rode twenty-five miles from Peachtree
to Buckhead Streets and beyond. On one ride, a barking dog with a head
of steam tore after them. The brothers enjoyed a good laugh until the dog
made a run at their ankles. Somehow the dog was pulled under Bobby's
rear wheel, flipping Bobby over the handlebars. The dog ran away yelping

but uninjured. Walthour went down hard, losing a good amount of skin and even more dignity.

Confident that McEachern was training well on his own, Walthour remained down south until December 6—three days before the start of the race. He and Blanche traveled to New York City by train with their two daughters, three-year-old Viva and one-year-old Nona.

The race was scheduled to begin at midnight on Sunday, December 8, 1901. By 9 p.m. five thousand people had arrived at Madison Square Garden, braving frigid temperatures to be there. By 11 p.m. the Garden was filled to capacity with twelve thousand fans. Among the spectators was N.C.A. president Amos G. Batchelder, who was seen limping on crutches into the racers' quarters. He had been injured while riding in an automobile with Frenchman Henri Fournier, the pioneer pacemaker who first brought a tandem motorcycle to the Garden three years earlier. The atmosphere was enhanced by two hundred amateur riders from the Century Road Club of America who circled the track while waving to the crowd. The crowd also included well-known cyclists—Harry Elkes, who arrived bedecked in a frock coat and a glistening silk hat, Frank Waller, Albert Schock, Major Taylor, Charles "Mile-a-Minute" Murphy, and Charles Miller, who was celebrating his second wedding anniversary. Jimmy Michael warmed up the crowd with an exhibition mile following the motorized pace of Frenchman Albert Champion, who was driving a "single." They brought the great crowd to its feet as they flew up and down the sharply banked track at nearly thirty-five miles per hour, completing the ten laps in one minute forty-seven seconds.

Walthour arrived at the Garden with his wrist wrapped from a sprain he had received in Boston months before. He was carrying a large brown jug, which he guarded diligently. The jug aroused the curiosity of his friends and fellow riders. "What have you got there, is it mountain dew from the old state of Georgia?" one man asked. Walthour winked at his questioner and, without a word, walked into his dressing room with the jug.[13]

One by one, the sixteen two-man teams were brought out in their brightly colored uniforms and introduced. The "Pan-American" team of Walthour and McEachern received a tremendous ovation. The French duo of Jean Gougoltz and Caesar Simar received the most enthusiastic reception among the foreign entrants. At five minutes past midnight, one man from each of the sixteen teams lined up, and world featherweight boxing champion William C. Rothwell, known as Young Corbett, fired the starting gun.[14]

The cyclists shot out in a long, unbroken line, their legs spinning in an unceasing rhythm as they rode around and around and up and down the steeply banked track. The low whirring sound of the wheels produced an almost hypnotic effect on the crowd. The Garden spectators became strangely quiet. The hush was punctuated now and again by a random shout from an excited spectator. Every so often a rider would break rank, stand up in his saddle and surge forward in an attempt to lap the field. Then the crowd would come to life, shouting and rising in unison, stamping their feet on the floor, and shaking down the dust from the rafters high above. For a few minutes the Garden was in bedlam until the pace relaxed again and the atmosphere calmed down.

Before twenty-four hours had elapsed, the top teams covered more than five hundred miles and four teams had dropped out, including the Gougoltz-Simar combination. Speaking in a thick French accent, Caesar Simar later told reporters he was sorry to have quit but that a pain in his heart forced him to stop. Fellow Frenchman Victor Breyer, a race promoter and editor of *Le Vélo* magazine, was attending the event to scout American talent, especially Walthour. In regard to Simar, Breyer offered a different opinion: "Simar has been around the Garden all day and is as well as any man here. . . . Naturally he may have felt ill, but what six-day racer does not at one stage or another? That is part of the game. To complain of that is as though a boxer should complain of one or two stiff punches. Nothing is wrong with Simar's heart except lack of courage. It was a plain case of quit."[15] As for the only French team remaining in the race—Chevalier and Fischer—Breyer said it was still too early in the race to give them strychnine or other stimulants, a common "therapy" in six-day races.

On the second day of the race, rumors filled the Garden that Walthour and McEachern would make a supreme effort to gain a lap on the field. They did indeed make several determined attempts to break away from the pack, but they could not lap other riders. Floyd MacFarland, sitting in a box close to trackside, remarked with a wry grin, "It is not so easy to steal a lap as it looks. I have tried it and I know."[16]

As a guest columnist for the *World*, Jimmy Michael wrote a vivid account of one of Walthour's attacks, which he called one of the fiercest he had ever seen:

> In an incredibly short time Walthour had opened a gap of half a lap and was driving every nerve into still more feverish effort. One by one he picked up in flashing speed McLaren, Chevalier, and Samuelson. The crowd that jammed the Garden went frantic. Hoarse yells and shouts from the men, shrill cries from the women, the waving of hats and of handkerchiefs heaped up a tumult that is rarely witnessed in the Garden. ... Human nature could not long sustain such an awful strain. The killing fight was kept up for two miles and then Walthour gave up the task and steadied himself down to ordinary plodding.[17]

On the fourth day an accident precipitated another of Walthour's surges. At 2 p.m., he surprised the field with a sudden and sustained burst of speed. The twelve thousand fans rose to their feet as relief riders for the other cyclists rushed onto the track from every quarter. Nat Butler came out to relieve his partner Hugh McLean, Fischer raced out to replace Chevalier, and George McLaren made an attempt to take over for his fellow Englishman Tommy Hall. On the narrow track, McLaren steered into Fischer's path, and the two partners, Chevalier and Fischer, collided and fell hard, bringing several other riders crashing to the pine with them. Fischer broke his collarbone, and Chevalier appeared paralyzed.

The collision happened right in front of Walthour as he was about to lap the field. He managed to avoid the wreckage and was confident that he had gained a lap. But the referee disallowed it. The decision so angered McEachern that the Canadian put on his street clothes and threatened to withdraw from the race. Walthour, meanwhile, kept riding around the 176-yard bowl, trying to calm McEachern down every time he passed his partner on the sidelines. McEachern rushed out of the building in a huff, but a short time later he reappeared on the track in his racing uniform, much to Walthour's relief. At the end of the day, 4 teams were tied for first: Walthour-McEachern, Butler-McLean, Maya-Wilson, and Babcock-Turville.[18]

More riders were injured the next day. As McEachern prepared to dismount, he rode into Johnny King, another professional rider who was not even in the race. Both riders hit the hard surface, and McEachern struck his head violently. He was dazed for a half hour, and the bump on his left temple grew to the size of a doorknob. The man from Toronto was tough as nails though, and he refused to quit. For the second night in a row, a foreign team was forced to retire because of a broken collar bone. Oscar Julius, who was teamed with Iver Lawson of the Swedish team, plowed into Michael Fredricks of the German team on the southwestern bank, and both went down. Fredricks suffered only a minor cut, but Julius landed hard on his shoulder and was forced to quit, leaving eight teams competing for cash and fame. By this time Walthour looked haggard, but each time the pace picked up, he rose to the challenge.[19]

With the final day winding down, the team of Fredricks-Jaak had no reason to continue because they were so far behind and left the track at 8:45 p.m. An hour later, Hans Jaak rode back onto the track, holding a pint of beer. He made no attempt to keep up with the others and toasted the amused crowd, shouting "*Prosit*" ("cheers" or, literally, "to your benefit") as the other riders looked on with envy. Immediately after Jaak's unscheduled ride, Albert Champion came out on a motorcycle for an exhibition of his own. Champion raced around the pine boards at nearly forty-five miles per hour, coming perilously close to the edge of the track. An alarmed Victor Breyer cried out, "*Mon Dieu!*" ("My God!") Champion will kill himself! He is going too fast for such a track." A few moments later Champion went barreling into a wooden railing, snapping it in pieces. The Frenchman was thrown down the track's slippery wood surface. The motorcycle continued its journey without the rider, and a few spectators in the box arena seats narrowly averted serious injury after the motorcycle crashed. Champion lay on the track stunned for a few moments but was able to stand up on his own. He had dislocated two fingers on his right hand and suffered cuts and bruises all along his right side. The humbled Frenchman slowly limped back to his training quarters while trainers wheeled the motorcycle wreckage away. Champion had gone beyond the speed limit of what the banking could sustain and paid the price.

The five remaining teams were tied for first place with 2,555 miles and 4 laps. They prepared for the final struggle at 10 p.m. Each team picked a rider to compete in a 1-mile sprint that would decide the entire 142-hour race. The five riders were Nat Butler, Benny Munroe, Lester Wilson, Oscar Babcock, and Bobby Walthour. At the crack of the starting pistol, Butler took the lead, followed by Wilson and Walthour. They loafed around the track, alert for any quick movement by the other riders. The excitement of the crowd built almost to the bursting point. Fans stood on chairs and railings for a better view. Walthour seized the lead in the second lap, but Butler forged back to the front on the fourth lap with the southerner hanging on his wheel. When the bell sounded for the tenth and last lap, Walthour bent over his handlebars. Displaying his marvelous sprinting ability, he shot out to the front with Wilson clinging on for dear life. The two flew around the track together, leaving the others to fight for third position. The crowd roared as Walthour crossed the tape seconds ahead of Wilson. Programs and hats were thrown in the air, and complete strangers hugged each other. Archie McEachern impulsively threw his arms around Blanche Walthour and kissed her.[20]

The *World* reported, "At the finish the scene in the Garden beggared description. Everybody was shouting and yelling. The swarming thousands broke through and surrounded Walthour, but he pushed his way along the crowded track until he reached his wife. 'Oh, Bobby!' she cried, and then she fell into his arms and kissed him again and again. McEachern and Walthour were shouldered and carried in triumph to the judge's stand. When the tumult had died down somewhat, all the successful contestants in the race, led by Walthour and McEachern, rode around the track and were again hailed by deafening cheers."[21] Blanche, heaped with roses and chrysanthemums, was led by police through the crowd.

In Atlanta the offices of the *Constitution* were crowded with Walthour's friends and family, who had gathered around the telegraph, anxiously awaiting word from Madison Square Garden. When the news ticked off that he had won, the excitement in the cramped room gave way to unbridled enthusiasm. Plans were made for a magnificent party to welcome back their hometown hero.[22]

After an impromptu reception at the Garden, McEachern, Walthour, and their trainers retired to a local Turkish bath. As Walthour was taking off his uniform, he called for service. "Have you any pie here?" The surprised attendant told him, "We don't usually keep it, but I suppose we could get some." The new six-day champion retorted, "Well, we have got to have pie. If you can't get pie, we will leave this place." The pies were delivered quickly, and Walthour devoured two pies himself.[23]

"Say, Bobby, tell us what was in that brown jug," said a happy man who had won a great deal of money betting on the Walthour-McEachern combination. Walthour replied: "Now that the thing is over I don't mind letting all of you in on the secret. That was Coca-Cola. I drank it because it refreshed me and at the same time there are no after effects like there are in other stimulants. You see those other fellows resorted to different kinds of drugs, but I took none at all. When I felt tired and worn out I just drank a glass of Coca-Cola and went back to work. It gave me strength, brightened me up and made me feel better generally."[24] Before 1903 a single glass of Coca-Cola contained nine milligrams of cocaine. "McEachern and myself used no drugs," said Walthour after the race, "all the reports to the contrary notwithstanding. Coffee was our strongest stimulant." The *New York Herald* confirmed Breyer's prediction that teams would use drugs later in the race. On Saturday at around 6 p.m., trainers were purported to give their riders "either tonic doses of cocaine, strychnine or some other powerful stimulant."[25]

When Walthour and his family arrived back at the Atlanta train depot, they were driven home in a carriage drawn by white horses covered with blue ribbons. Thousands of locals lined the streets to cheer the great cycling champion. Bobby and Blanche stood and held up their girls, Viva and Nona, for all to see. That evening Harry Silverman hosted a grand banquet for them at the Kimball House. Among the guests were Gus Castle and Zenus Fields.[26] Silverman, the man who hired Walthour as a young bike messenger and a man not known for being overly modest, took credit for starting Walthour on his career in racing.

Earliest known photo of Bobby Walthour, at right, circa 1894. *Buck Peacock Collection*

Walthour and Gus Castle, 1896. *Buck Peacock Collection*

Jack Prince. *Buck Peacock Collection*

Bicycle Race, Vailsburg, Newark, N. J.

Typical crowd at Vailsburg Track, Newark, NJ. *Buck Peacock Collection*

Charles Murphy rides a mile in 57.4 seconds, June 30, 1899. *Courtesy of Andrew Ritchie*

Bourotte derrière sa quintuplette.
(Coll. J. Beau. Archives photographiques du Touring-Club de France.)
LE SPORT AVANT 1900 : LES MACHINES MULTIPLES

Rider paced by a "quint." *Courtesy of Andrew Ritchie*

Henri Fournier, first to ride
a motorcycle inside Madison
Square Garden, 1898.
Courtesy of Andrew Ritchie

Major Taylor at the Buffalo Velodrome in Paris, 1901. *Buck Peacock Collection*

Walthour in Florida with Tom Eck, 1901. *Buck Peacock Collection*

Walthour training in
Florida, 1901. *Buck
Peacock Collection*

Harry Elkes on
chainless bicycle,
circa 1899. *Courtesy
of Andrew Ritchie*

Floyd MacFarland, Buffalo
Velodrome, circa 1905.
Buck Peacock Collection

Archie McEachern, circa 1901. *Buck Peacock Collection*

George Leander, circa 1902.
Courtesy of Russell Leander

Walthour's home on Woodward Avenue in Atlanta. *Buck Peacock Collection*

Harry Elkes's tombstone, Glens Falls, New York. *Photograph by Albert Fowler, courtesy of the Folklife Center, Crandall Public Library, Glens Falls, New York*

ROBERT WALTHOUR.   BEN MUNROE.

From Photographs Taken in Madison Square Garden on the Last Day of the Race.

Walthour and Bennie Munroe at the 1903 six-day race at Madison Square Garden. *Author's Collection*

Walthour and Gussie Lawson, Germany, 1904. *Buck Peacock Collection*

Left to right—Eli Winesett, unknown spectator, Lawson, and Walthour, Buffalo Velodrome, 1904. *Buck Peacock Collection*

Frenchman Paul Dangla at Parc des Princes, circa 1904. *Courtesy of Andrew Ritchie*

Robl-Walthour match race in Dresden, April 17, 1904 (Walthour held by Eli Winesett).
Courtesy of Andrew Ritchie

Walthour racing
in Germany
behind Lawson,
1904. *Courtesy of
Andrew Ritchie*

Thaddeus Robl bandaged
up and ready to go, 1904.
Courtesy of Andrew Ritchie

Walthour, 1904.
Courtesy of Andrew Ritchie

George Leander's postcard home, 1904. *Courtesy of Russell Leander*

POSTAL TELEGRAPH-CABLE COMPANY IN CONNECTION WITH THE COMMERCIAL CABLE COMPANY.

CLARENCE H. MACKAY, President.
J. O. STEVENS, Sec'y.   WM. H. BAKER, V. P. & G. M.

CLARENCE H. MACKAY, President.
ALBERT BECK, Sec'y.   GEO. G. WARD, V. P. & G. M.

CABLEGRAM.

The Postal Telegraph-Cable Company transmits and delivers this cablegram subject to the terms and conditions printed on the back of this blank.

Received, via Commercial Cables, at Main Office, Cor. La Salle and Washington Streets, Chicago.

AUG -- 1904

1004

12 CB. MC. 12

Paris 24

Leander

Chicago

Valuables 800 dollars cost sending body 400 dollars

Cable Quick

436am

No Inquiry respecting this message can be attended to without the production of this paper. Repetitions of doubtful words should be obtained through the Company's offices, and not by DIRECT application to the sender.

THE POSTAL COMPANY'S SYSTEM REACHES ALL IMPORTANT POINTS IN THE UNITED STATES AND BRITISH AMERICA, AND via COMMERCIAL CABLES, ALL THE WORLD.

Cablegram to Leander's family, 1904. *Courtesy of Russell Leander*

Letter from Victor Breyer to A. G. Batchelder, 1904. *Courtesy of Russell Leander*

Franz Hoffman and Walthour, 1904. *Buck Peacock Collection*

Tommy Hall paced by Henri Cissac, 1904. *Buck Peacock Collection*

{ 11 }

Sunday Preacher

fter the 1901 Madison Square Garden six-day victory celebrations, Walthour and Blanche settled back into their comfortable Atlanta home on Woodward Avenue. They enjoyed a family Christmas with their two daughters and took leisurely strolls through nearby Grant Park. Walthour tended to his chicken ranch. The roosters strutted while the chicks endlessly chased after the mother hens. Walthour needed some rest.

By late February 1902 Walthour had yet to touch his bicycle. He began working out to lose the weight gained after his 2-month layoff. He boxed using a punch bag, skipped rope, and wrestled. He also walked and ran for miles and miles. Finally, when weather permitted, he trained on his bike with his brother Russell on their favorite 25-mile ride from Peachtree to Buckhead as they had before the six-day race. He also practiced behind motor-pacers in Atlanta at Jack Prince's coliseum track, which was newly rebuilt with 2-inch oak planks. He started slowly, equipping his bike with a low 96-inch gear (46 x 13). On each successive day he changed the gear so that it was bigger and more difficult to spin. Soon, he was back comfortably to his old gear of 121 inches (54 x 12). He was able to follow Eli Winesett's motorcycle at more than 40 miles per hour as he had the previous fall.[1]

Victor Breyer, the editor of *Le Vélo*, had been impressed with Walthour as he had watched his six-day victory at the Garden. When Breyer returned to France, he discussed Walthour's achievement with Henri Desgrange. Desgrange was the manager of Parc des Princes, the 666-meter cement velodrome in Paris, and he would soon become one of the founding fathers of the Tour de France. Desgrange cabled Walthour in Atlanta with an offer to race in France in April behind the motorcycles at his track. Desgrange reasoned that Walthour would have plenty of time to return to America to start the 1902 season in late May. The offer called for Walthour to participate in 4 races in Paris at the Parc des Princes, with a guarantee of $2,000 (currently around $51,400). When Walthour refused, Desgrange countered with $2,400 ($61,700).[2] When Walthour again refused, Desgrange's final offer was a $3,000 ($77,200) guarantee for 3 races, with all expenses paid.[3] But Walthour would have none of it.

One explanation as to why Walthour would not go to Europe was the question of Sunday racing, because the main race day in France was on Sunday. Every race in Desgrange's offer was on Sunday. According to an *Atlanta Journal* article written by Walthour's close friend Gus Castle, Walthour supposedly guarded Sunday as a day of rest, and although Walthour was not formally a member of a congregation, he and his family attended the First Methodist Church in Atlanta. Castle claimed that when traveling, Walthour sought worship in Boston and New York and encouraged other professional riders to join him.[4]

In reality, however, Walthour's stance against Sunday racing may have been lukewarm. His position was certainly not as firm as Major Taylor's, who resolutely refused to race on the Sabbath. In fact Walthour had raced on Sunday many times and would continue to do so, although he once said that "money made on Sunday is bad money, and no good comes from it."[5] The reason Walthour stayed in the United States was, probably, that Blanche was pregnant with their third child. The article written by Castle was more likely a puff piece to foster Walthour's squeaky clean image.

Will Stinson, the undertaker's son from Cambridge, was one American who had no qualms—real or imagined—about Sunday racing and had accepted an invitation to ride abroad. Under the strain of a heavy riding schedule in Europe, however, Stinson had resorted to drug use to keep

himself going. A mixture of cocaine, strychnine, and other chemicals resulted in his temporary blindness. Stinson was unable to keep his March
engagements in Paris. The office of the N.C.A., desperate to make up for
the loss of Stinson, cabled an offer of $4,000 ($103,000) to Walthour to
take Stinson's place to represent the United States in Europe. The answer
from Atlanta to Al Reeves, the secretary of the N.C.A., was brief and to
the point: Walthour wanted $5,000 ($130,000) and refused to race on
Sunday.[6] As a result Walthour remained in the United States that spring.

With his Boston six-day win, his New York six-day victory, and his successful motor-pacing and sprint season, Walthour had netted well over
$10,000 ($260,000) in 1901. Not many athletes in the world could boast
they had made as much. Why would Walthour bother to travel to Europe
when money in the United States was good?

Oddly Walthour had difficulty finalizing a financial arrangement with
Jack Prince to race on his Atlanta track in the spring of 1902. A battle of
words erupted in the press. Walthour declared he would forgo Paris and
race in Atlanta, but only if Prince gave him a fair percentage of the gate receipts. Prince countered that Walthour owed him from the days when nobody had ever heard of Bobby Walthour, and now that he was "at the top,
he seems inclined to cause all the trouble he can," and Prince accused
him of not helping promote professional cycling in his own backyard.[7]

Eventually the two unlocked horns and reached an agreement. Walthour and Prince sat down at Harry Silverman's store and signed a contract. The first race was against George Leander from Chicago on March
7—three five-mile heats behind motor-pace. Forty percent of the gate receipts would go to the winner, plus a $400 ($10,400) side bet.[8]

Leander was a big, tough, handsome young rider with a soft side. He
frequently wrote to his mother and large family back in Chicago about his
adventures. Leander was forty pounds heavier than Walthour. In a photograph that appeared in the *Atlanta Constitution*, the two unsmiling riders
stood side by side in their dark training uniforms, their arms crossed. Walthour was nearly as tall as the six-foot Leander but much thinner.

In 1901 Leander was an amateur motor-pace champion who turned
professional later that year. In the months leading up to the showdown

with Walthour, Leander had been bruised and battered both in races and in fights. In January 1902 he got into an altercation with Floyd MacFarland at the end of a race in Boston. The brawl escalated into a conflict that included almost two hundred men—professional riders, trainers, and fans. Police used their clubs to stop the melee.[9] Later, after he arrived in Atlanta, Leander nearly came to blows again, this time with Connecticut-born rider Willie Fenn. The two were braced for blows at the track but were quickly separated. Leander was not a man who was afraid to stand his ground—not even in front of Bobby Walthour on his home turf.

Given time to heal, Leander was in good health for the race on March 7. In the first heat, at 9:55 p.m., Walthour quickly lost ground to Leander. On the fourth lap of the third mile, Walthour's pacing machine, driven by Winesett, slid wildly around a corner, causing Walthour to ram into the rear tire. He was thrown from his bike and flailed helplessly down across the grain of the steeply banked wooden track. The momentum of the bicycle sent it careening down until it upended into a railing. Those nearest to Walthour rushed to his aid. The smell of the dust stirred up from the bark that lined the inside of the track. Blanche Walthour, holding one of the girls in a trackside box seat, stood up and cried, "Oh my God, my God!"[10]

Walthour, with the taste of dirt in his mouth, was helped up by his trainers. Thick skin had been painfully torn away from the palms of his hands. A swath of bright red "road rash" was burned into both of his arms. An ugly five-inch-long gash on his groin started to bleed.[11] With Walthour hunched over in pain, the trainers carried him back to his quarters. When he returned to the track to resume the race—cleaned up and bandaged in white—the crowd gave a mighty cheer, and the band struck up "Dixie." He looked up, smiled, and waved his bandaged hand before walking to the spot where the accident had occurred. He retrieved the American flag he had worn around his waist. The crowd became even louder when he picked it up, and he acknowledged them by waving the red, white, and blue. On the track, waiting for the starting gun, he retied the flag around his waist. Walthour assured Blanche that he was all right, but she remained apprehensive and hid her face when the race restarted. The heat resumed from the point of the accident. Not surprisingly, Leander maintained his lead in the first heat and won by a half lap.

For the second heat, Walthour came out for revenge and did not appear to be bothered by his injuries. With his legs pumping furiously and his upper torso relaxed, he kept the pacing motorcycle only inches in front of him. Flying around the track, Walthour and Winesett leaned precisely together into the banked turns, as if the bicycle and pacing motorcycle were one. Sensing that Leander was gaining, Walthour shouted at Winesett to increase the speed. As Winesett gave his motorcycle more gas, Walthour pedaled harder and gained more ground. Blanche seemed to forget her husband's accident and waved her handkerchief, cheering him on. The crowd was thrilled by Walthour's grit and determination. To make more noise of approval and support, people beat on the floor with their chairs and feet. Walthour crossed the line the winner.

For the third and final heat another round of fierce betting began, and the band played "Dixie" once again. When the gun fired, the noise from the fans was deafening. Walthour forged to the front in what appeared to be a repeat of the previous heat. Unfortunately Winesett lost control of his motorcycle at forty miles per hour. On the steep banking, his tires slipped. Walthour was forced out from the protective draft of his pacing machine, and the huge gear he had turned to maintain forty miles per hour was suddenly as difficult to push as if he was going up a steep hill. Walthour stood up on the pedals and rocked the bike side to side, huffing and puffing, anxiously waiting for Winesett to come back around. Meanwhile Leander, being paced by Gussie Lawson, passed the unprotected rider and never looked back, winning by a lap and a half. Walthour could have taken advantage of his injuries as an explanation for his defeat, but he did not.[12]

Many people, including Jack Prince, blamed Walthour's accident and subsequent loss to Leander on the slipshod motorcycle riding of Eli Winesett. Rumors floated around Atlanta that Albert Champion would pace Walthour, but the southerner neither confirmed nor denied the talk.

❋

With his skin scabbing up four days after the accident, Walthour contracted with Gussie Lawson, the man who had paced Leander to victory, to pace him until the close of Atlanta's indoor season.[13] In a compromise, Winesett remained in the Walthour camp but strictly as a manager. With

Lawson riding the motorcycle, Walthour competed in several more motor-paced races that spring and won them all.

In 1902 Walthour's popularity continued to rise. That year he was the best drawing card for any cycling promoter. Across the eastern seaboard Walthour's gate receipts averaged more than $1,600 ($41,200) per appearance while other prominent riders were drawing $400 ($10,300) during his absence.[14] Attendance records were set and tracks records pulverized when Walthour arrived in town.

Much of his success came because Walthour retained the services of Gussie Lawson, who at only seventeen years old was one of the best motorcycle pacemakers in the game. Shortly after he first contracted to pace Walthour in Atlanta, Lawson learned that his brother John had died of pneumonia in Milwaukee.[15] The close relationship between Walthour and Lawson evolved from that point on. Although Gussie could not attend his brother's funeral, he felt cheered by his visits to the Walthour home, with little girls and chickens running around. Jack Prince and his wife, Annie, also sympathized with Gussie through the ordeal and invited him to stay with them.

Walthour's consistency in winning made betting on him nearly a sure thing. One night after the children had been put to bed, Walthour answered a knock at his front door on Woodward Avenue. Two strange men with trench coats and hats pulled down low over their eyes stood on the porch. They offered him $500 ($13,000) if he would intentionally lose a three-heat race. Walthour refused. They quickly upped the ante to $1,000 ($26,000). No thank you! They doubled the offer again. Walthour calmly but firmly told his visitors that $10,000 was not enough. In desperation they offered $500 for Walthour to lose just one heat. Walthour lost his patience and ordered the men off his property.[16]

Since Walthour's bike messenger days, his association with Col. Harry Silverman, one of Atlanta's biggest sports gamblers, was widely known. Silverman had been in a barroom brawl at the Kimball House days before the Walthour-Leander race.[17] The fight probably started when Silverman defended Walthour with a large bet. In addition, Jay Eaton, Walthour's former Madison Square Garden six-day partner, had been banned for life from professional cycling. In the fall of 1900 he was caught fixing a race with fellow rider Orlando Stevens in St. Louis.[18] It was not surprising, therefore, that these anonymous men chose to seek him out at his home.

Even within his family Walthour developed problems from his new-found fame. Walthour's identical twin brother Jimmy became involved in the music-hall theater, where he rode his bike on stage on a home trainer. The *Atlanta Constitution* reported Bobby Walthour was making an appearance in Philadelphia at a dime museum racing on a stationary bicycle. Large crowds gathered on the corner of Ninth and Arch for a glimpse of the famous rider from the South. In reality Bobby Walthour was home in Atlanta with his family.

Jimmy found he could make more money impersonating his twin brother than he could in theater work. Bobby was placed in the uncomfortable position of ordering his brother to stop the masquerade, and not for the first time.[19] In November 1901 the *Atlanta Journal* had reported that Jimmy fattened his wallet posing as his brother in another home trainer race.[20] In 1903 a misleading advertisement appeared in newspapers around the country, including the *Journal*, for Duffy's Pure Malt Whiskey; Jimmy probably earned money or at least a few cases of free whiskey from the company. The twins' surname was used in the advertisement along with a drawing of "Walthour" on a home trainer. However, no first name was mentioned to identify which twin.[21]

Jimmy was not the only Walthour with a less-than-clean public image. Although Bobby wanted to impress his many followers, many of his religious fans were aware that he *did* race on the Sabbath—contrary to his protests otherwise. That, along with his associations with gambling and the Walthour name being connected with hard liquor, tainted the choir-boy image he wished to maintain.

{ 12 }

American Champion

S printer Frank Kramer won the first of his many American professional championships in 1901 and was appalled at the many defec-
tions to motor-pacing among the ranks of the sprinters. But a lot of
prize money could be made riding behind the motors, and Walthour had
been one of the defectors. According to the *Atlanta Constitution*, Jimmy
Michael had earned more than $200,000 ($5,210,000 in current dollars)
since 1894, first by riding behind human-powered pace and later behind
motor-pace.[1] Fans were awestruck with the nonstop action of motor-pacing,
fascinated with the noise and addicted to its danger.

After Kramer lost his good friend Johnny Nelson, killed as a result
of motor-pacing at Madison Square Garden, he worked out in the off-
season with Johnny's younger brother Joe. "I don't like the hazard of that
kind of thing," said Kramer about motor-pacing. Floyd MacFarland made
light of Kramer's championship and implied that he won only because
motor-pacers who had opted out of sprinting had weakened the professional sprint competition in the United States. Kramer snapped back, as-
serting that whatever MacFarland might say, he was the worthy winner of
the championship.[2]

Walthour's four-year-old daughter Viva would have agreed with Kramer
about the dangers of motor-pacing. She loved watching when her father
rode—unpaced. From the porch of their house at 624 Woodward Avenue,

Viva waved goodbye to her father and her Uncle Russell as they set out on their morning road workouts. The brothers smiled and waved back under the shade of big Savannah oak trees as their tires crunched along the dirt driveway. But when Walthour took Viva to his workouts on the track, she cried at the sound of the motors. She knew that her father would be following them, inches behind at breakneck speed, and that he could be seriously hurt. He didn't have time to wave to her at that point. When Walthour's tandem steersman, Zenus Fields, held little Viva in his arms at trackside as Eli Winesett started the motor, she wriggled away and ran to her mother, begging for her father to stop.[3]

Whatever his daughter felt, Walthour kept on racing behind the big noisy machines. On March 24, 1902, less than three weeks after his loss to George Leander, Walthour was on Prince's track in Atlanta, working out and peddling faster than ever behind the precision pace-making of Gussie Lawson. Another professional rider from Chicago, Billy "Plugger Bill" Rutz, was working out on Prince's track at the same time as Walthour and Lawson.

One day Rutz was paced by R.G. Bennett riding aboard a motorcycle named the White Ghost. As Lawson and Walthour leaned into a turn along the steep banking, Walthour's front tire blew when Bennett was twenty yards behind him. Walthour veered off course from Lawson, who continued on at full speed. Near the top of the embankment, Walthour fell. Bennett, reacting with instinctual speed, saw that gravity would send Walthour down the banking and kept an outside line. Bennett went up high to the very rim of the bowl, disturbing the dust that had settled there. Rutz followed the motorcycle as best he could. They missed Walthour by only a few feet. If Bennett had panicked and gone to the inside, Walthour likely would have been killed. Instead Walthour added to his collection of scrapes and bruises by falling and sliding down the track.[4]

Archie McEachern, Walthour's partner from the 1901 Madison Square Garden six-day race, was becoming a good motor-pacer. On May 13, 1902, McEachern was training on New Jersey's newest track, the Coliseum in Atlantic City. He and his tandem pacers, Alf Boake and Bobby Thompson, set out to break the fifteen-mile track record in practice. Thompson, like McEachern, was from Toronto, and they had known one another for many years. The three men set out a hot pace and were closing in on the record. But with less than a mile to go, the tandem's chain snapped. The machine immediately lost its driving power and slowed from more than forty miles per hour. With the front of McEachern's wheel spinning downward and the back of the tandem's tire spinning upward, the tires touched. When rubber met rubber, McEachern's front wheel swung high in the air and cast the helpless rider up onto the embankment, crushing his chest and puncturing a lung, as well as breaking his collarbone. His neck caught a protruding board at the railing, which ripped open his jugular vein. On the other side of the track Thompson and Boake looked back to see if he was okay and were relieved to see that he was standing up. But as they came around closer to him, they saw blood pouring from his neck. He walked a few more yards and fell to the ground in a heap. Twenty-eight-year-old McEachern died on the way to the hospital, another victim of the dangerous world of motor-pacing.[5]

Two months later Walthour was at the Charles River track in Boston in front of more than ten thousand spectators, including Blanche and their two daughters. At the start Walthour shot between his two rivals—local man Jimmy Moran and Pennsylvanian Otto Maya. Walthour's great strength enabled him to push the big gear faster at the start than either Moran or Maya. He gripped the handlebar tightly and rocked his bike's creaking frame from side to side with his head down while his feet strained at the pedals.

At the end of the first lap, Walthour and his tandem were up to nearly forty miles per hour. The crowd stood up and cheered as they came around to the grandstand side of the track. Suddenly Walthour heard a metallic rattling sound. The big oily chain of his tandem pacing motorcycle had snapped and was dangling. His front tire touched the back tire of the tandem, just as McEachern's had done earlier. The effect was the same. In front of the grandstand where Blanche and his daughters sat, Walthour's front wheel popped up, and he was thrown above the head of his pacemaker—a full ten feet in the air.

A few terrible seconds followed when Walthour had no control over his body, and he did a complete flip in the air. He ended up in the grass and dirt on the inside of the track. His bicycle continued on without him and flew over a fence. After compulsive shrieks of horror, the stadium fell silent. All that could be heard was the drone of motorcycle engines. People covered their eyes and looked away. Surely Walthour must be dead.

John J. Donovan, a writer for the *Boston Daily Globe*, called it "the most sensational fall cycling has ever known. . . It was a miracle he was not killed."[6] Blanche was seven months pregnant; she went into hysterics and could not be consoled. Little Viva was sobbing and calling for her Papa. A mad rush of trainers and spectators went to help Walthour. He was found dazed but had miraculously escaped without broken bones. His only injuries were minor scrapes and bruises.

A week later Walthour returned back to racing at the Charles River track. This time he was paced by a belt-driven tandem, which he named Candy. There would be no more chains snapping for him. In the twenty-five-mile race, three other riders were each paced by a tandem: the little Englishman Tommy Hall, Otto Maya, and Benny Munroe. Walthour must have felt the effects from his fall a week before, but he did not show it. Maya took the early lead and held off several challenges from Walthour. At mile twelve Maya's tire punctured, and Walthour took command.

All four riders focused their attention on the back wheels of their machines, trusting their pacemakers implicitly. Each was at the limit of the speed of their pacers. Walthour's machine went faster though, and he was able to keep behind it. He beat Maya by a mile and set a new twenty-five-mile track record with a time of thirty-five minutes two seconds, more than forty-two miles per hour. Walthour had bounced back only a week after his sensational fall.[7]

Walthour went on to win thirteen straight races that summer. He set track records at nearly every major track in the country from Connecticut to Georgia. He almost had the 1902 motor-pacing title sewn up. The dark-haired Frenchman Albert Champion, who also had scored a number of impressive victories, was the only rider standing in his way. Champion beat Walthour's track record at Hartford. The two met twice in June. "I will race you any time for fun, money, or marbles," the Frenchman had said to Walthour, "but I am going to beat you and beat you badly."[8] He was right: in two events in June, Champion won against Walthour, who experienced mechanical difficulties. The American championship was to be settled between them on September 6 at the Revere track in Boston.

On every day of the week before the big showdown, Walthour worked out at Revere. He needed to know every bump and divot in the track's wood surface. He wanted to perfect his speed around the banking and be able to follow Candy, his motor-pacing tandem, with precision. During one of these workouts, Walthour's tandem blew a tire. The pacing machine went down right in front of him. Luckily, both he and his two pacemakers escaped injury. The machine thudded heavily into the wood track before it slid down the embankment toward the infield. In addition to scrapes, the tandem left behind a liquid trail, and the smell of gasoline permeated the wreckage. The redhot exhaust pipe ignited the gas, and Candy was soon engulfed in flames. Thick black smoke rose high in the air, and soon the track surface caught fire. A quick-thinking motorman, Watson Coleman, dashed for a fire extinguisher, and the blaze was soon put out, but not before Candy's tires and seats burned.[9]

Mechanics worked around the clock to find replacement parts then meticulously repair and clean up the motor tandem in time for the championship. Walthour was not mechanically inclined and made frequent visits to the mechanics as if they were doctors healing his child from some terrible sickness. They assured him everything would be all right and Candy would be ready.

On race day thousands filled the Revere stadium to overflowing. A sense of history making was in the air, and everyone was talking about whether the American motor-paced championship would go to a Frenchman or to an American. Walthour and Champion started the twenty-five-mile championship race at opposite sides of the 220-yard Revere track. The smell of freshly sanded wood was still in the air. The starting gun fired, and the crowd stood up as each rider caught his pace. Walthour held a slight lead after the first mile. Champion would not fade, though, as the riders climbed and plunged up and down the steep banking, following less than an inch away from their big pacing tandems at more than forty-two miles per hour—about ten seconds per lap. At eight miles Walthour nearly caught up to his rival and took a lead of a half lap, but the motor tandem suddenly lost power. Champion heard the machine cough and yelled out to his pacemakers, *"Allez! Allez!"* ("Come on! Come on!") Champion sensed that Walthour's tandem was in trouble, and his pacemakers summoned as much speed as they could. Candy's motor continued to sputter but maintained enough power to hold a tenuous lead. The big crowd was thrilled at the seesaw battle. Walthour managed to keep his margin and win the 1902 American motor-paced championship by nearly a half lap.[10]

The Boston crowd gave Walthour a tremendous ovation. The twenty-four-year-old former bike messenger from Atlanta sealed a victory and an American championship motor-pacing title that no one could take away. According to the *New York Times*, "[Atlanta] newspapers printed cartoons of him wearing the championship and proclaimed him candidate for Mayor."[11] When he arrived home, brass bands met him at the train station and played "See the Conquering Hero Comes."

{ 13 }

Back in Dixie

fter a long train journey from Boston to Atlanta with two young children and his very pregnant wife, Walthour happily extricated himself from their confined compartment. They arrived home on September 20, 1902. Walthour at once began to work on his training and racing schedule, in preparation for the defense of his six-day victory at Madison Square Garden in December. The largest and richest bicycle race in the United States was a scant ten weeks away. Walthour had to be fit enough to ride at twenty miles per hour, two hundred miles per day for six straight days. But first he needed a good rest.

Atlanta would not let the undisputed motor-pacing champion of America relax, however, and he was given a hero's welcome. Two days after he stepped off the train, Walthour was the star attraction in the Georgia Elks Association parade. Four hundred members from around the state marched in the streets, dressed in purple and white, the official colors of their fraternity. Mounted police, the Fifth Regiment Marching Band, Charles Vitter's drum corps, and the Governor's Horse Guard all joined in the magnificent procession, which started at the corner of Harris and Peachtree streets and wound its way through the downtown.[1] The rat-a-tat of the drums could easily be heard from the Walthour home. From a slow-moving automobile, Bobby Walthour, Atlanta's first sports superstar, stood waving and smiling to the thousands of people who lined both sides of the street.

Just days after the parade, the Walthours enjoyed a more private celebration. Robert Howe Walthour Jr. was born at 1:45 on the morning of September 27, 1902, and his proud parents received many congratulations.

But even the birth of his son did not deter Walthour from his training. His workout routine always started with a large breakfast of steak and eggs. Then he would drive his new electric car downtown for an egg sherry. This gentleman's drink consisted of raw eggs, sherry, cherry brandy, maraschino liqueur, and powdered sugar. The day before his son was born, however, he may have skipped his workout altogether in favor of one too many egg sherries. While he was driving through Grant Park on September 26, his car tires could not gain traction on the road, which was paved with loose stones. So he decided to drive on the smoothly paved sidewalk. All was going splendidly until an Atlanta Police officer spotted him. The officer wrote up a ticket for Walthour's riding on the sidewalk and ordered him to make an appearance before a judge.

On the same afternoon his son was born, he was expected in court about his traffic ticket. The courtroom was filled with fans of the famous rider. When the clerk called out "Robert Walthour," every eye turned toward the waiting room. But there was no appearance. Walthour was charged with contempt of court and eventually paid a court-ordered fine of $9.50 (around $245 in today's dollars).[2]

After the arrival of his son Walthour prepared seriously for the six-day race. Every morning he rose at 8 a.m. and tended to his chickens. Then he ate rare steak and eggs, with cereal and milk. After that he met one of his training partners, usually Gussie Lawson or his brother Russell, at the Y.M.C.A. They worked up a good sweat—playing a few furious matches of handball, hitting the punching bag, taking a three-mile run—then cooled off with a swim in the pool. Walthour returned home, ate a big lunch, and took a peaceful nap.

In the afternoons he met his motorman, ·Charles Turville, at Jack Prince's ten-lap wooden track at the Piedmont Coliseum. Turville led out with Walthour tucked in closely behind his latest single motorcycle, Candy Junior, at a steady medium pace for five miles. For the next five miles

Turville increased his speed each mile until the last mile, when he had the motorcycle going at full throttle. Walthour stayed right behind, looking as if he were being pulled by an invisible rope at forty-five miles per hour. They climbed and dived up and down the steeply banked turns. After a brief warm-down, Walthour went to the clubhouse for an hour-long massage. Then he went back home, where he ate a big supper and played with his children. After the children were in bed, he put on as many as four sweaters and ran five miles through Grant Park. As the weeks went by, Walthour kept to his routine but steadily increased his time on the bike to be ready for the six-day race.

The citizens of Atlanta didn't care about Walthour's workouts; they wanted to see Walthour race at home. Saturday, October 17, was officially declared "Walthour Day" at the Georgia State Fair. Traditionally the fair zeroed in on anything to do with horses, especially harness horse racing at the Piedmont Park track. An idea was hatched to promote Atlanta's greatest athlete and horse racing in the same event.

Walthour was put up against five harness horses, which would combine in a relay against the motor-paced champion paced by Candy Junior in a ten-mile race. Many years before, a much younger Walthour had seen Jack Prince race against horses at the same venue, so it was not an original idea. However, no beast had gone up against a man on a bicycle, paced by a motorcycle, in Atlanta. The dirt horse track was specially prepared for the event. A four-foot-wide strip on the inside was rolled and manicured for Walthour and Zenus Fields, who was to ride the pacing motorcycle.

Fifteen thousand people packed Piedmont Park's horse track. The presence of a great many college students made the atmosphere boisterous. The more daring students found seats on the grandstand roof. Down on the dirt track, Fields revved the engine, and Walthour prepared for a dusty race. The two inched close to the starting line with the first horse, a gray gelding named Keenan. A deafening roar from the great crowd echoed throughout the Piedmont hills at the sound of the bell. So much dirt was kicked up that Walthour's blue and yellow striped racing jersey could hardly be seen. The noise that reverberated from the fans was so loud that Fields and Walthour could not hear Candy Junior's motor until they came around the less populated back stretch. Betting odds were two to five in favor of Walthour, and when he came around the second turn in the lead, tucked in closely to the motorcycle's rear wheel, thousands were yelling, jumping up and down, pumping their fists in the air, and waving handkerchiefs.

Keenan pulled the sulky containing its driver with quick clopping strides and a marvelous dexterity. Walthour continued his tenuous lead. Once Keenan finished his two miles, a fresh horse pulling its sulky came out to catch Walthour. Near the end of the race, as the fifth horse was running, fans became frantic, especially those with good money on Walthour to win. He finished ten lengths ahead of the last horse, in a blaze of glory.[3] The crowd surged toward the finish line to greet the dusty rider, who wheeled his bike around in the uneven dirt with a toothy white grin. Walthour was the largest drawing card anyone could remember; he had become more popular than ever in the eyes of Georgians.

Walthour Day was a great success, but with the six-day race looming only weeks away, Walthour needed to negotiate a contract with the management at Madison Square Garden. Since he was the defending six-day champion and reigning American motor-paced title holder, his confidence was high. To the managing partners of the six-day race, Patrick Powers and James Kennedy, Walthour may have seemed to possess too much confidence. Walthour asked for a guaranteed sum of $1,000 ($25,700) plus expenses. He quickly rejected their counter offer of $350 ($9,000). The two sides eventually met somewhere in the middle, and Walthour began the difficult task of selecting a partner for the race.

Since Walthour's 1901 six-day race partner Archie McEachern had died tragically earlier in the year, he chose fellow southerner Benny Munroe from Memphis. Several weeks before in September 1902, Munroe had been injured in a motor-pacing accident in Baltimore. He had been thrown into the stands and had fractured his skull. He was not expected to live through the night, but the doctors at Johns Hopkins Hospital had removed skull fragments and succeeded in reviving him. Thereafter Munroe wore a protective leather cap for riding.[4] He was not the most talented motor-pacer, but he was a southerner, and he possessed a grit that could benefit Walthour in the six-day race.

On Tuesday, November 10, about four weeks before the six-day race, Walthour raced against Joe Nelson on Jack Prince's indoor track at the

Piedmont Coliseum. Prince had designed the track with the exact banking specifications of the Madison Square Garden track and the same
length—ten laps to the mile. Walthour had a perfect track on which to
practice for his defense of the New York six-day, right at home in Atlanta. But to enable Prince to pay for the lumber and the labor of at least
thirty carpenters, he needed races to be run and paying customers in the
seats. Walthour agreed to participate in several motor-paced races to help
Prince. Of course, Walthour would benefit financially from racing too.

The race against Joe Nelson, Johnny Nelson's younger brother, called
for the best of three five-mile heats. A sellout crowd of more than four
thousand fans pleased Jack Prince, who enthusiastically announced the
contestants in his charming British accent. Gussie Lawson was pacing for
Walthour as usual. He and Nelson's motorman started when the pistol
shot, and the race got underway. The revving of the engines, the noise
from the crowd, and the smell of the blue cigar smoke drifting up inside
the well-lit Coliseum added to the excitement. Around and around they
went at more than forty miles per hour, doggedly staying in the slipstream
of their pacing machines. The crowd went wild as Lawson nudged up to
Nelson and made a clean pass, with Walthour safely in tow. But a few minutes later Walthour's front wheel clipped the back of the motorcycle, and
suddenly he was thrown off his bicycle and rolling forty feet across the
track. Although Walthour was safe from Nelson and his motorman, the
fans were hushed at the sight of their hero going down hard. Walthour sat
up, holding his left shoulder in agony, as attendants ran to his aid.

Walthour was taken to Dr. Samuel Visanska, who X-rayed the shoulder
and found that not only was Walthour's collar bone broken, but it was a
rebreak from a previous accident. Dr. Visanska bandaged and wrapped
the area to make it immobile and sent Walthour home.[5]

"Nonsensical," said Jack Prince, when asked whether Walthour would
be able to defend his six-day title in New York City. He pointed out that
perhaps Walthour could go a day or two, but he would not be able to rest
nor feed himself while riding.[6] Also, six-day riders frequently went shoulder to shoulder, leaning against each other at high speeds, and did not
hesitate to throw elbows when they thought the referees were not looking.
A crash, not uncommon in six-day races, might have dire consequences

if Walthour did decide to race. Although he tested how the injury was healing by riding and even participating in a few motor-paced races on Prince's track, in the end he wisely chose not to participate in the New York six-day.

After he beat Albert Champion on September 6, Walthour was declared the official American motor-paced champion for 1902 by the N.C.A. But a brash challenge to the title came from New Hampshire, home of Harry "The Manchester Giant" Caldwell. Caldwell had raced against Walthour in Hartford, Connecticut, and won. He also had repeatedly beaten Walthour's chief rivals for the title, Albert Champion and Harry Elkes. Caldwell began signing his name with "World's Champion" appended to it.

When his shoulder had fully healed, Walthour could think of no more fitting rival than Harry Caldwell for his first motor-paced race of 1903. "I want to show the people of Atlanta that this fellow Caldwell did not beat me [in October] because he was a better rider than I am," Walthour said, "but that he won on a fluke."[7] He maintained that Caldwell had paid off Burroughs, Walthour's pacemaker at the Hartford race. Walthour claimed that Burroughs purposely rode Candy Junior around the Hartford track slowly.

To secure a contract with the 6-foot-6, 200-pound Caldwell to go against Walthour, Jack Prince traveled north to Boston. From there Prince went to Maine, where Caldwell was bear hunting. Prince found the hunting cabin, but Caldwell was fifteen miles higher up in the mountains. Undaunted, Prince rode on horseback through a fresh blanket of snow, found Caldwell, and brought him back to Boston. They drew up a contract for a race against Walthour and signed it before the N.C.A. Racing Board. Prince paid Caldwell's expenses to race against Walthour in Atlanta on March 11.[8]

When Caldwell arrived in the South for the first time, he stepped off the train wearing a Colt .45 on one side and a big bowie knife on the other. He told the press that he was a dead shot and wanted there to be no mistake that he was a genuine Yankee. Caldwell even named his pacing motorcycle the Monitor after the Civil War Union ironclad that went after its Confederate counterpart, the Merrimac. Caldwell had a week to train in the Piedmont Coliseum, which provided plenty of time for him and his motorman, Harry Sinclair, to adjust to the boards and angles.

A sellout crowd of four thousand men, women, and children came to see the big match race, which was built up by the press almost every day for two weeks. Prince's arduous journey up north to sign Caldwell finally was going to pay off. The race called for the best of three five-mile heats. Sinclair was ready for Caldwell, driving the Monitor, and Charles Turville was driving Candy Junior.

Prince fired the starting pistol, and the first heat was underway. The building shook from the pounding and shouting of the fans when Walthour appeared to take an early lead. But the gangly Caldwell, with his milk-white legs pedaling smoothly, quieted the home crowd by taking the lead. At the third mile Walthour and Turville forged ahead, and the four thousand fans lit up the Piedmont Coliseum once again. Walthour never wavered nor looked away, concentrating on the back wheel of Candy Junior, and he finished the first heat ten yards ahead of Caldwell.

Shortly after the first heat, Jack Prince brought out his unofficial adopted son and Walthour's best friend, Gussie Lawson, to the inside of the track. Most of the crowd recognized Lawson and quieted down to hear what Prince was about to say. Prince shot the firing pistol twice just to make sure everyone was listening. Prince announced that Lawson would race the winner of Caldwell versus Walthour.

For the second heat, Caldwell gained a quick lead again, but this time he put a quarter lap on Walthour. Suddenly the few in the crowd rooting for Caldwell took heart and started yelling and cheering. But when words were exchanged between Turville and Walthour at the four-mile mark, Candy Junior was cranked up. At first Walthour had trouble keeping within the slipstream of the pacing motorcycle and nearly lost his pace. He put his head down and rose off his seat, rocking his bike back and forth furiously as he pedaled faster and faster. Once he caught up to his motorcycle, the race was all but over. Walthour made up the quarter-lap difference unbelievably quickly and proceeded to gain a half lap on The Manchester Giant.[9]

When Gussie Lawson took to the track to challenge Walthour, he rode behind a pacing machine named Bonanza, ridden by Jed Newkirk. The race was a great opportunity for Lawson to begin his motor-pacing career, racing three five-mile heats against probably the best pace follower in the world. In the first heat Walthour held a slight advantage, but Lawson hung on and eventually closed the gap. By the fourth mile, Lawson was leading with a mile to go. Charles Turville gave Candy Junior a little more gas at the beginning of the fifth mile, and Walthour clung to his pacemaker for dear life, passing Lawson and Newkirk. Walthour finished twenty yards ahead, and the big crowd went wild, delighted with a close and hard-fought race.

The second heat of the Walthour-Lawson match race started in much the same way as the first. At the start of the fourth mile Walthour called for Turville to give Candy Junior more juice, and with a frightful speed they shot ahead of Lawson and Newkirk. Lawson was lapped already when Walthour called for more speed. Men threw their hats in the air and jumped on benches and women screamed; bedlam reigned supreme in the Piedmont hills.[10]

The victory inspired *Atlanta Journal* sports reporter Grantland Rice to write this poem:

> Paul Revere was a rider bold—
> Oft has his dashing sprint been told . . .
> But listen now while we recite
> The ride that Walthour made last night.
>
> He rode like a flash from the star-lit sky—
> Like the gleam of a meteor flashing by.
> With never a look to the left or right,
> On, on he sped like the spirit of night.
> No wonder young Lawson lost out in the race,
> For no living man could have held that pace.
> There may be riders living today
> Who can beat Walthour. Hidden away
> There may be others who even now
> Might snatch the wreath from the victor's brow.
> But none can rival the rider who
> Wears the Shamrock twined with the red white and blue.[11]

{ 14 }

Baptism of Blood

although Walthour had been unable to compete in the New York six-day race in December 1902 because of his broken collarbone, he benefited both physically and mentally from being home in Atlanta for almost eight months. He was able to rest completely and allow the break to heal. Traveling between New York, Boston, Hartford, Providence, Baltimore, and other cities was costly and disrupted his family life. In Atlanta Walthour was able to establish a routine and build a foundation of fitness with regular workouts. But he still had time to relax, play with his children, and tend to his chickens.

One of the last Atlanta races before Walthour went north to start the regular season of motor-pacing was held on May 8, 1903, against Harry Elkes. During the previous season Elkes had beaten Walthour five times in a row. Walthour, however, had come back to win the next six races against Elkes. Elkes knew his string of American motor-paced championship-level races was in jeopardy, so he decided to go to Europe and take advantage of the thousands of dollars on offer from European promoters. In 1903 Elkes hoped to reestablish himself as the best American pace-follower and take back the title from Walthour. Once he had realized this ambition, Elkes planned to retire a wealthy and happy man. He was newly engaged to be married and seemed to have his priorities in order. But he worried

about the hazards of the sport. "The game is getting dangerous," he told
a reporter. "[T]he odds are against coming out alive."[1]

Elkes held the five-mile record behind pace on the track, with a ride
of seven minutes eleven seconds, or about forty-two miles per hour. After Walthour he was considered the best American behind the motors.
To convince Elkes to travel south and race Walthour on his home track,
Jack Prince enticed the New Yorker with a $1,000 guarantee plus another
$1,000 (a total of $25,200 in current dollars) if he beat Walthour. The
prize money was displayed in the window at Schaul and May's jewelry store
in Atlanta on the corner of Peachtree and Decatur.[2] Thousands of citizens
came to gawk at the money—it was more than most earned in a year.

Jack Prince was thrilled that another capacity crowd of four thousand
had gathered at his track to see the two best motor-pacers in the United
States, if not the world. With Charles Turville driving Candy Junior and Elkes's pacer, Jed Newkirk, on Prince's pacer, "Dixie," both came out on the
track to warm up the engines. Turville and Newkirk astonished the crowd,
demonstrating the power, noise, and speed of the machines. When Walthour and Elkes came out waving to the crowd, all stood to acknowledge
the two great champions.

The race was a contest for the best of three five-mile heats. In the
first mile of the first heat, Walthour was timed at one minute twenty-three
seconds, a new track record at more than forty-four miles per hour. This
blistering first mile carried him to the finish line in seven minutes twenty-
two seconds, only two seconds off his own track record. But in the second heat Elkes took the lead and never relinquished it. Walthour brought
the crowd to its feet, however, by nearly catching Elkes at the line. Eager
men chewing on cigars, women nervously clutching their handkerchiefs
in both hands, and children jumping up and down to get a better look
were all rewarded with what they had paid for—a great race with two of
the finest tuned athletes in the world, men who competed at the edge of a
technological revolution.

In the deciding heat, the riders whirled around the track with all their
might, hugging the backs of their motorcycles, taking as much advantage
as possible of the draft. With Walthour ahead by a quarter lap after two
miles, the cyclists were attaining twelve seconds per lap, and another track

record was close to being broken. Near the end of the fourth mile the two kept up with their pacing motorcycles, traveling at a reckless forty-four miles per hour. Suddenly Walthour's rear tire burst, and his bicycle slipped out from under the steep banking. In a flash he fell, rolling and sliding fifty feet before he stopped on the inside of the track, where he was safe from the motorcycles flying around him at full throttle.

Elkes, who saw the accident, deftly slowed down, hopped off his bicycle, and was the first to arrive at Walthour's side. Except for the painful splinters imbedded in his left hip, Walthour said he was fine. Elkes put his hand out and helped his rival stand up, and Walthour crouched with his hands on his knees, wincing from the pain. The crowd was silent from the drama of the crash but responded with a torrential ovation, acknowledging Elkes's great sportsmanship and showing their relief that Walthour had not been seriously hurt.

Gingerly Walthour remounted his bicycle with the help of an assistant and gained confidence as he rode around the track for a few test laps. He waved to the crowd and received a rousing cheer. The race resumed from the point of the crash just before the four-mile mark. Walthour was able to maintain his lead for the final mile and won a great victory and $1,000.[3]

To give Elkes a chance to prove that he was at least Walthour's equal, another race was scheduled for a few days later at the Piedmont Coliseum. Rather than the familiar formula of the best of three five-mile heats, a single race of ten miles was slated. By the sixth mile Elkes seemed sure to win. But Turville gradually gave Candy Junior a little more gas and reduced Elkes's lead. By the end of the eighth mile Elkes and Walthour were riding neck and neck. The hushed crowd watched as the cyclists raced at an incredible speed, and the rear wheels of both motorcycles slipped on the turns. Walthour did not have a clear lead until the last mile, and when he came across the tape almost a half lap ahead, the Coliseum became a scene of wild celebration. Walthour finished the ten miles in fourteen minutes thirty seconds, setting another track record.[4]

❋

Walthour's first race north of the Mason-Dixon Line for the 1903 cycling season was at the newly refurbished Charles River track in Boston. The old three-lap-to-the-mile cement track had been ripped out and replaced with a modern wooden five-lap-to-the-mile track. The surface was twenty-five feet wide with turns banked at thirty-eight degrees. The open-air grandstand at the start-finish line could seat eight thousand spectators, and the bleachers that wrapped around the remainder of the track could sit at least six thousand more.

Memorial Day, May 30, was a beautiful spring day. More than fifteen thousand people including Blanche Walthour and the flaxen-haired Walthour children—Viva, Nona, and eight-month-old Bobby Jr.—crammed every available inch of space to see the first race at the updated facility. Four of the best paced riders in the country—Walthour, Elkes, Will Stinson, and Jimmy Moran—were set to race behind the fastest motorcycles available. The technology of gasoline engines was improving by the month, and motorcycle speeds spiraled up at a dizzying rate. The Charles River track had been purposefully designed to withstand record speeds. In practice a few days before the race, both Walthour and Elkes had clocked a mile behind motorcycle pace in one minute thirteen seconds at Charles River—almost fifty miles per hour.[5]

The featured Memorial Day event was a twenty-mile race. Seconds after the starting gun the four riders caught up to their pacing machines. The roar of the four motorcycle engines combined with the screaming from fifteen thousand spectators was deafening. At one point the pace was too hot for Walthour, and he pulled back from his machine. Elkes yelled at his motorman, Franz Hoffman, for more speed. By mile fifteen he had a three-lap lead over Walthour, who was in second place. At mile sixteen Elkes again called for Hoffman to pick up speed. Hoffman turned around to tell him they were going fast enough.

At that moment Elkes's bicycle chain snapped. "I looked back and saw him wobbling along and thought he was going up after his other wheel," said Hoffman. "I came around and could not see him. The next time around I called for Harry and someone hollered back something that I could not understand. The next time I called out loud, 'Come on Harry; hurry up' and someone said Harry is dead. I could not believe it and when I came around again I called for him, but again they said he was killed. I thought they were fooling me."[6]

Just as Hoffman had turned to look back, Elkes coasted safely down the backstretch. But his broken chain became entangled in the spokes of his back wheel, and he was thrown off his bicycle, landing directly in the path of Stinson's fourteen-horsepower pacing machine driven by Frank Gatley. At nearly fifty miles per hour, the big motorcycle ran over the rider lying helplessly on the track and pulverized Elkes's body with a sickening thud.

Lying on the smooth board surface were the motorcycle, the two bicycles, and the entangled figures of Elkes, Stinson, and Gatley. Blood poured from the wounds of all three. Elkes was limp and senseless, his head horribly crushed. Stinson looked almost as bad, covered in blood from a deep gash in his head. Hundreds of people jumped from the bleachers onto the backstretch and rushed toward the tangle of machines and men. Gatley sat up holding his left foot; his toe was almost severed. Doctors were summoned from the crowd, and willing hands carried the injured to the training quarters. An ambulance rushed twenty-five-year-old Harry Elkes to the Massachusetts General Hospital. On the way there, he died without having regained consciousness. The *Boston Daily Globe* called the race at the new Charles River track "a baptism of blood."[7]

Many feared Stinson would lose his left eye, but doctors carefully stitched up the injury. Two days after the accident and against his father's wishes, Stinson put on his coat and hat and walked to Charles River from his Cambridge home on Greene Street. His face was full of stitches, and he had the wounds uncovered to give them air and allow them to heal better. Near the park entrance he attracted more than one hundred people, who gathered around the big rider, amazed that he had brushed up against death and had survived. "I feel badly battered and am very sore, but what bothers me most is that owing to my upper lip being split clear to my nose I am unable to open my mouth except a little bit on the right side. . . . I cannot comprehend Harry Elkes is dead and that I will never race him again. It seems hard, for when they go they are always good ones, Johnny Nelson, Archie McEachern, and Harry, all good fellows and fast game men and whenever they were booked to start the public was always sure of a race."[8] The incident profoundly affected Will Stinson—both physically and mentally—and he did not race much for the next three years.

James Kennedy was the comanager of the Madison Square Garden six-day races along with Patrick Powers, and he was also Elkes's trainer and manager. Kennedy sent the tragic news to Glens Falls, New York, where Elkes's father, William "Pop" Elkes lived. His father was too distraught to come to Boston and sent his brother, Harry, in his place. Elkes's body was transported to Glens Falls on the train and laid to rest in the Bay Street Cemetery. A great tombstone was erected in his honor. Under his name a bicycle wheel with a wing was carved out of the stone. On the back it read, "Champion Cyclist of the World. 1878–1903. Erected to His Memory by His Boston and New York Admirers."

❋

Although Walthour had not received a scratch at the Memorial Day race, his mental state, like Stinson's, was severely affected. His schedule included races within days after the disaster, and his performances were lackluster at best. On June 1 Walthour was soundly defeated by Hugh McLean—to whom he rarely lost—in a twenty-mile race at the Providence track. Walthour quit after sixteen miles, claiming that his tire had punctured.[9] The next day he rode against Joe Nelson and Harry Caldwell in another twenty-mile race, again on the Charles River track. The *Boston Globe* reported that when Walthour seemed to have a victory well within his grasp, his tire punctured. Rather than look frantically for a new wheel and return to the race as he usually did, he sat down and appeared not to worry whether he continued or not.[10]

He finally pulled out of his apparent depression with a convincing victory over McLean and Nelson at Charles River. The race was the best of 3 5-mile heats, which were thought to be safer than the longer races without heats. Walthour was timed in 6 minutes 17⅕ seconds in the first heat, a new world record for the distance. His last mile was 1 minute 12⅗ seconds, another world record. For the third heat Walthour set a blazing pace behind his motor and never backed off, finishing with one more world record timed in 6 minutes 6⅕ seconds—nearly 50 miles per hour for 5 miles.[11]

Although motor-pacing continued unabated with faster and faster speeds, the growing number of injuries brought new safety measures. Some pacemakers, such as Benny Munroe, wore leather helmets. Motorcycles appeared on some tracks with a roller attached to the back of the machine. Walthour did not like the roller idea, because it prevented him from being as close as possible to the pacing machine, maximizing his protection of the motorcycle's slipstream and minimizing air resistance.[12]

As motorcycle speeds increased, so too did motor-paced cycling records. On July 12, 1903, Albert Champion, as good a motorcyclist as he was a motor-paced cyclist, went to the Charles River track with a leather helmet, corduroy pants, and wool sweater and cranked up his 4-cylinder motorcycle. In front of thousands of screaming fans, Champion sliced through the wind, leaning down over the long machine, and negotiated a mile in 58.8 seconds, a new motorcycle speed record on a circular track.[13]

Walthour was always intrigued by the powerful motorcycles that paced him. But he rarely, if ever, rode motorcycles; he left the pacing to the experts. Not long after he broke the mile record on the Charles River track, Albert Champion was at the Washington, D.C., Coliseum wooden track with his famous four-cylinder motorcycle. Champion was there to help pace George Leander, who was practicing for a race. Walthour was at the Washington track too, squinting in the bright, hot, humid sunshine. He had ridden several laps unpaced to limber up his muscles and sat waiting for Charles Turville to come out and pace him. Leaning against the stands next to him was Champion's motorcycle. Champion and Leander were in the training quarters getting a rubdown. Walthour was not an experienced motorman, but he straddled the machine. He balanced the big bulky motorcycle between his legs, looking down, poking at levers, and pulling at the clutch. He started it up and checked around to see if anybody was watching him. The coast was clear. He gave it some gas and took off down the track, not going fast enough to go up the banking very far on the turns. He gradually understood how the motorcycle functioned then sped up. From the training quarters, Champion recognized the sound of his prized possession and ran out onto the track wearing only a towel around his waist.

Walthour laughed and sped by when Champion cursed at him in French. After a few laps more Walthour decided he had enough fun and attempted to return the motorcycle to its rightful owner. But the throttle mechanism would only speed up the machine and not slow it down. He circled the track much faster than he wanted, forcing the motorcycle high up the turns. On the straightaway Walthour gave Champion and the others that had assembled to watch a signal that there was a problem. Walthour looked as if he were going to jump off. The half-naked Champion grabbed Nat Butler's pacing machine and went after the pale-faced Walthour. Little by little, Champion gained on the runaway machine, which was luckily not at full speed but was still going more than fifty miles per hour. Champion expertly matched the speed of his own machine, and around the track they went side by side. Champion precariously leaned over and pressed the lever to slow the machine down. The two came in safely, and everyone congratulated Champion. Walthour swore off motorcycles forever.[14]

Days before Champion rode his powerful motorcycle a mile in under a minute, Walthour raced George Leander and Basil de Guichard, an up-and-coming motor-paced rider from Denver, in a race at the Charles River track. Walthour was paced by Charles Turville, and he won the race by three-quarters of a lap from Leander. It was a great win, but Walthour created a sensation by reeling off the last mile in 1 minute 7 seconds, a speed of nearly 55 miles per hour. Turville recklessly tested the limits of the track, and Walthour displayed an absolute lack of fear. For the entire distance Walthour was timed in 17 minutes 29⅕ seconds and set motor-paced world records from 1 to 15 miles.[15]

For Walthour there was no slowing down, and it seemed that no one or nothing could keep him from defending his American motor-paced title, except possibly death itself. On August 22, 1903, Walthour raced fellow southerner Benny Munroe and Hugh McLean at Revere, Massachusetts, an eight-lap-to-the mile open-air wooden track in an hour-long contest. With less than half the time covered at the seventeenth mile, Walthour was leading comfortably when the rear tire of Turville's motorcycle unexpectedly peeled off. Rubber debris shot up in Walthour's face. The motorcycle's rim dug into the track's wood surface and carved a smooth impression down the banking. Turville was thrown clear of the wreckage and the motorcycle crashed, sending sparks, splinters, and motorcycle parts far and wide.

Walthour went down hard as well but like Turville was safe. The motorcycle came to a rest on its side and almost immediately caught fire. A cry came from the thousands of spectators who lined the stadium when the McLean and Munroe teams came around, but they, along with their pacemakers, were able to avoid the blaze. People ran out to help douse the flames as Walthour calmly stood up and wiped the blood off his legs and arms. The motorcycle was quickly dragged off the charred, blackened surface of the track. The clock continued ticking, and Walthour mounted a new bicycle. But he had lost many laps to Munroe, who had continued to ride and won.[16]

Down south, rumors spread like the flames on the Revere track that Walthour had been killed.[17] With the deaths of Johnny Nelson, Archie McEachern, and Harry Elkes, such news might not have been such a surprise, and many believed the rumors were true. In fact Walthour was better prepared and more determined than ever to win the 1903 American motor-paced title, and he would not allow tragedy and setbacks to stand in his way.

{ 15 }

Dixie Flyers

obby Walthour often threatened to retire from the motor-pacing game, just as Harry Elkes had done. Walthour was as vulnerable as any motor-pacer but had an uncanny ability to avoid serious injury. He was fearless and thrived on the excitement. He thought nothing of furiously pedaling a huge gear and following a pacing machine going over fifty miles per hour. Walthour did this in front of sell-out crowds, wearing no protection and knowing full well that a technical mistake or an unexpected accident could put him in the morgue. Riding behind the motors could have killed him as it had done his contemporaries, but it also kept him alive. From his earliest days as a bike messenger, Walthour had achieved fame beyond all expectations and was making more money than he had ever dreamed was possible. Above all he was doing what he loved and was dedicated to the sport. In spite of his public threats to retire, he privately left the worrying to his wife; Blanche was the one who had constant fears that he would be injured, disabled, or killed.

❋

In the fall of 1903 while preparing for the Madison Square Garden six-day race, Walthour signed a contract with his cycling mate, Eli Winesett, to manage his professional affairs through January 1, 1905.[1] Walthour arrived home in Atlanta on September 9, 1903, having finished the motor-pacing season. He had won thirty-seven of his fifty races on the northern tracks.[2]

At a time when the average American annual salary was significantly less than $1,000($25,200), Walthour's guaranteed salary, prizes, and endorsements netted him at least $20,000 ($503,000 in current dollars) in the three and a half months since the end of May. By comparison Honus Wagner, who was one of the best hitters in baseball during that time, earned a salary of $4,200 ($106,000) playing for the Pittsburgh Pirates in 1903.[3] For motor-paced men and professional sportsmen of the day, betting on themselves to win was not at all unusual and was in fact almost expected. With Walthour's fabulous winning percentage, he undoubtedly cleared a substantial amount above and beyond his appearance fees and winnings by wagering on himself. Given his "superabundance of wealth," as *Bicycling World* put it, to retire from racing would have been difficult.[4] Like many professional football players today, Walthour wanted to make the most of his potentially short athletic career, especially given the possibility, indeed the *probability*, that he would be killed or permanently maimed.

"The Manchester Giant" Harry Caldwell won twenty-three out of his forty-four motor-paced races during the 1903 season, putting him second in the running to Walthour on the N.C.A.'s prestigious championship chart. Walthour had beaten Caldwell six out of eight times, so no question actually existed about who had won the championship, which was awarded on an aggregate basis rather than for one specific event. However, Albert Champion had begun racing late in the 1903 season and had beaten Walthour three straight times. Consequently Champion publicly claimed the 1903 American motor-pacing title for himself.[5]

With the northern circuit completed and cyclists gearing up for December's big six-day event in New York, Walthour and the other six-day invitees began to train longer distances to increase their stamina. But Champion wanted to prove his claim, and Walthour wasn't about to let a little interruption in his training bother him if he could stay in Atlanta and make money at the same time. For Champion to travel south to race against Walthour on the ten-lap-to-the-mile track inside the Piedmont Coliseum was not an easy proposition for track promoter Jack Prince. Prince had to produce as much money as he had when Harry Elkes raced in Atlanta in May—$2,000 ($53,000).[6] Never one to shy away from a risky venture, Prince signed a contract with Champion to race Walthour in Atlanta.

On September 17, 1903, thousands squeezed their way inside the cozy and smoky atmosphere of the rollicking Coliseum to see the best of three five-mile heats to decide who was the best motor-pacer in America. Prince expected nothing less than a great sellout crowd. From the center of the track, with his derby hat tilted to one side, his arms wildly gesticulating, and a big smile on his face, Prince's loud voice reached every ear in the arena as he introduced Champion. On cue Champion rode onto the track wearing his white racing uniform with the French fleur-de-lis tied around his waist. The crowd gave him a standing ovation as he circled the track waving.

The people who paid fifty cents to fill the stands did not mind the foul smells or the poor ventilation of the building. But they had not come for Albert Champion. They took great pride in drowning out Prince's introduction of Walthour. Of course, he needed no introduction and rode onto the track just as Champion had done, except with the Stars and Stripes wrapped around his waist and bandages on his arm from a recent crash.

Champion was paced by Jed Newkirk and Walthour by Gussie Lawson. The motormen both came out to the track roaring and revving their engines to the delight of the spectators. As the contestants lined up the crowd quieted down. But when Jack Prince shot the starting gun, they became rowdy once again. In the first heat Champion lost his pace and crashed to the board surface at forty miles per hour before the first mile, but he was not hurt. The race was restarted and Walthour won in seven minutes twenty-five seconds.

In the second heat Champion took the lead at the crack of the pistol, and by the halfway point Champion was nearly a halflap ahead of Walthour. Before being caught on the backstretch, however, Lawson gave Candy Junior a little more gas. Both motorcycle and Walthour responded magnificently, and they gained on Champion. By the fourth mile the crowd stood up in unison as Walthour nearly caught up to Champion. Eventually Lawson moved his machine past Champion. Walthour was inches behind his pace, pedaling fluidly, his upper body hardly moving and his attention focused on nothing but the back wheel of Lawson's motorcycle.

Walthour won by a half lap in seven minutes seventeen seconds, breaking his own track record by three seconds and averaging more than forty-one miles per hour. Champion showed true sportsmanship and gave the hometown hero a hearty handshake for his victory as they rounded the track together. Champion lifted Walthour's arm up to give him a victory salute. The crowd showed its appreciation with a huge ovation for both riders.[7]

✸

Although he had already been invited to attend, Walthour still needed to negotiate a contract for the December six-day race at Madison Square Garden in New York. In October managers Kennedy and Powers made Walthour an offer. He countered it, and a contract was drawn up. Walthour was to receive $500 ($12,600) to start the six-day plus $60 ($1,510) for each day he remained in the race. Walthour's popularity was never greater, and he was arguably the best rider in America, but Powers and Kennedy had an upper hand in the negotiations. Worldwide attention was given to the race at Madison Square Garden; to win meant fame and money. It was one of the most publicized sporting events in the world, a forerunner of modern commercial sporting events.

Walthour hired Bobby Thompson as a manager specifically for the six-day race. Thompson was a boxer and cycling pacemaker who had managed the winning team in 1902. He also had managed Walthour and McEachern when they won in 1901. Walthour again chose fellow southerner Benny Munroe as his partner for the continuous 142-hour race.[8]

Munroe, Walthour, and Gussie Lawson moved to Savannah to train for a few weeks. Once there they came up with the team name The Crackers, but later changed it to The Dixie Flyers. They were away from their homes, wives, and children, and although Walthour was a teetotaler and did not smoke (he said it gave him a dry mouth), Gussie Lawson was known to drink heavily at times. Perhaps through Lawson's influence, they had more than a few nights out in Savannah. Walthour admitted that the trio rested more than they rode and arrived in New York "overweight and under trained."[9] As usual several teams from Europe had assembled to race at Madison Square Garden, as well as a large domestic contingent. The foreign delegation included Jean Gougoltz, Lucien Petit-Breton, Arthur Vanderstuyft, and Jimmy Michael, and they arrived in New York by steamship along with African American Woody Hedspeth from Chicago.

With the blatant racism in the United States, Hedspeth, like Major Taylor, was forced to race in Europe. Although he was never as dominant as Taylor, Hedspeth had a successful European campaign in 1903. After he crossed the Atlantic back to the United States, he was paired with Melvin Dove in the 1903 six-day race. Dove was another African American who was just breaking out of the amateur sprint ranks.

On December 6 the doors of Madison Square Garden opened at 7 p.m., and a continuous stream of humanity flooded the great arena until fifteen thousand people jammed every space. In the box seats close to the track the scent of freshly sawn wood was quickly replaced by the heavy odor of cigar smoke. At five minutes past midnight, ex-heavyweight boxing champion James "Gentleman Jim" Corbett fired the shot that sent seventeen riders on their long journey round and round the yellow pine saucer. With help from the 69th Regiment Band and a large assortment of throats, megaphones, sirens, whistles, and rattles, the Garden girders shook, and the Eleventh Annual International Championship Six-Day Race was under way.

Frank Kramer, who had recently won his third straight American sprint title, wrote for the *World*: "There will be dangerous riding in this race from the start to the finish. I know the temperament of the men and know that within the ranks there is the bitterest rivalry. Between Walthour and Munroe, the Southerners, and Dove and Hedspeth, the colored men, it will be a war to the knife."[10]

Gaining even one lap ahead meant the difference between winning and losing the entire race, and many unsuccessful attempts at stealing a precious lap were made. During one such attempt Walthour, John Bedell, and Jean Fischer rode desperately hard, digging into their pedals and gripping the handlebars tight so that their bike frames squeaked under the strain. The three riders failed to gain a lap, but they collided in that burst of speed. Bicycles flipped lengthwise, scraping and pounding the wood surface of the track. The riders were tossed to the track—one slid on his belly. Fortunately, no one lost any laps from the accident, and miraculously none were hurt. They all brushed themselves off, received new bikes, and continued with the race.

Hugh McLean, who was partnered with Jimmy Moran, did not have such luck. He crashed into James Bowler and injured his face and head so severely he was rendered unconscious. An ambulance was summoned while doctors attended to McLean, who sat in a daze, bleeding. Since McLean was forced to withdraw, under the new rules Moran could replace him with another rider from the field. Fortunately for Moran, Patsey Keegan's partner suffered from dizziness, and Moran was able to form a new partnership with Keegan. By forming a new team, the rules declared that Moran and Keegan would lose a lap to the field. After the first day nine teams, including the Dixie Flyer team, were tied at first place with 506 miles.[11]

On the second day Walthour and Munroe remained tied with seven other teams for first place. Frank Galvin, who came out on the track after a previous wreck, was not in any condition to ride, but he insisted on giving his partner a well-deserved rest. After only a few laps Galvin was unable to maintain a straight line and took a hard tumble, bringing down four other riders with him. Two flipped over their handlebars and flew into a box. A woman nearby fainted when a rider was flung unconscious into the seat next to hers. Police did all they could to avoid a panic, and the big crowd calmed down after several minutes.

After 3 days, 8 teams were tied for first place at 1,275 miles. The Dixie Flyer team of Walthour and Munroe was the favorite among the New York crowd, but the odds makers put them at seventh place at 5 to 1 as likely winners. The Leander-Butler team was the 2-1 favorite to win.[12] A large pall of smoke hovered over the great arena, and riders at the far end of the track appeared as ghosts through a blue fog. A powerful smell from the hot dog vendor's busy stand permeated the Garden basement, and patrons of Steven's bar queued up for thirst-quenching beers. Any significant noise from the arena crowd created a rush of excited fans back to the track closure above.

During one of the days' many attempts to gain a lap, Eddie Root, who was partnered with young Oliver Dorlon, came very close to lapping Benny Munroe, the tail-end rider of the leading eight teams. If Root had passed him, Walthour and Munroe would have then been second behind the seven leading teams. But Munroe crashed immediately before Root was going to pass him. The referees investigated whether Munroe had thrown himself intentionally to avoid being lapped, because according to the rules, no lap could be gained in the event of an accident. The lost lap was eventually rewarded back to Munroe and Walthour, but all the riders were warned that from this point forward no deliberate falls would be tolerated.[13]

On the morning of the fourth day Munroe insisted on having a large automobile horn attached to his handlebars and honked it continuously, yelling for riders to "clear the way." He also shouted incoherent statements such as, "Here's where I go to the electric chair!" At the side of the track Frenchman Lucien Petit-Breton coughed up blood. From these incidents and others, and according to the *New York Daily Tribune*, rumors spread that "dope" was being administered to some of the riders and that the Health Department might interfere to cancel the race.[14]

The riders continued to circle the small track day and night, but they were not the only ones at the Garden behaving strangely. Much to the amusement of the surrounding crowd, two women got into an altercation; one had a large chunk of brown hair torn from her head, and the other woman suffered from a deep cut on her lip from flying debris being thrown at them. Police separated the women but then were forced to run upstairs to break up another fight between two men on the second balcony. One officer was taken to the hospital after having been bitten on the thumb.[15]

Thursday rolled into Friday, and the fun continued. Floyd Krebs, who was partnered with Frenchman Jean Gougoltz, rode around the pine oval, muttering unintelligibly while wearing a women's hat. Two trainers came to blows on the infield over a water bottle. A veiled woman kept handing George Leander dollar bills each time he came around. When teams were not trying to steal a lap the riders plodded along at a slow pace, drinking water or a broth tea concoction from rubber-tubed containers handed to them by their trainers. Overall, they were three hundred miles behind the record established four years before by the Miller-Waller team. The slow speed was especially evident on the fifth day, and it was clear the riders were saving themselves for the final one-mile sprint, which would ultimately determine the winners, unless one of the teams succeeded in lapping the entire field before the end of the race.[16]

Just after midnight, with less than twenty-four hours to go, the seven leading teams reached the two-thousand-mile mark: twenty thousand laps.

The teams were Contenet–Petit-Breton, Leander-Butler, Krebs-Gougoltz, Newkirk-Jacobson, brothers John and Menus Bedell, Bowler-Fischer, and Walthour-Munroe. The oddsmakers still had George Leander and Nat Butler as 11-5 favorites against the field.

Leander's training assistant, who had reportedly slept for only four hours during the entire race, fell asleep on Leander's cot. Needing to sleep himself, Leander shook the dozing trainer, who promptly jumped to his feet and caught Leander in the face with his fist. The big temperamental Chicagoan, too weak to retaliate, seemed not to mind the blow, threw himself on the cot, and fell fast asleep.

Walthour was accustomed to having his restorative sleep, and he typically slept for ten hours plus a daytime nap. But during the six-day race, to catch one or two hours of shut-eye at any time was an accomplishment. The riders' cots had been carried up from the basement to the trackside so the resting men could be close at hand if anything happened. The riders were so tired they did not seem to be bothered by the overhead lights and the thousands of noisy New Yorkers in the stands. At noon Julian Samson crashed his bicycle close to the cot on which Walthour slept soundly. The crowd nearby rushed to the spot where Samson lay stunned. As each person pushed forward for a better look, the support railing gave way and sent the mass of people onto Walthour's cot. Walthour woke up with a scream. Fortunately Blanche was close by and succeeded in settling him back down on his cot.

At 9:55 p.m. it was announced that, among the seven teams tied for first place, a mile sprint would be ridden to decide the race. The teams not in the top seven left the track, and the others picked their sprinter. With his past experience as a sprinter and because of his six-day victory two years earlier, the easy choice for the Dixie Flyer team was Walthour.

The gun went off for the final ten laps, and the crowd of 15,000 hysterical people cheered for their favorite team. Walthour, in his blue uniform with an American flag tied around his waist, rode a Columbia sprinting bicycle fitted with a 104-inch gear and French-made racing tires. He moved to the front at the first lap but was overtaken by Floyd Krebs, who led the next two laps. Walthour took back the lead on the fourth lap, and Leander went to the front on the fifth, sixth, and seventh laps. With each succeeding lap the crowd grew louder and the speed faster. Walthour took the lead on the eighth and was followed closely by Leander, Krebs, Fischer, Newkirk, Petit-Breton, and John Bedell.

Walthour dug in for a supreme effort and increased his slight lead. Swiftly and abruptly Petit-Breton's front wheel collapsed under the strain, and he fell heavily, taking down Bedell, Fischer, and Newkirk in a writhing heap. A shriek of dismay went through the vast arena. Petit-Breton and Bedell were knocked unconscious, but the remaining riders quickly remounted and finished the race.

The rules for the final mile sprint stated that falls should not count in favor of the fallen rider. Walthour crossed the line ahead of Leander, and the Dixie Flyer team had won the great six-day race at Madison Square Garden. The crowd was in ecstasy, and Blanche Walthour ran out to greet her victorious husband. Many spectators left their seats for a better look at the winners, broke through the railings, and slid down the embankment of the track. Full scale chaos was narrowly averted as Walthour and Munroe took their victory lap.[17]

When news of Walthour's victory was first announced on the ticker tape at the overcrowded offices of the *Atlanta Journal* Walthour's former trainer and mentor, Gus Castle, jumped over three chairs in celebration and may have gone through the window if he had not been restrained. Other impromptu celebrations were held in cigars shops and bars as news spilled out into the streets of Atlanta. Walthour was the toast of the town. The next morning newsboys fought to supply extra editions to the Atlanta public. The newspapers sold almost as fast as the boys ran out with arms full of the latest edition.[18]

Walthour received $750 ($18,900) in double eagle gold pieces for his share of the winnings plus his $500 ($12,600) to start and $60 ($1,510) per day thereafter. In addition he was promised lucrative appearances at theaters in New York City.[19]

Race managers Powers and Kennedy estimated that Walthour and Munroe cleared $5,000 ($126,000) for their victory. Powers and Kennedy may have intentionally given a high estimation to disguise the fact that they made an absolute killing. Expenses for the six-day race were $35,000 ($755,000). But with box-office receipts of $90,000 ($2,260,000), each manager made well over $25,000 ($629,000) apiece.[20]

The haggard riders finally slept as they pleased without disturbance, ate when they wanted, and tended to their wounds. No longer would they be subjected to a noisy and nerve-racking existence, hear the monotonous drone of the wheels going around the yellow pine, or ride through thick layers of blue tobacco smoke. Most riders stayed at the Putnam House across from the Garden on Fourth Avenue, but Walthour and Munroe spent the night at Walthour's mother's house.

Bobby and Blanche arrived in Atlanta on December 21 and were congratulated by many friends. Walthour was alert and well rested and told the gathered crowd:

> I feel as well as ever and am fit to ride another six-day race next week if it is necessary. I had already planned to go to Paris in May before I won the six-day race. After this event I was much sought after by managers of bicycle tracks in Paris who wanted me to come at once. I had many things to attend to, however, and will not be able to leave for Europe until February 10. I also desire to ride before the people of Atlanta before going to France. I think that I have demonstrated to the satisfaction of all that I have a good claim to the title of champion of the world. And as I understand that there are several in France who think that they can win from me I intend to give them a chance. I am very thankful to my friends in Atlanta for the many telegrams received, and these gave me great encouragement in my [six-day] race. I won far easier than expected, and when I finished I felt as fresh as one could possibly be who has ridden one week on a stretch. My time for the last half-mile was caught at 54 seconds, which is faster than Kramer had ridden in his exhibition trials during the week. Munroe is one of the best partners I have ever had.[21]

❋

1903 was the first year of the Tour de France and of the Harley-Davidson company. These two sacred institutions, mere fledglings at the time, would have their day in the sun. But 1903 was Bobby Walthour's year in America.

{16}

L'Imbattable Walthour

O n November 20, 1902, Georges "Géo" Lefèvre originated the idea for the Tour de France while he was having lunch with Henri Desgrange and Victor Goddet. Desgrange was the editor of *L'Auto*, a Parisian sports journal printed on yellow paper. Goddet was the financial manager and Lefèvre was the journal's chief cycling reporter.[1] With the Madison Square Garden six-day race in mind, Lefèvre suggested a one-lap race around France, using their country as a sort of gigantic cycle track or velodrome. The rest is history. Today the Tour de France leader's yellow jersey, or *maillot jaune*, remains a symbol that not only represents the yellow paper of *L'Auto* but signifies the highest echelons of sporting excellence.

Desgrange also served as the director of the Parc des Princes, which was an outdoor 666-meter velodrome in Paris, as well as director of the Vélodrome d'Hiver, the first permanent indoor velodrome in France, located near the Eiffel Tower. In the promotion of French cycling Desgrange was one of the kings. Victor Breyer and Robert Coquelle, who brought Major Taylor to Europe, were two other active promoters. Although skeptical of most American cycling talent, Desgrange wanted Walthour. "I have been trying for two years among the Americans [to engage] the man who can race with our boys. Since the regrettable death of Elkes, only two names have fixed my attention, Kramer, three times champion of America, and Walthour."[2]

In the weeks before his first European trip, Walthour painstakingly conditioned himself with light weights under the supervision of James W. Barton, a doctor who was associated with the Atlanta Y.M.C.A. Walthour credited "Professor Barton" as being the best athletic trainer in the world. He had worked with Barton since December 1902, during which time his physical development improved remarkably. At the age of twenty-six, Walthour was 5 foot 10 inches, and his weight fluctuated from 150 to 160 pounds. Since he had been training under Barton, he had never felt fitter and had added five pounds of lean muscle to his slender but powerful frame.[3]

On February 9, 1904, before he left Atlanta, local fans presented Walthour with a silver loving cup as a good-luck token for his European adventure. The silver trophy was the brainchild of restaurateur Henry Durand and purchased by more than two hundred and fifty citizens of Atlanta. Walthour accepted the beautiful and gleaming gift from Lowry Arnold, a well-known Atlanta attorney, who made an interesting and humorous presentation at the Bijou Theatre House in front of the largest audience ever assembled there. After the roaring applause subsided, Walthour faced the crowd, stammered, and then regained his composure. "I thank Mr. Arnold for his remarks. I am not a public speaker, however, and do not wish to take up your time. In closing, I wish to thank Mr. Durand for his kindness and every one for the interest they have shown in my plans."[4] In addition to the cup Walthour took a United States flag to Europe, which he wore around his racing jersey.

Cold and heavy rain welcomed Walthour, Eli Winesett, and Gussie Lawson to Paris on the morning of February 22. Although his presence on French soil was highly anticipated, only Robert Coquelle and his assistant, Truchot, who were writers for the French sports journal *Le Vélo*, met Walthour and company at the Saint-Lazare station.

Walthour, Lawson, and Winesett brought two enormous multicolored cases, assorted team luggage, and equipment, which they tried to shelter from the rain. After the Frenchmen and the Americans exchanged pleasantries, Walthour told Coquelle that he had rested well on his journey and desired to work out at the Buffalo track immediately, even though the rain poured down outside. Coquelle was taken aback. Walthour did not ask to see the Eiffel Tower or inquire as to the whereabouts of the catacombs or the Notre Dame Cathedral. "*Tout de suite?*" "*Ce matin même.*" ("At once?" "This same morning.")[5]

They arrived at the track two hours later. Victor Breyer managed Buffalo Velodrome, which was located at Neuilly-sur-Seine, a heavily populated suburb of Paris. The track's name came from Buffalo Bill Cody, whose circus had performed there. The sun came out briefly, and fellow American and sprinter Walter Bardgett gave Walthour a tour of the beautifully crafted 300-meter board track with cream-colored railings. The men stepped lightly to avoid soaking their feet in the saturated turf inside the track, which was normally a field of well-manicured grass. Walthour visited with other professionals, including Frenchman Lucien Petit-Breton, who had raced against him at the Madison Square Garden six-day race a few months earlier. To understand the track better Walthour took a ten-mile spin while Eli Winesett and Gussie Lawson busied themselves readying the pacing motorcycle, Death Dealer.

In a letter home Walthour wrote:

These Frenchies could not understand that I should get to work so quickly, but I told them I had come over to clean them up and not see Paris, for as far as Paris is concerned, give me good old Georgia and I am hungry to see the good red hills again. . . . I got lost once and walked myself to death and when we would ask someone where we were they would shrug and say, 'No compre.' When I go to the drug store to buy soda I get what I want after great trouble and then open my pocketbook so the man can help himself, but I am getting wise to the money over here now and they do not fool me. . . . I am up early in the morning and training twice a day and go to bed at night with the chickens. These Frenchmen do not understand why it is I am not out for a good time, but I tell them I am out for the money and to win instead. I cannot get onto their jumble talk here and I don't want to, for Georgia English and Atlanta is for me. But I am going to show these fellows a few things about riding bicycles.[6]

Grantland Rice, sports editor for the *Atlanta Journal*, regularly received cables from Walthour. One of the first cables Rice saw, however, was addressed to Jack Prince from Gussie Lawson. The cable said that there was heated discussion over who would have the honor to race Walthour first on French soil. Rice wrote in the *Journal*:

> It seems that the match was first arranged with [Henri] Contenet, as he was the national French [motor-pacing] champion. Then [Paul] Dangla arose in wrath and stated that as he held the one-hour record he should be given first choice and so for a while the turmoil was something fierce. Mustaches were twisted and bent beyond recognition and the fierce gesticulating and side stepping of the frog-eating people seethed for several days. Absinthe flowed like Bourbon in Kentucky while the debate was in progress and it was finally decided to allow Dangla and Contenet to draw lots. Dangla won out and so he will be the first to tackle the local champion at the Buffalo track. Contenet will be taken on several days later.[7]

Frenchman Paul Dangla was an overwhelming favorite to beat Walthour. On October 18, 1903, on the Parc des Princes, Dangla set the coveted hour world record behind pace: he had ridden 84 kilometers and 577 meters (52.4 miles).

Walthour's European debut occurred on March 17 in front of fifteen thousand spectators at the Buffalo track. Several photographs were taken at the starting line that show manager Winesett towering over Walthour, who crouched low over his handlebars. A short trainer holds Dangla's bicycle steady. Dangla, with his flat nose, heavyset frame, and thick dark hair, looks more like a German boxer than a French cyclist.

The match race was for the best of three heats. Both Walthour and Dangla were on bikes with front wheels that were three to four inches smaller than the rear wheels. Their forks were straight with no forward rake, and they were at the same angle as the steering tube. The small wheel and the straight fork ensured that the rider's body came inches closer to the motorcycle, thus enabling more efficient drafting.

Lawson rode Death Dealer and drew away from Walthour at the start of the first heat, which was ten kilometers long. Many in the Buffalo stadium scoffed, thinking Walthour had lost his pace already and that the first heat was going to be an easy win for Dangla. But the fair-haired American bent low and pushed his huge sprocket gear as hard as possible and quickly caught up to the back of his pace-making machine. Walthour breezed past Dangla almost as if to trick him. Walthour maintained his lead throughout, averaging over forty-six miles per hour. Dangla finished a full lap behind. The big crowd did not know what to think of this American and became strangely quiet. In the second twenty-kilometer heat Dangla tried to duplicate his competitor's sneaky move at the start. But the attempt backfired, and Walthour led from the beginning, winning the second heat rather easily.[8] The French spectators politely and quietly applauded Walthour—nothing like he had ever heard from such a mass of spectators.

In a stadium more packed than his first race but with large black clouds overhead, Walthour's second race on French soil, three days later, was on a Sunday. Most of the locals thought that Walthour's victory against Dangla had been a fluke and could not wait for Walthour to go up against their national motor-pacing champion, Henri Contenet. In the first heat, a twenty-kilometer race, Walthour led from the start. But the great stress he put on the chain from pushing so hard on the cranks caused it to break. The broken chain nearly became tangled as it rubbed against the spokes, making a rhythmic metallic clank, but a few seconds later it slinked safely onto the track. As Walthour coasted down the embankment, looking for a new bicycle, Contenet passed him and won the first heat by a lap and a half.

In the second heat Walthour led again, but his chain broke once more. By the time he returned to the race Contenet was two laps ahead. "I got crazy mad to think of my hard luck," Walthour wrote in a letter to his mentor, Gus Castle. By then he was way behind, and Walthour shouted to Lawson above the noise of Death Dealer's engine to let the motorcycle go for all it was worth. Flying around the track, Walthour eventually caught Contenet and gained one of the two laps. Pushing his legs and lungs to their limit, Walthour rode up behind Contenet again and made a challenge for the lead. But Contenet had the pole and fought the American off. Lawson and Walthour took all kinds of chances to try to pass the Frenchman.[9]

Remarkably Walthour stunned the huge crowd by finally overtaking Contenet and winning the second twenty-five-kilometer heat. Even with the misfortune of needing a new bicycle, Walthour averaged forty-four miles per hour. In the third and deciding heat, Contenet, who reportedly suffered from a cold, left the track after riding only half the distance. This time Walthour's victory made a great impression on the French public, and he rode around the track for *plusieurs tours d'honneur* (several laps of honor).[10]

Walthour cabled Grantland Rice shortly after his incredible victory. "We are whooping things up for old Atlanta over here. . . . I won from Contenet, the national French champion, yesterday in easy style, taking both straight heats. I could have lapped him but am taking no chances. Nearly 15,000 people were present and the American colony tore things up for a few minutes after the race. I am in fine shape and expect to win every race and establish new records from one to fifty [miles]. The tracks here are lightning fast. . . . There is big money in the game over here."[11]

❀

Walthour traveled to Berlin for his third race. The cement track at Friedenau Sportpark had been built in 1897 and was five hundred meters long. The stadium could seat more than forty thousand spectators, but Walthour considered it one of the worst tracks he had ever ridden. He liked smaller tracks with high banking, but Friedenau was long with low banking. The worst problem was that the cracks on the Friedenau surface became wet and froze in the cold winters. In the summer the repaired cracks created unavoidable and dangerous bumps.

Thaddeus Robl, who was the European and German motor-pacing champion, knew every bump and crevice at Friedenau and was undefeated there. Robl was from Munich, a dashing, dark-haired man with muscular legs and comparatively skinny arms. He was the darling of Berlin and was considered by many Germans to be the greatest sportsman ever. When Walthour arrived in Germany, his victories in France and the United States were of no consequence to the Germans. Just as he had been in France, Walthour was definitely an underdog in Germany—especially against Robl.

Rather than train for their upcoming fifty kilometer race on Easter Sunday, April 3, Robl chose to make a formal complaint about Gussie Lawson's leather suit. Robl thought the suit gave Walthour unfair draft protection. The Friedenau officials, however, ruled that Lawson was allowed to wear his protective gear, which included a football-style leather helmet. Walthour meanwhile trained diligently on Friedenau, becoming accustomed to its rough surface.

The day of the race was windy and the track slippery and damp. More dangerous than the track conditions was the extremely congested field. Six bicycle riders and six pace-making motorcycles would crowd the track, making almost as much noise as the huge crowd. In the race were Robl—by far the favorite—and fellow Germans Bruno Salzmann and Bruno Demke. Fritz Ryser from Switzerland was making his debut in motor-pacing in the race. Frenchman Raoul Buisson and Walthour himself rounded out the competition. In the first ten kilometers the lead exchanged half a dozen times, often causing the largest crowd Walthour had yet experienced rise to its feet. When Robl wheeled off the track with mechanical problems at the thirteenth kilometer, Walthour was in the lead. Ryser and Demke fought for second place. Walthour had an easy victory against his five competitors, and his time of forty-three minutes six seconds was a remarkable one considering the wintry conditions.[12]

The next day Walthour raced again at Friedenau against the same group of riders, except Demke. In the hour-long race, with Walthour ahead at the 5 kilometer point, Robl made a rush for the lead. The crowd of 40,000 stood in unison, anticipating that their hero Robl would pass the American. But the celebration was short-lived. Lawson hit Death Dealer's throttle, shooting clear of any attack, and Walthour dug into his pedals furiously. Robl was unable to pass the American, who remained safely in control in Lawson's slipstream. In spite of the continuing heavy winds, Walthour set a track record by 250 meters.[13]

Spectators swarmed the track and put Walthour on their shoulders. When the enthusiasm died down, Friedenau track director Ferdinand

Knorr asked Walthour if he would not mind riding around the track a few times to oblige the spectators who had remained in the stands. Walthour agreed. In a letter home to Atlanta, Walthour told Gus Castle that the applause was louder than inside Madison Square Garden at the end of the six-day race in 1903. He went on to tell Castle, "I have big contracts here with bicycle and tire makers and plenty of races to keep me busy all the year. If I live I will be home about September and will hardly expect to race any in the north, as it will be fall and the season ended when I get back."[14]

❉

Walthour's string of victories in Europe continued. Back at the Buffalo track on Sunday, April 10, when he crashed to the boards at fifty miles per hour, Walthour stood back up and won in straight twenty-kilometer heats against the Frenchman with the Italian name, Eugenio Bruni.[15] On April 17 Walthour was victorious in Dresden on a four-hundred-meter cement track, where he beat Robl a third time.[16] On April 24, in spite of what Walthour called an "irrational" moment—the result of which he was fined one hundred francs for throwing his bicycle[17] —he won the Roue d'Ore de Buffalo, a fifty-kilometer race against Frenchmen Charles Albert Brécy and Bruni.[18] On May 8 he won the first edition of Le Grand Prix de la Republique at the Parc des Princes,[19] and four days later he won the second edition of Le Grand Prix de la Republique at Buffalo against Paul Dangla.[20]

Not since Major Taylor's run of sprint victories in 1901 had an American come over to Europe and decimated the competition as Walthour had that year. Amazed by his speed and quiet confidence the French press began labeling him "*L'imbattable Walthour*" (the Unbeatable Walthour) and "*Champion du Monde*" (Champion of the World). Chairman of the racing board of the American National Cycling Association Amos G. Batchelder received a cable from a high-ranking French official (either Victor Breyer or Henri Desgrange) indicating that Walthour was the "best ever seen in Europe and by far the best that has ever come from America, and is distinctly superior to all other riders now following mechanical pacing machines."[21]

On May 1 in Dresden, Walthour went up against Robl for a fourth time in a one-hundred-kilometer race. Walthour started out in the lead, but Death Dealer's engine lost power, and Lawson was forced to pull off the track. A spare motorcycle came out to pace him, but it developed a mechanical problem as well. Walthour rode unpaced and lost a great deal of ground by the time Lawson came out again. Slowly Walthour, with his smooth, powerful pedaling action, began gaining back the distance he had lost to Robl. As they neared the finish Walthour had almost closed the gap. The crowd, sensing that a sporting miracle was about to happen, cheered for Walthour to catch Robl. But as the excited crowd reached a fever pitch, Walthour's thin tire blew with a loud explosion. Walthour skidded down the embankment; with his incredible bike-handling skills, he stayed upright. He was desperate to find a new bicycle, but time had run out, and Robl finally had his victory against Walthour. In a letter to Gus Castle Walthour wrote that the "audience called out 'bravo,' as I was really the winner."[22]

Before he returned to the United States Walthour wanted to add one more notch to his European belt—the hour world record, behind pace. Londoner Tommy Hall did not look like a world-class athlete; he was thin and short, with pale skin and big sleepy eyes. But Hall had shown his mettle when he beat Dangla's hour record in October 1903 by riding 87 kilometers and 393 meters (54.2 miles) behind a huge belt-driven motor-cycle ridden by Frenchman Henri Cissac.

On May 15, 1904, Walthour had the opportunity to snatch the hour world record from Tommy Hall. Eugenio Bruni, Hall, and Walthour were to race for an hour at the Parc des Princes, where Hall and Dangla had set their records. A sellout crowd of more than twenty thousand people bought tickets to witness the grand battle. Walthour started in third position but quickly overtook Hall and Bruni and continued putting distance between himself and his rivals. He was benefited further when Hall and Bruni both had punctured tires. Walthour's first ten kilometers was relatively slow only because of the standing start, was seven minutes twenty-eight seconds. His second ten kilometers, however, was a blazing fast six minutes fifty-three seconds, or about fifty-five miles per hour. The judges posted his times on a big mobile chalkboard that was displayed in the infield for everyone to see. He reached the thirty-kilometer point in twenty-one minutes twenty-three seconds, right on pace for the world record.

The crowd braced itself for history to be made. On the next lap, Walthour came blazing around the banked turn and was fifty meters from the starting line when his tire exploded. With fearless dexterity, traveling at more than fifty miles per hour on a flat tire, he yanked his foot backward out of the toe clip and quickly placed his foot on the fork, and using the sole of his shoe as a brake, Walthour stopped ten inches short of a pole that would have surely sent him flying over his handlebars.

An extra bicycle was produced quickly, and Walthour returned to his place behind his pacing motorcycle. In less than 30 seconds, Walthour was up to full speed and still way ahead of Hall and Bruni. Walthour's fourth set of 10 kilometers was timed in 8 minutes 12 seconds, incredible considering the bike change. His next pair of 10 kilometers was reeled off in 6 minutes 53 seconds and 6 minutes 47 seconds, again averaging 55 miles per hour. Not a single person in the stands remained seated. The French were deeply appreciative of the American's valiant efforts, but the world record was not broken that day, owing to that flat tire. Walthour finished the hour going 82 kilometers and 666 meters (or 51.4 miles).[23]

The attempt at the hour record was his last race before Walthour returned to the United States, and he arrived in New York on May 24. In all Walthour won eleven of twelve races, capturing worldwide attention and proving his European critics wrong. No professional athlete could have dreamed of better results.

{ 17 }

On Top of the World

W althour's first European adventure in the spring of 1904 had been a resounding success, financially. His guarantee to race in Europe had been at least $5,000 ($124,000 in current dollars). In addition, for each race he won Walthour averaged about $1,000 ($24,900). Endorsements to ride a French bicycle called J.C. and to fit Pector tires and a French saddle added another $100 ($2,490) a week. During the two months he had raced in Germany and France, Walthour earned approximately $15,000 ($373,000). Walthour did have expenses though; the purchase of two new pacing motorcycles along with Winesett's and Lawson's salaries made sure of that.

Although the money was spectacular, Walthour may have wished for more. Around the time he boarded the steamer on February 10 and crossed the Atlantic to Europe, Mrs. Grace Mallory filed suit against the Georgia Interstate Fair Association, Jack Prince, Gus Castle, and Bobby Walthour for $15,000. The suit, filed through her attorney, J. W. Preston, was for damages resulting from the death of her eighteen-year-old husband, Charles Mallory. The petition set forth that Mallory died a day after riding in a race on August 25, 1902, at the Piedmont Coliseum track in Atlanta. A boy running across the track caused the accident responsible for Mallory's injuries. The petition claimed that the defendants were duty-bound to provide a clear and unobstructed track.[1] Walthour may have known about the Mallory suit while he was in Europe, but in either case, eventually he would be cleared of all charges.

Walthour was homesick, however, and he missed his wife and children. With his European fortune partially realized and his confidence high, he sent for them in late March. Blanche, Viva, Nona, and Bobby Jr.—along with their grandmothers, Blanche's mother, May Kah, and Bobby's mother, Sarah Hall—arrived in Europe in late April.[2] A clear and warm spring day greeted Walthour's family to Paris race season on Sunday, April 24, 1904. The Buffalo Velodrome was filled to overflowing, and Walthour's family sat in the best box seats at the finish line. The sun shone bright and glaring as they waited to see their first race in Europe, a three-man, fifty-kilometer affair with Walthour up against Eugenio Bruni and Charles Albert Brécy.

The enormous crowd around the track stood as the riders powered up to speed in less than a minute. The board track was fast and smooth. A hard tire rolling over its surface was like a billiard ball rolling along the felt of a pool table. Walthour pedaled in a perfectly smooth cadence at fifty miles per hour. He concentrated on relaxing his breathing while he focused his attention on the back of Lawson's leather jacket, the screaming crowd a blur on his right-hand side. Without warning early in the race, one of Bruni's highly pressurized, paper-thin tires blew. His bicycle slid out from under him, and he hit the board surface at fifty-one miles per hour. The force caused Bruni's body to pitch forward like a rag doll and somersault twice, finally leaving him motionless and slumped on the track. A doctor was immediately on the scene and found Bruni's wounds to be superficial. But the rider remained unconscious. As the race continued, officials removed Bruni on a stretcher and transported him to the Beaujon Hospital where, ultimately, he did recover.

By that time Walthour was so far ahead of Brécy that he could have walked his bike to the finish line. But he was on a track record pace, so he continued unabated at lightning speed, tucked in inches away from the roller that protected his front tire from the rear tire of Lawson's machine. Coming upright from the steep turn and nearing the finish line at more than fifty miles per hour, Death Dealer's tire punctured. Lawson and the motorcycle swerved and crashed to the boards. Thick chunks of wood were gouged out of the beautiful track surface by the motorcycle's foot-rest. Walthour overturned and slid on his back along the track surface. But apparently uninjured, he sprang to his feet. On the grass inside the track, he picked up his bicycle by its bent handlebar and flung it through the air. The French crowd, until that moment enamored with the Ameri-can, hissed at Walthour—not understanding that this was how he took out his frustration. Meanwhile Lawson was laying still while medical men attended to him. Although he was not seriously injured, Lawson was taken away on a stretcher into the riders' quarters. Walthour was provided with another bicycle, finished the race, and won without pace.[3]

✳

Walthour and his family left Europe with Eli Winesett and Gussie Lawson. They boarded the steamer *Kronprinz Wilhelm* and arrived in New York on May 24.[4] During the voyage Walthour's mother-in-law, May Kah, fell on the ship's deck and slammed her head.[5] After the big steamer an-chored in the New York harbor, Blanche, the children, and her mother—still suffering from the effect of the fall—traveled back to Atlanta by train. Walthour, Winesett, and Lawson stayed behind to fulfill racing contracts in Boston.

Once they were on American soil, the managers of the Revere Beach and Charles River tracks in Boston immediately contacted Walthour. He was now able to dictate most of his own terms, and his ego started to in-flate like his high-pressure tires.

> "Hugh McLean is a good rider," Walthour said, "but I believe James Moran is the man who should meet me in my first race on this con-tinent. But as my manager, Mr. Howe, agreed that McLean should meet me next Saturday evening, and as the advertising for the meet is out for McLean to meet me, I will give McLean a chance. . . . I intend to sail for France the latter part of July, for I have a contract calling for ten races for $5,000 and a percentage of the gate for every race I win, and I don't intend to tarry here.[6]

In spite of this posturing, Walthour debuted in 1904's American sea-son against Hugh McLean on May 28 at the eight-lap-to-the-mile Revere

Beach track. McLean was not happy with Walthour's comments to the press, and during the warm-up, they exchanged heated words. However, the bitter rivals returned to their warm-up without further incident and readied themselves to race twenty miles in front of five thousand frenzied fans. Gussie Lawson wore his trademark leather suit and helmet, and McLean's pacemaker, Billy Saunders, protected himself with bulky sweaters. Both men were in control of big ten-horsepower motors. After six miles Walthour held a slim lead as he stuck to Lawson's rear wheel, spinning his huge gear smoothly and seemingly without effort. McLean managed to avoid getting lapped for some time, but Walthour shot through a gap with Lawson's machine at full throttle. In the twelfth mile he set a new track record of one minute nineteen seconds for a mile, or forty-five miles per hour. The speed was too much for McLean, and by the end Walthour had lapped his rival ten times.[7]

Walthour's next stop was three days later at the larger, faster, five-lap-to-the-mile Charles River track against George Leander, Nat Butler, and Will Stinson. All the riders followed motorcycles fitted with 16-inch "windshields" attached at the rear that reached from the saddle to the ground. The windshields offered significantly more draft protection than normal, and the riders could go much faster. Leander sprinted out in the lead, but Walthour turned loose and passed the big man from Chicago with hair-raising speed. With each lap he increased his speed and constantly lapped the field. The faster he went, the more fiery orange sparks shot out from under Lawson's engine, which delighted the huge crowd that packed the stadium. Not one of the riders could keep up with Walthour's blazing speed, and he finished the thirty miles in a track record time of thirty-three minutes fifty-two seconds—averaging an astonishing fifty-three miles per hour.[8]

As Walthour arrived back home in Atlanta and stepped off the train from New York wearing a Parisian steamer cap made of striped silk, an impressively large crowd had assembled to greet Georgia's most famous athlete. Officials escorted Blanche to her husband. After being separated for a few weeks, they shared a long, tearful embrace. The Walthours climbed into a waiting barouche pulled by four white horses and decorated with the Stars and Stripes waving high above the German and French flags.

From the open carriage Walthour told the crowd, "I had a great time and a great trip, but the best of all is getting back to dear old Atlanta. . . . I saw great cathedrals and wonderful art galleries, and all kinds of things, but the best of all to me was the architecture of the old union [railroad] car shed, for that meant home and Atlanta."[9]

After his impromptu speech while the horse's hooves clopped along, pulling the barouche through the streets of Atlanta, the Walthours had some private time in spite of the crowds of people who lined the streets. Blanche told Bobby about the condition of her mother. May Kah had suffered an attack of paralysis, probably as a result of her fall on the ship, and was being treated by a doctor. Her health had improved somewhat, but the family was still very concerned.

Walthour settled in at Woodward Avenue and was happy to be at home with his wife, children, and his chickens. In a subsequent interview with the *Atlanta Journal* Walthour said that he rated Frenchman Paul Dangla, the very first cyclist he had raced in Europe, the best non-American behind the motors.[10] The two had become friends in France. Only ten days after that interview, on June 12, 1904, Dangla was involved in an accident while racing in Magdelburg, Germany. He was speeding at nearly fifty miles per hour when he took a horrific spill, causing head and leg injuries. Twenty-six-year-old Dangla died two weeks later.[11]

❁

On Wednesday, June 15, Walthour and Albert Champion had a race in Atlanta on the eight-lap-to-the-mile wooden track at Piedmont Park designed by Jack Prince. In the by-now familiar format, the races were to consist of the best of three five-mile heats. Walthour raced behind Bushet, one of the two pacing motorcycles he had brought with him from Europe. Bushet had a powerful twenty-horsepower motor and was considered too big to drive on the tight turns of the Piedmont track. But Walthour and Champion had decided to forgo the smaller four-horsepower machines in favor of more power. As usual, Gussie Lawson paced Walthour, and Billy Saunders paced Champion. In the first heat, mile after mile was reeled off at track record pace. Piedmont was not designed for such speed and heavy machines. In reckless fashion Champion led and forced Walthour to his limits. But Walthour caught and finally passed him with a mile to go, winning the first heat by twenty-five yards. As Champion crossed the finish and began to slow down, one of his tires slipped off its rim. Champion cascaded down and slid across the track. He writhed in pain on the ground; a splinter had penetrated deep into his stomach. He was rushed to Grady Hospital, where doctors extracted the splinter in a painful operation.[12] No further racing took place that day.

Two weeks after Champion's crash, on June 30, Atlanta enjoyed a motor-paced race between Basil de Guichard, Benny Munroe, and Walthour. The young de Guichard was paced by Fred Shultz, for Munroe was Franz Hoffman, and as usual Walthour followed Gussie Lawson. The three riders started together, standing up on their bicycles, each pushing their huge fixed-gears as the motorcycles came around the track. The riders scrambled to catch their machines. After four miles Walthour had lapped his opponents twice and was closing in on passing them for a third time. Hoffman, riding a belt-driven machine, looked behind and saw Lawson coming on strong on the outside. Hoffman steered his machine high up the embankment, leaving his man Munroe in the middle of the track. Seeing there was no space to cycle through, Lawson was forced to hit the brakes. Walthour plunged into the back of Lawson's motorcycle and was thrown high up the track embankment.

The impetus of his body was so great that his shoulder broke two 3 x 6-inch pine posts. Blanche, who made a habit of never watching her husband during a race, had her eyes hidden. At the crack of the wood, people shrieked in horror, and a hush fell over the crowd. Blanche made a mad dash to Bobby's side as he was being helped by willing fans. Police held off the crowd and pushed people away. Blanche had a difficult time making her way close to him, but when she did, she was certain Bobby was dead. He hung unconscious over the railing with his feet dangling over the track. Blanche held him in her arms, doing the best she could to comfort him.[13]

Walthour was taken from the track to the dressing room, then back to his home, where his injuries were evaluated. Dr. Visanska diagnosed a broken left collarbone. Bobby's right elbow and fingers of his right hand were badly bruised and torn, as were his hips and legs. He had a large wound on his abdomen. "When a man is suffering from a shock of this kind," declared the doctor, "all the symptoms do not show up at once. I have carefully examined Walthour, but do not know whether his injuries will be serious or not. It is impossible to tell yet whether he has received internal injuries. If he rides at all, it will be several months before he is able to get on his wheel. The fracture of his collarbone will be set tomorrow."[14]

News of Walthour's narrow escape from death spread quickly through the cycling world. He received anxious phone calls at his home, and telegrams came from distant cities. The very next night, with his arm in a sling, his body swathed with bandages, and unable to stand up, reporters asked him whether he expected ever to race again. With firm resolve and indomitable will he answered:

> I must admit that I will if I get over the result of this accident. I know some people, when they meet disaster, are quick to swear off, but I will be candid and truthful and I say I intend to keep on racing as long as I think there is no man to beat me. If I knew there was a man who was a better and faster rider than I was I might quit the track for good. There is no man in my class who has come up against me yet. . . . As is known, Lawson, who was pacing me, attempted to pass Munroe and de Guichard, and Hoffman, who was pacing Munroe, ran up the bank and left no room for Lawson to pass. Lawson had to slow up and I struck his motor. Hoffman had a right to run up on the bank if he did so in order to pass de Guichard, but if he did it to keep me from passing, it was wrong. Of course, we cannot tell what his intention was.[15]

After such a serious accident, Walthour's recovery was remarkable. Only two weeks later he went on to race and win. Death, however, was drastically thinning the ranks of the motor-pacing specialists. Paul Dangla, Harry Elkes, Johnny Nelson, and Archie McEachern were all gone. Specialists such as Major Taylor and Frank Kramer refused to be sucked into the profitable, hazardous game. Yet younger riders kept coming up through the ranks. When Walthour had been gathering laurels in Europe, George Leander emerged as his possible American motor-pacing successor. In June 1904 Leander signed a contract with Victor Breyer, the manager of the Buffalo Velodrome. He steamed for Europe soon after his May 31 race against Walthour in Boston. But Leander was apprehensive. He told his friend Sol DeVries that he wished he could call the trip off. The twenty-one-year-old Leander confessed, "I am sure something is going to happen to me."[16]

But Leander had great success in Europe. By August he had achieved his sixth straight victory. Walthour was also back in Europe in August with Blanche and Bobby Jr. after winning twelve of thirteen races in the United States. For the year Walthour had won all but two of his twenty-five races. With the two Americans now dominating the increasingly popular sport of motor-pacing in Europe, the promoters decided to pit them against each other on foreign soil. The showdown was set for August 21 at the big Parc des Princes cement track. More than twenty thousand Parisians came out to see the one-hour race. *L'Auto* described the sellout crowd as the "most insane mob which can be imagined."[17]

In addition to Walthour and Leander, Eugenio Bruni competed. Walthour came to Europe with Franz Hoffman as his motorman instead of Gussie Lawson. Hoffman was on a one-cylinder, sixteen-horsepower motorcycle. Leander rode behind Henri Cissac, who drove a two-cylinder, twenty-six-horsepower machine, and Bruni had Reimers riding a two-cylinder, twenty-four-horsepower motorcycle. The sport had become a contest of motorcycle technology, as well as a test of the courage and athletic ability of the riders.

The three lined up, the gun fired, and after two hundred meters, Leander broke a toe clip. Track officials restarted the race, and Leander blasted off to an excellent start. After only four minutes Leander lapped Bruni. Walthour lost one and a half laps to Leander, because he was forced to swap pacing motorcycles. While Leander pedaled his bicycle with amazing speed, however, Cissac's jacket started to flap in the breeze. Immediately programs started to fly through the air as the crowd, under the impression that Cissac's jacket was creating an unfair drafting advantage for Leander, started to protest angrily.

The referees waved pacers and riders off the track and stopped the race. Cissac's jacket buttons had been ripped off, and the referees decided that the race should continue at the point at which they had stopped it, but they required Cissac to remove his jacket. The race resumed with Leander continuing well in command; he gained even more ground on his two rivals.

Shortly after the thirty-kilometer mark, Cissac attempted another pass at Bruni. Leander was going with all his might to keep up with his pacemaker, his legs churning furiously. But as he tired, a slight distance developed between him and the safety of the motorcycle's draft. At more than fifty-five miles per hour, Leander began to wobble just as Charles "Mile-a-Minute" Murphy had done five years earlier when he had nearly lost contact with the slipstream of the train that was pacing him. Leander rode into the banked turn with blinding speed and lost control of his bike. He went over his handlebars and flew twenty yards through the air. He hit the cement head first, and his body rolled until it had no more momentum, and he came to a stop, unconscious at the side of the track.[18]

Officials transported Leander to Beaujon Hospital, where doctors found he had a broken right clavicle and multiple contusions. He never regained consciousness, and he died thirty-six hours later from a brain hemorrhage.[19] This was the second fatality that Walthour had witnessed on the track in only two years.

❋

Shortly after Leander's funeral at the Temple de l'Avenue de la Grande-Armée, Walthour crossed the English Channel and headed for London, site of the world championship at Crystal Palace track. Walthour was as likely to have been killed as any of his motor-pacing rivals, and such obvious dangers must have preyed on his consciousness. The first day of the championship, under the auspices of the International Cyclists' Union, featured the professional one-hundred-kilometer motor-paced event. The competitors' pace-making motorcycles were restricted by weight, thus eliminating the heavy tandems. For Walthour, who preferred to race behind single-seat motorcycles, it was a perfect scenario.

On Saturday, September 3, seven thousand people braved the rain to see the races at the Crystal Palace. Fortunately the low sun broke through the pink clouds before the six riders lined up with their machines late in the afternoon. The field included Caesar Simar (France), Arthur Vanderstuyft (Belgium), Axel Hansen (Denmark), Edmond Andemars (Switzerland), Giovanni Gerbi (Italy), and Walthour. The American bolted out to the front and steadily increased his lead until his motorcycle was forced to take a pit stop. In the meantime Simar passed the unpaced Walthour, who was struggling to spin his big gear. But Hoffman was quickly back out onto the track. Walthour called for more pace from Hoffman and gained on Simar. By the twentieth lap Walthour and Simar were on even terms, and the two alternated the lead several times.

When the race was nearing its end, the belt of Gerbi's pacing motorcycle came loose, slipped off, and tangled into the Italian's front bicycle wheel. Gerbi sustained severe road rash from falling onto the cement at more than forty miles per hour. Many onlookers feared he was dead. For five days the nineteen-year-old remained in a coma at the hospital, but he did make a complete recovery.[21]

Walthour had a relatively easy time winning the world championship by 4¾ laps. Simar's pacing machine had developed problems. Walthour finished the 100 kilometers in 1 hour 33 minutes 57.6 seconds.[20] Walthour took a lap of honor, waving to the London crowd in near darkness. First prize for the motor-paced world champion was not much in cash terms—only 80 English pounds. But Walthour also received a heavy gold medallion. On its face was a globe surrounded by the words "Union Internationale World's Cycliste Championships." The opposite side was inscribed with, "100 kilometers professional championships, 1904; won by R. Walthour."[22]

Walthour wasted no time at all in returning across the rough waters of the English Channel. He appeared in France the very next day to race at the Parc des Princes. An editorial article in *La Figaro* opined, cynically, that poor Leander's death had been forgotten already and that the crowds in Paris were still hungry for another dreadful and enthralling spectacle, such as the one in which Leander died.[23] This was getting to the heart of the motor-pacing sport—fast, noisy, exciting, sensational, and brutal—a sport for hard men and modern spectators hungry for drama, a bit like gladiators in the ring in ancient Rome.

Three Frenchman—Albert Champion, Eugenio Bruni, and Charles Albert Brécy—lined up with Walthour, "le champion du monde," on the cement for the start of an hour race behind the motors. Sixteen thousand fans crowded the stadium. Most Parisians hoped for a French victory, but they were becoming acclimated to the American's undeniable bicycle skills. The time Walthour had spent traveling from London to Paris did not seem to effect him, and he took the lead from the start. Compared to London, the fall weather was fine, and Walthour lapped his rivals over and over in the warm sunshine. He rode the hour in 77 kilometers and 393 meters, a new track record in competition. His nearest competitor was Brécy, who was over 4 kilometers behind. Champion placed third but seemed to ride without conviction, although perhaps his stomach injury from Atlanta bothered him.[24]

Walthour kept traveling. Three days later he rode a one-hundred-kilometer race on the Friedenau track in Berlin for the Grand Prize of Europe against Dutchman Piet Dickentman, German Thaddeus Robl, and Englishman Tommy Hall, the owner of the prestigious hour record behind pace. These three riders had refused to ride in the world championship because neither big tandems nor windshields were allowed on the London track. Undoubtedly the three were better than Walthour's competition in London. Friedenau director Ferdinand Knoll labeled the race "the real championship." Both Dickentman and Robl used tandem-pacing machines; Robl's rear man was so padded that he could barely squeeze through a doorway. In addition, Robl's machine was fitted with windshields, whereas Walthour had no windshield and was paced only by a single motorman, Franz Hoffman.

With the red flags down and the motors grouped behind on the banking, the bombardment of Friedenau began with a pistol crack. Dickentman's tandem duo let out yelping cries to let Walthour know they were close to him, and off they went into the lead. Walthour rode off in second followed by Robl. Although Robl unleashed several attacks to dash by the American, Walthour would have none of it. There was a roar from the crowd when Robl appeared to lose his pace, but he quickly regained it. Another tremendous cheer came from forty thousand throats when Walthour passed Dickentman for the lead. By seventy kilometers, Walthour had gained a full lap on Dickentman. Eli Winesett smiled, and the cool-headed manager remarked, "Wal, we've got the lead now, and I guess we'll keep it. If nothing goes wrong, Bab won't get bumped today." Robl was forced to quit after Walthour had covered ninety-four kilometers, and Dickentman placed a distant second.[25] *Bicycling World* reported:

> The usually unexcitable Germans were immensely pleased at Walthour's victory, and they swarmed onto the track after the race finished. They took the champion from his bicycle and carried him around the track on their shoulders, and, as Walthour says, "They gave me the greatest ovation I ever had in my life." Walthour says he has become very popular in Germany, especially at Berlin, and he thinks it is partly due to his being blonde. "I do look something like a German with my light hair, and that must be the reason they like me so much," he said. When Walthour escaped from his admirers an immense crowd gathered around his "cabin," as the riders' quarters were called, and waited for him to come out. He made one attempt to get away, but so many insisted on shaking hands with him that he had to go back, nor did he get away until 9 o'clock, when he escaped by crawling out of a window.[26]

In one of Walthour's last races in Europe for 1904, in front of thirty-thousand German fans at Leipsic (Leipzig) track, Walthour lost his motor-pace because Hoffman's tire punctured. The defeat inspired Grantland Rice, who went on to become one of America's great sportswriters, to write another Walthour poem:

> Ach Gott! Vot choy in Chermany,
> Ven Bobby Walthour lose—
> Vot matter if he puncture tire
> Or motor fail to fuse.
> Herr Robl snatch his blond haired scalp
> And beat him twenty lap;
> It vas der Dutch who von der race—
> Von Hoffman took a nap.
> No matter vat de reason vas,
> All Leipsic's vild mit choy.

Dot even mit a punctured tire
Dey beat der Georgia boy
No matter if he lose his wheel
And haf to valk around—
Jus' so der Dutch can beat him vonce,
Der choy is much profound.[27]

❋

For Walthour 1904 was the kind of career year that few professional athletes ever experience. Contrary to today's trend and the overwhelming attention given to the Tour de France, in 1904 road racing was not as popular as track racing, and no other rider in the world could sell out a track stadium like Walthour. For a few years he ruled as king of the cycling world, and a very dangerous world it was.

That year the Tour de France seemed to be on its way out. Vexed by a scandal in which the first four riders were disqualified for cheating, including the inaugural winner, Maurice Garin, along with his brother, César, Henri Desgrange was afraid the Tour de France would not continue. "The Tour de France is over," he wrote, "and its second celebration will also, I deeply fear, be its last. It will have been killed by its own success, by the blind passions that it unleashed, and the slurs and filthy suspicions worthy of the ignorant and malicious."[28]

{ 18 }

Sputtering Skyrocket

Walthour had arrived in the United States on October 20, 1904, accompanied by Blanche, Bobby Jr., Gussie Lawson, and a small bulldog intended as a present for Alfred Reeves, the manager of the Columbia cycling team. The voyage was rough, and Bobby had been sick for two days, but as they disembarked they all looked healthy and refreshed. Blanche wore a dress in the latest Paris fashion with an oversized hat. Bobby sported a London bowler hat and a brown velvet vest with agate buttons. His world championship medal was attached to his watch chain. Two-year-old Bobby Jr., in his father's arms, played with the heavy gold medallion, feeling its smooth contours with his fat little fingers, slobbering on it, and biting it. Porters helped with the luggage, which consisted of one trunk for Blanche, one for Bobby, and a third for his bicycles.

Several people had been waiting for them as they departed from the *Deutschland*, including Patrick Powers, manager of the six-day bicycle race at Madison Square Garden and founding president of the National Association of Professional Baseball Leagues; Walthour's mother; and stepfather; and a reporter for *Bicycling World*.[1]

The news was not good. Walthour had been forced to cut short his European engagement after he learned that his mother-in-law's health had deteriorated. In fact, May Kah had died suddenly on October 15 while the

Deutschland steamed toward New York. Bobby's mother gave Blanche the news, and it was a crushing blow, because Blanche had been close to her mother. Mrs. Kah had appeared to be healthier after her fall aboard the ship months earlier. She had agreed to look after the Walthour girls while Bobby, Blanche, and Bobby Jr. traveled in Europe.

May Kah's funeral was delayed until the Walthours arrived in Atlanta. Services were held at their small home at 624 Woodward Avenue on October 23. Among the six pallbearers were Walthour himself and his old friend Zenus Fields.[2]

Although the return to Atlanta was bittersweet, Walthour had achieved a phenomenal list of professional triumphs, winning the world's championship and beating the best in Europe and the United States. In 1904 he had won forty out of forty-four races, a winning percentage almost unprecedented in bicycling or other professional sports. Counting his appearance fees, winnings, gate receipts, and product endorsements, by mid-October Walthour had earned at least $60,000 ($1,490,000 in current dollars). If his personal investments and winnings from betting on himself were factored in, he may have cleared more than $100,000 ($2,490,000).

❋

After his mother-in-law's funeral Walthour immediately renewed his training. The annual six-day race at Madison Square Garden was to start on December 5, and of course he wanted to defend his title. He mapped out a daily training program. Every morning, after sleeping for ten hours, he rose and had his egg sherry. Afterward, with coffee or tea, he ate a high-protein breakfast of boiled eggs and rare steak. To build up his stamina for the six-day race, Walthour cycled between twenty and forty miles in the morning—more than he usually would in training for motor-pacing competitions. For lunch, he consumed more steak and a few pints of ale. In the afternoons, he cycled again for about twenty miles, sometimes with motor-pace. Then, after a few games of billiards, he lay on the "rubbing board" for half an hour to relax before his daily massage. "As to massage," Walthour said, "this is most desirable, and you've got to find the right man to do it. Some masseurs do you more harm than good, for, instead of easing and freeing the muscles, they tire them." Last in the day was dinner at 7 p.m.—more steak with no vegetables. He was usually in bed by 10 p.m.[3]

Walthour could have selected just about anyone as his partner for the six-day race. Harry "The Manchester Giant" Caldwell had understood that Walthour picked him as a teammate. Hugh McLean also had assumed that he and Walthour were to be a team. But Benny Munroe, Walthour's partner in their winning race the previous year, actually arrived in Atlanta for some November training. Walthour found that Munroe, the southerner who rode with a leather cap, was in surprisingly good shape. "I try to shake him by going mile after mile at this clip [two minutes twelve seconds per mile unpaced], but when I look around I find him in back of me smiling. I call to him to come up and take his share of the pace, and there he is with the goods."[4] The Dixie Flyers were reunited for the 1904 Garden six-day race, and Caldwell and McLean were left to find other teammates.

Walthour also was booked for a different event at the Garden—race Jimmy Michael behind pace on December 3, 1904. The duel was the main attraction in the exhibition races on the Saturday preceding the big six-day event. Michael was only a year older than Walthour, but he had been elevated to a world-class professional at an early age. Michael was eighteen in 1895 when human-powered multicycles were still used to pace riders rather than motorcycles. That year Michael earned $63,000 ($1,660,000) and by all standards was widely reported to have been the most popular and wealthiest cyclist in the world. But in 1903 Michael endured a horrible accident on the Friedenau track in Berlin that almost killed him. Franz Hoffman had been Walthour's motor-pacer for much of the year and paced Michael that day in Berlin. Michael's tire exploded, and he landed hard on the cement track. Recalled Hoffman, "One of the other motors came along and struck him in the face, tearing the flesh open from his mouth to his ear." Michael spent six months recovering in a Berlin hospital.[5]

By 1904 twenty-seven-year-old Jimmy Michael was broke and desperately trying to make a comeback in the sport that had once made him rich and famous. Even before his Berlin crash Michael had lost most of his fortune gambling on horse races. His comeback was not producing great results, but he did manage to negotiate the race against Walthour at Madison Square Garden. The buildup featured a battle royale between a former great pacing champion and the current world motor-pacing champion. In November Michael and several European professional riders were crossing the Atlantic from England aboard the French steamer *La Savoie.* They were on their way to the races in New York City. All the riders enjoyed a wonderful meal prepared by the ship's chef. They also consumed plenty of alcohol as they reminisced and told one another funny stories. Michael was in his element. At 3 a.m. in the morning, after the happy dinner, Jean Gougoltz, who was booked to compete in the six-day race, heard a disturbance coming from Michael's stateroom. Michael had experienced a violent seizure, and his wife was in a panic. Doctors rushed in, but it was too late; the great rider from Wales was dead.[6]

From headlines in newspapers and magazines, the news of Michael's death shocked the cycling world; it was the cover story in December's issue of *La Vie Au Grand Air.* Major U.S. cities including New York, Boston, Chicago, and Atlanta carried the tragic news. *Cycling,* Britain's premiere cycling magazine, printed a piece by Stella Bloch in which she wrote, "Jimmy Michael was not only, in my estimation, the best man Great Britain has produced, but his remarkable powers, that for so many years kept the two hemispheres in breathless admiration, stamp him, perhaps, as the greatest distance rider the world has ever seen—aye, many of us look upon him as the most brilliant man in the whole of cycling history."[7]

Hugh McLean, who was generally recognized as the second-best American pace follower after Walthour, was substituted in place of Michael, and thousands flocked to the Garden on Saturday, December 3, to watch the "curtain raiser" events of the six-day race. A fifteen-mile motor-paced race between McLean and Walthour was the feature of the evening. When Walthour and his pacemaker, Gussie Lawson, were introduced, they received tremendous applause. McLean and his pacemaker, Charles Turville, who had worked with Walthour in the past, were cheered as well but not with the same vigor. At the start, Turville could not start his motor running. Hugh's brother, Alex McLean, made many attempts by pushing Turville around the ten-lap track. At first the crowd found humor in their misfortune. But as time wore on, the McLean brothers and Turville still could not start the engine. Even Gussie lent a hand. The crowd grew impatient and began shouting catcalls. Somehow the engine finally did come to life.

The gun fired and after a few laps they were at full speed at more than forty miles per hour. Tucked inches behind the motorcycles, they rounded the track, speeding up and down the steep banked turns. Walthour took the lead. After several miles Walthour noticed that the rubber on his front tire had worn away. Rather than risk a blow out, he came down off the track to replace his bicycle. Unfortunately his spare did not have any toe clips, and he was forced to find another bicycle. By the time he reentered the race and picked up his pace, he was six laps behind McLean.

At the thirteenth mile McLean crashed and slid down the embankment. He immediately untangled himself from his bicycle and stood up to find a replacement bike. The rollicking crowd, especially those with money on Walthour, thought the southerner might still have a chance at catching McLean. Yet amid the great excitement during his bike change, McLean lost only four laps. Two laps were too much even for Walthour to make up, and McLean won the race.[8]

✳

"They're off!" shouted fifteen thousand cycle-mad New Yorkers in unison at seven minutes past midnight on Monday morning, the very moment Congressman Timothy Daniel "Big Tim" Sullivan fired the shot that sent off eighteen colorfully clad two-man teams, who would circle the yellow pine saucer for six straight days. Amid the mass of sounds, a great pall of blue tobacco smoke, and the smell of hot dogs, the walls of Madison Square Garden shook as the great international six-day race got underway on December 5. Those who had not been to a Garden six-day, including some of the riders, were afraid the roof might cave in. The initiated simply smiled. Enthusiastic youths in the upper gallery with tin horns and grinding rattles attempted to drown out the band performing ragtime tunes. The *World* reported, "Every seat was taken and the center of the track was almost impassible until it looked as though not another fan could squeeze into the enclosure. But still they continued to arrive and got in somehow to add a little more noise to the turmoil that reigned."[9]

The race was a rolling start, and the first mile did not count. But as soon as the second mile came into play, Walthour was at the front, standing on his pedals, digging in for all he was worth. From the topmost rafters containing unwashed and unsupervised youths in turtleneck sweaters and golf caps all the way down to the trackside box seats with distinguished men in white shirts and ties, New Yorkers loved Walthour. The other competitors, however, defended against any advantage right from the start that he might have, and Walthour failed to gain a lap on the other seventeen teams.

With the six-day race underway for half an hour, Frenchman Jean Gougoltz, who was the last man to have seen Jimmy Michael alive, was extremely fit and anxious to set a hot pace. "To beat me ze first hour zey will have to—what you call—splinter ze track."[10] While the riders accustomed themselves to going around and around the 176-yard track the first day, mostly it was a slow-paced affair. Walthour's partner, Munroe, crashed on the first day and tore his ear from sliding down the steep wooden bank. Fortunately the injury was not severe and had no effect on his riding ability, and he was able to continue. By 2 a.m. Tuesday, 13 teams were tied at 517 miles and 8 laps but had averaged only 20 miles per hour.[11]

Into the second day the relative positions of the teams remained the same. During a prolonged period of slow riding, the *World* reported, "Not that the racers are suffering torture other than the mental strain which comes from the deadly monotony of doing one thing over and over again without ceasing and without variation in the way of the doing. But the spectacle presented by the haggard riders dressed in motley and the evident fascination of the thousands of spectators who hang over the rail and never cease their bewitched staring is enough to make any observer think that the whole thing is some sort of gigantic punishment destined to go on eternally."[12]

Shortly before 3 a.m. on Wednesday, those in the Garden woke up with a start. Oliver Dorlon of the New York team came down off the banked turn, stood on his pedals, shot away from the field, and quickly took a half-lap lead. The other seventeen teams rode after Dorlon in a hurry. In what was a well-choreographed attack, Dorlon's partner, Eddie Root, came out for relief. Root sprinted so fast with his body hunched over that it appeared his head might graze the front wheel. Root was much fresher than the rest of the riders, and by the time the teams' better-rested riders entered the race, Root pulled farther ahead and managed to put a lap on the entire field.

To gain a lap on an individual team was very difficult unless that team had some misfortune. But to gain a lap on the entire field was as rare as a no-hitter in baseball. The exhausted riders leaned over the handlebars, their eyes squinting. They sucked in huge quantities of impure air; they coughed and hacked. But the teams continued on. During this recovery period the Belgian-Holland team of Arthur Vanderstuyft and Johann Stol saw an opportunity. They began relieving each other at shorter intervals and also pulled ahead. The field, however, made no effort to catch Vanderstuyft and Stol because they recognized, along with most of the crowd, that the pair had been lapped twice by Dorlon and Root; in other words, they had already been left behind the bunch.

Soon after the official scorer announced that the Root-Dorlon and Vanderstuyft-Stol teams were tied for first place. Down on the track the riders were asking whether Vanderstuyft and Stol *should* be tied for first. The majority of the riders agreed that only the Root-Dorlon team were one lap ahead and that the Vanderstuyft-Stol team were tied for second with the rest. An hour later a protest was put up by some of the riders that Vanderstuyft and Stol should not be tied with Root and Dorlon.

The four teams of Walthour-Munroe, Nat Butler–Jimmy Moran, John Bedell–Menus Bedell, and Otto Maya–Jed Newkirk demanded to be placed on even terms with the Vanderstuyft-Stol team and threatened to walk out on the race if they were not. When the representatives of the N.C.A. refused to take the lap away, the four teams quit the track, and Walthour became their spokesman. The team of Hugh McLean and James Bowler also left the track under protest.

At 7 a.m., Patrick Powers was summoned from his bed at the Bartholdi Hotel. The disheveled race manager quickly arrived at the Garden and conferred with the ten striking riders. Powers suggested that they continue to race under protest, with the understanding that the Board of Control of the N.C.A. would convene a hearing immediately.

That morning an executive meeting of the N.C.A. was held inside the Garden at 9 a.m. They stuck with the judges' decision; Vanderstuyft and Stol had gained the lap fairly and were on even terms with Dorlorn and

Root. In addition, the judges agreed that the protesters would be suspended from racing.

Meanwhile the crowd was in an uproar. Half the spectators taunted the "quitters," and those sympathetic to the cause of the protesters hissed and booed management. The factions became so vehement that police sent for patrol wagons. Rumors spread throughout the big hall that one of the striking riders had been beaten up. A fight broke out on the enclosure of the track, and Joseph Sullivan, a trainer of one of the riders, had four teeth knocked out by a local prizefighter named "Kid" Hannon. The crowd believed that one represented the quitters and the other management.[13]

With the excitement happening above them, the ten strikers had taken refuge in the riders' training headquarters in the basement. Walthour, confident that all would work out, took a nap. Harry Pollack, Powers's managing assistant, entered the racers' quarters and shook Walthour awake. Pollack ordered Walthour and the others out of the building and told them the N.C.A. had suspended them.[14]

Walthour was nonplussed. He hunted down Powers, the same man who had greeted him and his family at the New York harbor seven weeks earlier. The two argued, shouting with their reddened faces inches away from one another.

"I don't have to do any more six-day riding," Walthour exclaimed. "I'm worth $100,000 ($2,490,000) and you know that."

Powers retorted, "I'll bar you from every track all over the world."

"What! You bar me? Why do you know that out of your action this morning will come the Independent Bicycle Riders Association, and another six-day race, which will be fair, will be held here in February? Remember that. Independent riders will take part, and I will be in charge."[15]

According to *Bicycling World*, Walthour then "babbled like a crazy man, and sputtered charges and threats whenever he could obtain a listener. He vowed that he would attach the box receipts; that the race was not on the square; that last year's contest—which he won—was a fake; that he had been paid to participate; that he would organize an independent racing men's association—in fact he called on every one and everything in the heavens above and on the earth below to witness the terrible things he would do."[16]

The next day, after Walthour had calmed down and had a chance to rest, he arrived at the Bartholdi Hotel seeking a conference with Pat Powers. The two met for an hour. Shortly thereafter, Walthour, the ringleader of the ten striking riders, issued a written declaration:

> The statement attributed to me regarding the six-day bicycle race now in progress at Madison Square Garden, in which I was quoted as saying that the race was a "fake" is absolutely false. In the heat of passion over what I considered my wrongs I may have made several statements that could have been construed into attacks against the honesty of the six-day contests. I never took part in a "fake" race and I was never approached in any way by P.T. Powers or any one else connected with six-day racing at Madison Square Garden as to how I should ride. There was never any agreement that the riders should not steal a lap, either between the riders themselves or between the riders and the management. In all my dealings with Mr. Powers I was always treated with the utmost fairness and honesty.[17]

Meanwhile, the six-day race continued without the striking riders. The Root-Dorlon and Stol-Vanderstuyft combinations remained tied after 142 hours. A one-mile race was set up to determine first place and second place. Eddie Root rode for his team, and Johann Stol was chosen for his. The gun fired, the two riders went out slowly away, and the crowd went wild. Stol took an early lead, but the slow pace continued until the seventh lap, when Root went by in a flash. Stol did his best to keep up, but Root won by twelve lengths. The fourteen thousand spectators "were all on their feet and yelling like mad, gave Root a send off that seemed to make the iron girders shake."[18]

On December 14 the Board of Control of the N.C.A. Chairman R. F. Kelsey, after consideration of the ten dissident riders, announced their ruling. Walthour and Moran, as the two ringleaders, were each suspended for one year. Otto Maya and James Bowler were suspended for six months.

Hugh McLean was suspended for six months but given the option to pay a $100 fine ($2,490) instead. Nat Butler, Jed Newkirk, Menus Bedell, John Bedell, and Benny Munroe were suspended for six months or could pay a fine of $50 ($1,240).[19]

From Atlanta a defiant Walthour was quoted by the *Atlanta Constitution* saying that he had expected Moran and he would receive heavier punishment then the other riders "while we were no more in the wrong than the rest." Walthour envisioned a group that would "purify" cycle racing in the United States and called it the American Cyclist Association. "We are backed by men of wealth," he said, "and the association is already an assured success. I believe that all the riders will live up to their agreement and refuse to agree to the suspensions of the National Cycling Association. We have the best riders in America, and besides we have been joined by Lawson, Turville, Saunders, and a number of others."[20]

A prominent cycling official told the *New York Times* that "Walthour's defiant attitude and utterances are not improving the situation and it begins to look as if he was out of cycling for good. Had he displayed a contrite spirit after the excitement of the affair had passed and accepted his punishment quietly he would have been able to ask for a lightening of the sentence after six months had passed."[21]

Jimmy Moran, who was more apt to accept his punishment quietly, announced that he would appear before the N.C.A. in February and ask for a modification of his sentence. Until the matter was resolved Moran attended to his milk dealer business with his two brothers.

While serving his one-year N.C.A. suspension back home in Atlanta, Walthour had time to think, relax, catch up with family and friends, and tend to his chicken ranch. He invested in a bowling alley and practiced at the lanes nearly every day. He also spent anxious time working on his reinstatement. A letter received by Gus Castle from A.G. Batchelder, the president of the N.C.A., stated that Walthour needed to patch things up with Pat Powers. Unfortunately both Walthour and Powers had large egos, and Powers lost the most as a result of Walthour and Moran having quit the New York six-day race. In early January Walthour wrote Powers a letter, hoping it would persuade the N.C.A. to reinstate him. Walthour's threat to "smash the N.C.A. to smithereens" and form a rival organization was put on hold indefinitely.[22]

French newspapers and the *Boston Globe* printed articles confident that Walthour's suspension would soon be over. Of the news surrounding his possible reinstatement he said, "If I am reinstated, I expect of course to be fined. I have heard nothing of that rumor and do not know whether it is true or not. Whether I pay the fine or not depends on how large it is."[23] Of all the suspended riders of the six-day revolt, only Walthour and Moran remained suspended. The others had simply paid a small fine for their reinstatement.

Walthour considered an offer from Barney Oldfield to race in an automobile. Oldfield, now a cigar-chomping race car driver, had befriended Walthour in the 1890s when the two rode in professional cycling competitions together.[24] Oldfield made the switch from cycle racing to automobile racing, and in 1903 he won the AAA Indycar Championship. Oldfield was passing through Atlanta on his way to New Orleans for a race during the Mardi Gras festivities. He asked Walthour to join him, and although Walthour was tempted, he declined the offer. Instead of heading to New Orleans with Oldfield, Walthour traveled to New York to make a personal appeal to the N.C.A. Board of Control.

The seventh annual meeting of the N.C.A. was held at Hotel Bartholdi in New York City on March 1, 1905. Walthour asked the Board if he and Moran could pay a fine instead of having the lengthy suspension. Walthour swallowed a great deal of pride coming north, but Powers was not in a forgiving mood; Walthour's appeal was denied.

Two days later, Walthour was back in Atlanta and told the *Constitution*:

Well, I have been racing steadily for seven years and I can afford to take a rest. There is in fact nothing else for me to do. The new association planned some time ago is no more, as all the other riders have been reinstated. I have a good paying business here and there is no real reason why I should not be content with life. I do not intend to give up racing, however, and will start training very soon in order to keep in condition. It is possible of course that something may turn up, which will result in my reinstatement. We have the right if we desire of carrying this matter to the board, but I am inclined to let it rest where it is. The National Cycling Association was willing enough to let me race again, and the question of my reinstatement was up to Powers. He was busy with his baseball league, however and we had little time to talk over the situation. You know I was considering going to New Orleans and driving an automobile there in a race with Barney Oldfield, as stated in the *Constitution* some time ago. I see that in the race in which I would have taken part the machine was wrecked and the driver nearly killed. So I was lucky in going to New York.[25]

Walthour's primary concern about his suspension was how it would affect his racing contracts in Europe. He was afraid of a pact between the N.C.A. and European delegations. With the exodus of many U.S. riders to races abroad, the N.C.A.'s incentive was to keep the best in the world riding on American tracks. At the beginning of the year, two of the United States' best riders, Iver Lawson and Floyd MacFarland, had gone to Australia, tempted by the money. Frank Kramer, the reigning American sprint champion for the previous four years, arrived in Europe with his trainer Jack Neville on March 20, 1905.[26] Hugh McLean, the United States' second-best pace follower after Walthour, also went overseas earlier in the year.

Walthour kept himself in riding form by working as he had done for years. The public voiced various opinions of his predicament. Even the flamboyant Jack Prince weighed in on the matter: "I would have come on to Atlanta at once had Walthour been reinstated, but you know how things went and I was very sorry. But I hope that in a few weeks when the board of appeals meets that the pressure that will be brought to bear on them will square matters up all right for Bob. I will go to this meeting and do my best for him. I am glad Bob is training, for it will be well for him to keep in condition in case the board gives him another chance which I hope they will."[27]

On March 31, 1905, it was reported that in spite of Walthour's one-year suspension, Nat Butler and Frank Caldwell had raced in Richmond, Virginia, for the right to compete against Walthour. Had Walthour been reinstated? It seemed only a short time before Walthour's suspension days would be over.[28]

Jack Prince arrived in Atlanta on April 5 with the welcome news that Walthour's suspension was indeed over. In fact, Walthour was already scheduled to race in Boston on April 19. Prince's announcement was not the primary reason for his visit to Atlanta. He worked on his proposal to lease the indoor coliseum at Piedmont Park. He planned build a track and hold races in the winter and spring.[29]

Walthour wrote an article in the *Atlanta Constitution* on April 16. Included was a photo of him being held up by a trainer at the outdoor portion of Piedmont Park. He had been training there since late March and also was spotted on the roads of Atlanta yelling for more speed from his pacemakers. The photo showed a huge front sprocket. By today's standards, it appears to be close to a sixty-tooth monster.

Walthour and Moran's suspensions were changed to a fine of $100 apiece, conditional upon future conduct. Both men were required to participate in certain races at the Charles River and Revere tracks in April, May, and June. The final reinstatement stipulation was that they agreed to ride in New York's next six-day race in December 1905 without the usual appearance money but only "if Powers would desire them," according to the *Boston Daily Globe*.[30]

Rare was the occasion when Walthour's temper flared, and unfortunately it came to a boiling point at a time when his stock was at an all-time high. If he had stayed in the race and won, what would have happened to the Walthour legend? But perhaps what he needed instead was to relieve the stress and take a break from his great whirlwind of success.

{ 19 }

Déjà Vu

he winter of Walthour's suspension had been a bitter cold one for those living in the northeast. Frigid temperatures sent Boston residents scurrying to the Charles River track, not to see races but to carry away, piece by piece for their wood stoves, the fence that surrounded the stadium. The spring weather was not much kinder. On April 19, 1905 Walthour raced at Charles River track against two other six-day strikers, Nat Butler and Jimmy Moran. The race was Walthour's first in five months and the first since his reinstatement by the N.C.A.

The freezing northwest wind that came off the Charles River whipped around him as he rode at forty miles per hour, inches behind Gussie Lawson's pacing motorcycle. To protect himself Walthour formed an echelon behind Lawson's machine as he came around the first turn for the straightaway. Walthour's red hands froze to the handlebars, and his ears felt as though they would break off. Only his churning legs kept him warm, and occasionally he received bursts of heat from Lawson's tailpipe. If he had stopped at any point during the thirty-mile race, he would have had trouble remounting. Walthour was a warm weather rider, but he had a lot to prove in this race.

Both Moran and Butler experienced pacing and mechanical problems. But the thousands who bundled up and paid admission to the fenceless track agreed that Walthour would have won regardless of whether his competitors encountered problems. Considering his forced layoff, Walthour appeared to be in fabulous form, finishing the thirty miles in forty-four minutes fourteen seconds, averaging nearly forty-one miles per hour.

Had Walthour not been suspended and gone to Europe in February and March (as was his intention, as he had done the season before), he would have likely cleared at least $20,000 ($503,000 in today's dollars) for the two months. And although he took a big hit to his wallet, the absence from racing gave him time to reflect on how much he enjoyed what he did for a living. "I am glad, of course, that my suspension is at an end," he said before traveling north to Charles River, "not so much on the account of the money I intend to make from my European engagements as on the account of the mere pleasure of riding." But *Bicycling World* suggested that Walthour's statement was certainly intended to be sarcastic and commented, "It is not stated whether he laughed when he said this."[1]

According to the guidelines of his reinstatement, Walthour was required to remain in the United States until July 4, 1905. He would have loved to go to Europe where cycling—and motor-pacing in particular—had grown into a very popular sport. In Germany cycling enthusiasts could not build stadiums fast enough or big enough. Walthour understood that interest in cycling was waning in the United States and that baseball was emerging as the national game. "Here in America we consider it a big crowd to have 5,000 people at a race, an immensely profitable afternoon even at a big league ball park to count 15,000 to 25,000 people, but there in Europe over half a hundred thousand piled their way to see one race."[2]

Immediately after his first victory in 1905, Walthour and Lawson returned south to race on Jack Prince's newest creation, an open air track at the Coliseum in Piedmont Park. Six months had passed since Walthour had raced in Atlanta, and fans were anxious to see the hometown sports hero compete against Jimmy Moran. A purse of $1,000 ($25,200 in current dollars) was set up for the winner in best of three five-mile heats.

On April 27 big-winged beetles dodged the lights that lit up the orange-brown wooden track in the warm and humid night air as thousands filed in to see the high-speed excitement and hear the terrific noises that motor-pacing generated. In the first heat on the track, which was damp from the recent rains, Walthour won by nearly a full lap. The second heat was do or die for Moran, and he was forced to follow a fast pace from the start. Twice Lawson's front tire crossed Moran's rear tire, but Walthour called for him to back off and not make the pass. Both times, "the largest crowd that ever saw an open air bicycle race in Atlanta," according to the *Constitution,* stood up ready to cheer for Walthour. With a few laps to go, Lawson moved forward again with Walthour inches behind, and this time there was no questioning whether they would attempt the pass. But at that moment Walthour's foot slipped out from the toe clip, and he lost contact with his pacer. Walthour finished behind Moran by pedaling his fixed-gear bicycle with one leg. In the third and deciding heat, Walthour was able to make a quick start. Moran had overexerted himself in the second heat, and Walthour was victorious at his homecoming race.[3]

❋

Gussie Lawson had been a loyal friend to Walthour for years. Their professional partnership was considered one of the best in the motor-pacing world. Their verbal and nonverbal communication on the track was second to none. Pacing Walthour within inches behind his rear wheel, Lawson had an innate sense of when he needed to slow down or speed up for tactical reasons or because Walthour was fresh or tired. Likewise Walthour knew exactly what to do if Lawson had mechanical problems, or if heavy traffic was ahead or behind. As a professional bike rider, Walthour had the fame and fortune. But like a good caddy in golf, Lawson shared in that success. Walthour gave Lawson a salary that was similar to what a typical professional caddy got—about 10 percent of the winnings. Lawson had extraordinary talents on a bicycle, but he did not have that killer instinct of a champion. Nonetheless, his talents on the bike did transfer over well to pacemaking.

There were signs, however, that Lawson's drinking was getting the better of him. He was not only prone to drink—he was quite accomplished at it. Louis Darragon, a French motor-pacer, described Lawson sitting on his motorcycle at the side of the track, waiting to pace Walthour or another rider, taking pulls from a whiskey flask and toasting a variety of people, including anyone coming round the track or President Roosevelt or the German Kaiser. That same afternoon, all the motor-pacers and pacemakers went to a bar, and Lawson continued to drink beer and cocktails faster than anyone.[4]

Lawson may have been the first motorcyclist ever to use leather clothing for protection. From his big boots to his pants to his big jacket and football-style helmet that he wore on the track in Europe in 1904, Lawson was resplendent in cowhide leather. He called it his "safety riggin'." For his ingenuity, according to *Bicycling World*, Lawson had long been the butt of many jokes.[5] But he continued wearing his trademark gear.

In May Nat Butler arrived in Atlanta to compete against Walthour in a twenty-mile motor-paced race without heats. At the start Walthour stood up on his pedals and pushed his bicycle from side to side, catching up to the well-protected Lawson at twenty miles per hour. They gradually reached their cruising speed of more than twice that. Butler and his pacemaker were slightly slower, losing ground on each lap. Directly above the finish line in the grandstand, Blanche hid her face on the shoulder of a companion as her husband was just about to hand out another beating on Prince's track.

With one mile to go and coming round high up the steep banking toward the grandstand in a commanding lead, Lawson's rear tie suddenly burst. He tried to maintain balance, but the motorcycle slid wildly out from under him with its engine still revving. People in the stands drew back, afraid that it would come crashing toward them. Instead the momentum sent the motorcycle to the inside of the track, and Lawson flipped straight over its handlebars. His head and shoulders hit the track at over forty miles per hour, and his legs and arms flayed about in contorted positions.

Walthour's front wheel hit the gas tank, and he catapulted twenty feet through the air—enough to go over Lawson and the entire wreckage. Blanche peered over toward the smashing sounds to see both Lawson and her husband lying motionless. Seconds later Walthour moved. Instinctively he pushed himself up, and in a dazed state he looked around. As attendants came running toward him, he asked, "Is Gussie hurt badly?" Meanwhile Butler and his pacemaker continued on and won the race.[6] Lawson eventually regained consciousness, and remarkably, both he and Walthour escaped serious injury. Lawson credited his leather gear for saving his life.

❋

Before leaving for Europe, Walthour won eight of eleven races in the United States. The three losses were because of either mechanical problems with pacing or crashes. He was anxious to get to Europe, where he could make the most money. "My contract with Promoters [Robert] Coquelle and Victor Breyer calls for three months' racing in Europe," said Walthour, "for a return of a guarantee of $15,000. This is the minimum sum that I can receive for three months' work, and if I manage to win all my races, I will make in the neighborhood of $25,000 [$629,000 in current dollars]."[7]

By comparison, fellow Georgian Ty Cobb, who was about to make his professional debut with the Detroit Tigers in August 1905, made only $1,500 ($37,000) in his first full season. Not until he had become a full-fledged superstar in 1914 did Cobb's annual salary reach $15,000 ($332,000).[8]

Walthour's last race before he left for Europe was at the Revere Beach track in Boston, on the Fourth of July. Four of the best motor-pacers in the United States were there: Jimmy Moran, Hugh McLean, Harry Caldwell, and Walthour. The race was the last to satisfy Walthour's "forced" stay in the United States by the N.C.A. Hopefully, Walthour would have enough time in Europe to prepare and defend his prestigious world motor-pacing title in Antwerp on July 24.

The race at Revere was an unusual one. Traditionally, motor-paced races at Revere were either hour-long contests or between twenty-five and fifty miles; this one was for six hours. The timing couldn't have been worse for Walthour because he and Lawson had to catch a night train to New York, to meet his family and Zenus Fields in order to board the steamer heading for Europe the next morning. Walthour pleaded with the Revere management to cut the time of the race. They agreed to a start time of 1 p.m., and that the race would be three and a half hours instead of six.

Hugh McLean crashed out at fifty miles, and the other three cyclists continued on. The fans, like the riders, were not used to such long contests, and the clock began to drag. As mile after mile was reeled off in syncopated fashion, Walthour got more worried that he and Lawson would miss the train for New York. He regretted the 4:30 ending time and wished it was an hour earlier. Missing the train was not an option, because not only would he miss the steamer, but his family and Zenus Fields would not know what to do if he failed to arrive at the harbor in time. In addition, $3,000 had been paid in advance to take everyone and their luggage and equipment to Europe in grand style.

By about 3:50 p.m., Walthour could stand it no longer and pulled off the track. He yelled for Lawson to do the same. They quickly donned their street clothes and scurried off to the train station. They were booed out of the stadium.[9]

The two companions were lucky to leave when they did because they barely made the train to New York. Their welcome to New York was much more enjoyable than their humiliating exit out of the Revere stadium. Walthour happily embarked on his third trip to Europe surrounded by his best friends and family.

❀

Walthour and company arrived in Paris, after some delay through Liverpool as a consequence of the pea soup fog the United Kingdom was famous for. They all checked into the swanky hotel Joli-Sejour. Blanche was four months pregnant, and the three Walthour children admired the beautiful chandeliers that graced the hotel lobby.

Although Walthour's arrival was big news in Paris, not all the press reports were good. Much was made of the great American sprinter Frank Kramer, who had arrived earlier and cleaned house. Walthour hoped to do the same. A writer from *Les Sports* pigeonholed Walthour as a greedy American and claimed that his only motivation in Europe was to earn money by taking part in as many races as possible. Conversely *L'Auto's* Robert Coquelle praised Walthour as "Le Champion des Champions" and wrote of his enormous courage and beautiful form. Coquelle noted that whether he raced on wood or cement, rode behind pacing, or rode with or without windshield protection, Walthour was almost always victorious. Coquelle declared that he knew of no sportsman better than the rider from Atlanta.[10]

Rain delayed Walthour's European debut for 1905 at the outdoor Buffalo track in Paris, and Walthour's first competition was on July 20 against fellow American Nat Butler and Frenchman Cesar Simar. Because of more bad weather, the event was reduced to only two heats: a ten-kilometer race and a thirty-kilometer race. Butler surprised many spectators by winning the first heat with a superb performance from start to finish. A rusty Walthour was five hundred meters back in second, and the French hopeful finished four laps back. In the final heat Walthour nearly crashed at forty-five miles per hour when he misjudged the rollers that angled out directly behind Lawson's rear tire. Despite the anxious moment Walthour won wire to wire. Simar was two hundred meters behind most of the way and could not make up any ground on Walthour.[11]

Walthour and Lawson had four days to travel to Belgium to prepare for the world championships in Antwerp. They were able to arrive early enough for a few days' worth of rainy practice runs over the four-hundred-meter Zurenborg cement velodrome. In contrast to the world championships the year before in London, where only small engines were allowed to pace the riders, in Antwerp no limits were placed on what kind of power the motorcycles could possess.

The professional one-hundred-kilometer event on July 24 was in front of fifteen thousand Belgians, including the King of Belgium and Prince Albert. The track was damp from the day before, and ten riders lined up at the start as their pacing motorcycles revved up one hundred meters away, waiting. Along with Walthour the contestants were Willy Schmitter, Peter Gunther, and Anton Huber (all Germans); Tommy Hall (English); Paul Guignard (French); Piet Dickentman (Dutch); and three Belgians, Ivan Goor, Louis Luycken, and Arthur Vanderstuyft. An Italian named Bianchi (possibly Eduardo Bianchi, who founded Bianchi Bicycles in 1885) held Walthour steady as he fidgeted with pedals. Walthour cleared his throat several times and was given plenty of water.

All ten started at the crack of the pistol, and each needed to find his pacing machine. Tommy Hall, a small man with dark hair and sleepy eyes from Canningtown, was first to pick up his machine, ridden by Franz Hoffman, who had paced Walthour to his world championship in 1904. Dickentman picked up his powerful forty-horsepower tandem, which had the suction of a train. Walthour picked up Lawson's comparatively smaller machine.

Rowland Janson, an editor for *Cycling*, wrote, "[T]he noise was terrible as the men rushed by. Should someone fall we shudder to think." Walthour, with his head down as usual, cranked his pedals using a huge 58-tooth chain wheel in the front and a tiny 11-tooth cog in the back. He rode his feather-light steel bike with no brakes at more than 46 miles per hour. He relied on Lawson to serve as his eyes while they negotiated through a crowded field of ten riders.

After twenty-five kilometers an injury Hall had suffered weeks earlier became too painful, and he was forced to quit. Hall's manager pleaded at the side of the track, but the Englishman could not continue. With Hall and his pacemaker out, Lawson took advantage of an opportunity. He realized his pacing machine was not powerful enough to beat Dickentman, and as was his prerogative, he summoned Hoffman onto the track to help Walthour. Walthour changed pace from Lawson to Hoffman with remarkable skill and at once went to work to catch the leader Dickentman, who was by then several laps ahead.

Walthour and Dickentman rode side by side for three laps until they came close to passing two others. Then all four were together. Walthour lost his pace momentarily and fell behind one hundred meters. The crowd cheered madly for Walthour to catch up again. The tumult was loud enough to be heard above the nine pacing motors. In spite of the initial success and speed of Dickentman's tandem, it may have been the source of his undoing, because he could not endure the speed, and eventually he was forced to change to another, less powerful motor. Walthour saw his chance. "Are you ready?" he asked. With confirmation from Hoffman, Walthour said, "Let it go." With magnificent ease and speed Walthour sped around Dickentman. Another great roar came up from the stadium. Walthour continued on the attack and showed no mercy. When all was finished, Walthour won by four laps in one hour eighteen minutes fifty-four seconds. Paul Guignard passed a tiring Dickentman and took second. With no limits on the pacing motorcycles in Antwerp, the time for the one hundred kilometers was fifteen minutes faster than it had been in London, the site of the 1904 world championships.

"I never felt so good in all my life," declared Walthour after his second straight world championship victory. "[M]y legs never felt it, only my arms, and when I saw that fat German guy on the back of that locomotive of Dickentman's get his 'I am saved, brother' smile on, I felt just mad, and meant to do it. I said to Gussie, this morning, I reckoned I could beat the Dutchman, and am happy he did not win; his tandem should never have been allowed."[12]

Nobody could have denied that Walthour was the best of the bunch at Antwerp that day, but nevertheless a small controversy followed. Track officials questioned whether Tommy Hall had withdrawn on purpose to allow Hoffman to pace Walthour. Hall strenuously repudiated the claim that he was in any way connected with Lawson's decision to request Hoffman's assistance.[13]

The inquiry was dropped, and for the second year in a row Walthour was declared the best in the world at the incredibly competitive and lucrative cycling sport of motor-pacing. *L'Auto* wrote, "Bobby Walthour is the champion of the world for 1905. No victor could be more agreeable to the sportsman, no matter from what country, than this wonderful rider, who recently landed in Europe, has for the second time written his name on the glorious list of champions of the world."[14]

{20}

An American Superstar in Paris

Zenus Fields came back to the United States before the Walthours and Gussie Lawson. He was home in Atlanta in early November 1905 with the welcome news that Walthour had won fifteen of eighteen races overseas. Walthour had hired Fields in the summer of 1905 as a mechanic for his motorcycles and bicycles.

Fields had not previously been to Europe, and he was in awe of the great cathedrals, citadels, castles, and bridges, designed and built centuries before. The natural beauty of the landscape, from its flowing rivers to its beaches, green valleys, and snow-capped mountains had inspired him. But what most amazed Fields was how Walthour had been treated like a king in these foreign countries. Walthour's conquering style in front of massive crowds astonished Fields. He could not speak the language, but he shared the French cycling fans' deep appreciation for Walthour's athleticism. In what became an almost commonplace event involving those in the cycling business—as if Fields himself were famous because he worked directly for Walthour—a French tiremaker told Fields to take whatever he wanted from a huge stack of rubber tires.[1]

Although Walthour was a bona fide star attraction in the United States, his status did not pack the punch at home that it did in Europe. Walthour knew that baseball in the United States attracted more crowds than cycling. He was quoted by the *Atlanta Constitution*: "Here baseball is the national game, [in France] they don't know the horsehide game, but have adopted bicycle racing as the greatest of all the sports. Why, over there in France, I am as well known and as well liked as if I were a Frenchman. In fact, to them I have ceased to be an American. I am a Frenchman. They care more for me I believe than they do here in Atlanta."[2]

Fields left Europe too early to see Walthour's last European race in 1905, which was on November 12 at the Vélodrome d'Hiver in Paris, where a high-banked wooden track eight meters wide and 333 meters long could be seen comfortably from most of the twenty thousand spectator seats. Ever since George Leander had been killed at Parc des Princes French bicycle race promoters were reluctant to host motor-paced races with the ungainly and powerful motor tandems. But German national motor-pacing champion Thaddeus Robl refused to ride against Walthour in France unless he was allowed to use his huge hulking tandem, similar to the forty-horsepower monster that Dickentman had used in the world championships in Antwerp. Management relented and allowed Robl to bring whatever machine he wanted.

Walthour could have done the same, but he chose a more nimble and less powerful single-seat motorcycle to pace him. Walthour therefore was not obligated to pay two people to pace him, and besides he had one of the best pacemakers in the business. He did, however, need to invest in and keep up with the ever-changing motorcycle technology. Before the race with Robl, Walthour bought two French twin-cylinder pacing machines, on which Lawson could power up to sixty miles per hour. The new motorcycles offered little protection from air resistance compared to Robl's, which included giant windshields, but Walthour used them anyway.

Three individual heats of ten kilometers, twenty-five kilometers, and fifty kilometers were scheduled, with 2,500 francs ($500) for the winner, as well as a gold medal that was to be presented by Jules Dubois, the first human-paced national champion of France, who had won that honor as early as 1885.[3]

In the first heat Walthour beat the ten-kilometer track record by thirty-one seconds for a time of seven minutes ten seconds. The sellout crowd stood and gave him a loud and prolonged cheer. Robl's time was under the former track record as well, but he was nineteen seconds behind Walthour. In the second heat Walthour again smashed track records, averaging more than fifty-two miles per hour and leaving Robl hopelessly behind. For the fifty-kilometer final Walthour finished nearly three minutes ahead of Robl in thirty-six minutes ten seconds and beat the fifty-kilometer track record by more than a minute.[4]

Walthour's victory created a sensation in Paris, and in *L'Auto* Robert Coquelle wrote:

> We had yesterday in the meeting between Walthour and Robl all the emotions that we had been promised and all the interest that we expected. So brilliantly has Walthour ridden in the last three races he has won, in which he was opposed by the champion of Germany, that we can truthfully say that the conquered as well as the conqueror have pulverized all the records of the Galerie des Machines. I believe that Walthour was never in such brilliant form as yesterday. He had that easy and powerful manner of men in full possession of all their power and of whom one can demand anything.[5]

Walthour played down the great victory and instead took the opportunity to voice his opinion on the dangers of the big motors. "I have a wife and four small children to support," he said, "and I want to enjoy a long and prosperous racing career and I do not intend to take any more chances behind those death-dealing big motors. Just as soon as my present contract is [finished] I am done with the big motors and will follow the smaller ones."[6] Shortly thereafter the Walthour family and Gussie Lawson boarded a steamer for New York. With them were the two French pacing motorcycles.

❋

The four-month stay in Europe in 1905 had earned Walthour a phenomenal profit; Walthour cleared 40,000 francs ($8,000 in today's dollars).[7] In contrast, Louis Trousselier earned a lesser 6,950 francs ($1,400) when he won the three-week long Tour de France in 1905.[8] This was at a time when the average U.S. worker earned 22 cents per hour and the average speed limit in American cities was ten miles per hour.[9]

After a short stay in chilly New York on November 25, Blanche and the children took a train back home to the warmer climate of Atlanta. Walthour, Lawson, and the motorcycles remained. He prepared for the long-distance rigors of riding in the big six-day race at Madison Square Garden, which was to start on December 4. As well as training he also spent time looking for a suitable partner. Walthour wanted Jimmy Moran, but Moran was already teamed up with Hugh McLean. If Walthour was unable to team with any other rider, he had little choice but to drop out of the race.

However, he cut a deal with Patrick Powers, the manager of the six-day race. Walthour would ride motor-pacing exhibitions during the six-day race, paced by Lawson aboard one of his new French motorcycles. In addition, as Frank Kramer and Jimmy Michael had done before him, Walthour wrote celebrity guest columns for the *World* during the race. Between the exhibitions and the writing Walthour probably made more money than if he had split the $1,500 prize money for winning the actual race. But what Walthour failed to accomplish by not riding was the prolonged winter training that had prepared him for spring racing in previous years.

As always, thousands flocked to the Garden to see the six-day race, including millionaire celebrities Alfred Vanderbilt and Harry Payne Whitney. The usual popcorn and candy vendors walked up and down the aisles, hawking their wares in thick New York accents. Spectators stayed at the edge of their seats in anticipation that a team would break away suddenly in an effort to gain a lap. They witnessed the magical speed of the brightly colored riders going around and around like squirrels in a cage. Despite introduction of some safety measures, some fans were bloodthirsty and looked forward to riders crashing and sliding down the steeply banked bowl while their bikes bounced and ricocheted off the track. The band played upbeat tunes within the tracks' inner circle. Various dramas arose as well, such as accusations of riders' drug doping with strychnine, which was not illegal at the time but certainly was out of favor, unlike in earlier times.

Walthour shared his expertise in his daily articles. "One who has never ridden in the race cannot realize the strain, but it is far from torture and does not hurt the riders. The first two days are the worst and then the riding becomes easy."[10]

Youngsters high up in the rafters called out Walthour's name, as if he were circling the yellow pine track below with the others. But until Gussie Lawson came out on to the track for the first time in his trademark leather suit and gunned the two-cylinder beauty, the audience had not really expected Walthour. The six-day race was put on hold for a few minutes for the exhibition ride.

Lawson took a few warm-up laps, steering up to the highest point of the banking and risking an accident if he went over the rim. When Walthour appeared with a United States flag tied around his waist and waved to the crowd, the noise of the twin-cylinder engine could not be heard. Walthour was as popular in New York as he had ever been. He rode one mile (ten laps) so close behind Lawson that they appeared attached by an invisible rope. Going up and down the steep banks at more than forty miles per hour stirred up a pall of blue smoke, creating almost a tornado inside the building. The crowd unleashed a wild burst of cheering.

❋

Walthour spent the remainder of December at home in Atlanta with his family and took a rest for the holidays. The Walthours were overjoyed to welcome their fourth child, Blanche Annabelle, on December 17.

Then on February 6, 1906, he and Lawson left New York harbor for Paris, and their ship steamed directly into an oncoming storm. In a letter to Blanche, Walthour wrote about the power of the waves that tossed the *Kronz-Prince Wilhelm*, but they arrived safely in France six days later.[11]

In his first contest of the year Walthour was in a twenty-four-hour race at the Vélodrome d'Hiver on February 19. At first he had declined to race. But when management offered him veteran French sprinter Edmond Jacquelin as a partner, Walthour could not refuse as he had done in New York. Of the dozen teams, Walthour and Jacquelin were the clear favorites among the Parisians. In the twentieth hour of the race, however, Jacquelin fell and injured himself. Their chance for victory was instantly dashed along with the hopes of the majority of the twenty thousand fans who had bet large sums of money on the team. Walthour helped his French partner off the track and accompanied him to the hospital.

Meanwhile thousands inside swarmed the track and threw glass bottles, papers, and umbrellas at the other riders. A riot was narrowly averted when the referee wisely called all bets off. In Atlanta reports stated that Walthour was involved in the mob scene, but the error was dispelled once his family received a letter that explained everything.[12]

For the honor to race the world champion in the first motor-paced race of 1906 at the Vélodrome d'Hiver, four riders rode ten-kilometer heats on February 25. The German Peter Gunther beat Arthur Vanderstuyft, and Frenchman Charles Parent beat his countryman Louis Darragon. This set the stage for the fifty-kilometer race between Walthour, Gunther, and Parent. Walthour took the lead immediately and accelerated up to fifty miles per hour. He pulled ahead so far in the lead that the only contest was for second place. Gunther finished enough ahead of Parent for second but was three laps behind Walthour. Paced by Franz Hoffman, Walthour averaged nearly fifty miles per hour, finishing in thirty-eight minutes eight seconds.[13]

Walthour's stay in Europe on this occasion was short compared to his previous trips. He did, however, manage to rub shoulders with a veritable who's who of professional road racing men, including Henri Cornet, who won the scandal-filled 1904 Tour de France, and also Louis Trousselier, who won the 1905 Tour de France. Just as baseball was emerging as America's top sport, road cycling was emerging in France, although track racing—in particular motor-pacing—led in popularity. Walthour's body type, heart, and lungs made him well-suited to endurance road races. Certainly he would have been able to climb mountains with the best had he trained for that sport. What a different history the Tour de France might have had, especially as it relates to Americans, had Walthour considered racing in the Tour. As it was, Walthour was motivated by money, and the Tour did not offer enough money for him. Not until 1981 when Jacques Boyer first participated in the Tour de France did the United States have an entry in the Tour de France. Five years later Greg Lemond won America's first Tour.

❋

Walthour arrived back in America on April 11, 1906, accompanied by Lawson and Tommy Hall. Hall had recently set the world hour record behind pace with fifty-four miles and six hundred yards at Parc des Princes. He accompanied Walthour and Lawson to Atlanta as Walthour's guest.

Thaddeus Robl behind his tandem pacer. *Courtesy of Andrew Ritchie*

Jimmy Michael, circa 1904. *Buck Peacock Collection*

Walthour barely visible behind Lawson—making a pass at 1905 World Championship in Antwerp. *Courtesy of Andrew Ritchie*

Left to right—Willie Schmitter, Piet Dickentman, and Walthour in Cologne, July 30, 1905. *Courtesy of Andrew Ritchie*

At left, Walthour with Lawson, then Robl, Peter Gunther, and Bruno Demke, Steglitz, 1905. *Courtesy of Andrew Ritchie*

Louis Darragon behind his pacer, 1904. *Buck Peacock Collection*

Walthour, circa 1905. *Buck Peacock Collection*

Gussie Lawson and Walthour, circa 1906. *Buck Peacock Collection*

Left to right—Mettling, Nelson, Dangla, Brecy, Leander, and Elkes. *Author's Collection*

Nat Butler, circa 1909. *Buck Peacock Collection*

Bobby Jr. and Margaret Walthour, circa 1928. *Courtesy of Robert Walthour III*

Bobby Walthour Jr. and Bob III, circa 1930. *Courtesy of Robert Walthour III*

Walthour family in Santa Monica, circa 1939. Left to right—Bob III, Bobby Jr., Patricia, Margaret, and Richard. *Courtesy of Robert Walthour III*

Bob Walthour III, circa 1933. *Courtesy of Robert Walthour III*

Aftermath and devastation of fiery motor-pacing accident, circa 1909 (Walthour was not in this race). *Courtesy of German Sport University Cologne, Fredy Budzinski collection*

Hall, like Fields before him, was amazed at how much attention Walthour received. Atlanta newspapers cataloged his every move; even the Walthour family dog made the news because a neighbor became upset at the constant barking of the St. Bernard. The Walthour children adored the big dog and rode it around the yard as if it were a horse.

While in the South, Walthour continued winning motor-paced races, including one against Hugh McLean, the reigning American paced champion. Until Walthour beat him, McLean had won seventeen straight races.

In late May Walthour headed north to the Revere Beach track in Boston, which had recently been given a makeover. The track was resurfaced, and the training quarters were rebuilt and brought up to modern standards. Walthour enjoyed the new facilities, working out with Hugh McLean, Tommy Hall, brothers Menus and John Bedell, and Will Stinson, back in racing after a three-year layoff following the death of Harry Elkes.[14]

At Revere on June 2 Walthour participated in a twenty-five-mile handicap race against Stinson and Hall, who were each given a four-lap head start. Yet before the beginning of the race, the race organizer announced that the handicap was six laps. Walthour was well within his right to protest but decided to let things stand. Lawson paced Walthour, Charles Turville paced Stinson, and Carl Rudin paced Hall. By mile thirteen Hall was hopelessly out of the race and left the track. Walthour had gained two and a half laps on Stinson, but then he punctured a tire at mile sixteen. Stinson put another lap on his rival while Walthour changed his bicycle. Walthour had little time to settle in on his pace before his second bike gave out under him. He was compelled to change to a third one. In the meantime Stinson pulled ahead five laps and showed his old-time form; he looked to be the sure winner.

But Walthour kept plugging away. By mile twenty-two Stinson was under more strain than he could handle and lost his pace while Walthour rode faster and faster. The crowd realized that he might make a comeback. Around and around he flew, tucked in behind Lawson's slipstream, continuing to lap Stinson, who had caught up again behind his pacer. Walthour overcame both his six-lap handicap and terrific odds and beat

Stinson by one and a quarter laps. His finishing time was thirty-six minutes fifty-six seconds.[15]

Walthour reflected on the race two weeks later: "Probably my hardest race, where I was forced to let myself out to the limit and exert myself to the utmost to win, was one I rode recently in Boston with Stinson and Hall."[16]

Walthour's biggest race of the year was yet to come. The world cycling championships in 1906 were to be held in Geneva, Switzerland. For him to win a third motor-pacing world championship in a row would be a great achievement. Winning a world title would not earn Walthour much money, but it guaranteed lucrative future contracts, especially in Paris and Berlin.

July 29 was the day of the motor-pacing world championships, and Walthour was hoping for the best of luck on the day. He had raced and trained in Dresden in the weeks leading up to Geneva. The Germans were impressed by how seriously Walthour took his workouts. He cycled in ten-kilometer intervals every evening at more than fifty miles per hour and was in peak physical condition.[17]

Many other great riders were at the one-hundred-kilometer championship race, including Tommy Hall, Louis Darragon, and Arthur Vanderstuyft. Walthour, the lone American, bolted off the line first and pulled neatly in behind Lawson. Darragon was paced by Franz Hoffman, and he passed Walthour at the ten-kilometer mark. Suddenly, Walthour pulled off the track with a flat tire and was forced to change bikes, losing more time to Darragon. Meanwhile Vanderstuyft slipped into second. By sixty kilometers, Walthour was too far behind, and just like that, he lost his world championship to Darragon.[18]

Despite his losing the world championship, the French race-going public remained enamored of the American and considered Walthour the best behind pace, chalking up his defeats to bad luck. At the Buffalo Velodrome on August 15, a light rain caused the wooden track to be very slippery. As a result management announced to the packed venue that no racing would be held that day and no refunds would be given. The fans, hungry for some entertainment for their money, released their frustration on the stadium.

They tore up the seating, threw rocks at the lights, and destroyed the judge's box. Some protesters made their way to the riders' quarters, and Walthour came out calmly onto the racing platform. The ruffians suddenly became starstruck at seeing the famous American so close. They gave Walthour an ovation and began chanting, "*C'est Walthour, Walthour, qu'il nous fait!*" ("It's Walthour, Walthour that we need!") Happy to see their hero, they stopped their destruction, but once Walthour left they attempted to light a fire in the middle of the damp track. Eventually the authorities controlled the situation, and the stadium was emptied without too much further damage.[19]

Walthour, despite his loss of the world championship, came back strong with a number of impressive victories in Paris, including an hour-long race at Parc de Princes on August 19 in which he captured the American record held by Harry Caldwell for three years. Walthour rode fifty-one and a half miles in the hour, beating his nearest competitor in the race by six miles.[20]

Walthour was a genuine superstar in France and in Europe, and he knew that to continue with his great success, he should move permanently to Europe at some point. But for now he was willing to travel thousands of miles to be with his family and also to compete at his sport's highest level.

{21}

Crash and Burn

throughout his more than ten years as a professional cyclist, Walthour had been fortunate. With a combination of pure luck, remarkable bike-handling skills, and superior fitness, he avoided many high-speed accidents. But he never managed to avoid them completely. In 1906 Walthour crashed twice in Cologne, first on August 5 and next on September 23. On both occasions he hit the cement surface at more than fifty miles per hour. At that time, especially in Germany, sports reporters were not interested in more minor injuries, such as cracked ribs or broken fingers. Riders did not want to advertise that they were hurt, either. To do so could prevent them from being signed up to a big money contract. Walthour made fabulous money—more than any other professional athlete of his generation—and he could not allow a few dings or a little dent in the fender bother him. Yet every time he took to the track, the possibility of more serious injury awaited him.

❋

On November 23, 1906, Walthour and his family boarded the *Lorraine* in Cherbourg, along with a large delegation of foreign riders scheduled to race in the Madison Square Garden in December. The *Lorraine* steamed into New York harbor on December 1, giving Walthour a week to train before the six-day festivities began. Earlier, while in France during October, he had caught up with his friend and fellow American motor-pacer Hugh

McLean. It was there they agreed to ride together as partners in the six-day race.

Although Louis Darragon had been crowned the official world motor-paced champion in Geneva in July, the *New York Times* incorrectly announced the preliminary races on the Saturday before the six-day grind began: "The race between Walthour and Guignard will be the principal feature of the night, as it will decide the world's championship for 1906. Guignard holds the world's record for one and two hours, covering 59 miles and 80.5 yards, or almost a mile a minute. Walthour will have an advantage over the Frenchman, owing to the short saucer-like track in the Garden, of which Walthour knows every inch."[1]

In reality Walthour and Guignard lined up at opposite sides of the track, preparing for the hundred-lap (ten-mile) motor-paced race. As usual a crowd of thousands crammed the Garden. Guignard gained a quick start, but by lap twenty-eight Walthour nearly caught him. Around and around the yellow saucer they rode at a dizzying pace, testing the limits of the tiny track. Blue flames spurted from the exhausts, and their motors roared like Gatling guns. At lap thirty-four Walthour overtook Guignard for the lead, and the noise from the crowd nearly raised the roof. Walthour crossed the line a winner at sixteen minutes forty-nine seconds amid wild cheering—a full six laps ahead of his rival.[2]

Twenty-four hours later twelve thousand fans jammed the building to see the start of the great six-day race. A guest columnist from the *World* was Charles Miller, the former New York six-day winner and a former Walthour partner. Miller observed before the start:

> As I saw Bobby Walthour, elongated Floyd MacFarland, and Jimmy Moran stretch themselves and mount their wheels to line up opposite the boxes on the north side of the high-banked saucer-shaped board track, I felt like getting back into my own. There was the crowd packed to the very steel girders in the roof of the huge amphitheater; the six-day waltzes screeching from the owl-like phono machines in the oval made by the track; a wreath of foul tobacco smoke crowning every one present, and the well named all-nighters,

with their tell-tale eyes swollen from a store of sleep to last them through the week.[3]

A few hours into the race, as McLean was riding at the top of the banking, he suddenly shot down the incline in an attempt to jump the field. McLean did not leave enough room as he sped through a pack of four riders, and they all went down in a heap at the bottom of the track. Blood streamed from McLean's head, and Dr. Joseph Creamer put eight stitches in the gash. He was taken to the hospital with a possible skull fracture. The amphitheater buzzed with rumors that McLean might die. But the crowd later was told he was out of danger, and the fans calmed down. Hours later McLean arrived at the Garden with his head heavily bandaged and received sustained applause from the masses. McLean acknowledged the crowd, bowing and waving. He also shook hands with Walthour, wishing him the best of luck.

Without McLean as his partner Walthour rode solo until he could acquire a new partner among the other competitors as the rules allowed. A short time later Menus Bedell crashed at "dead man's curve," so named after Johnny Nelson, who had lost his life at the same spot years earlier. Bedell's injuries included a badly lacerated scalp and a broken collar bone and he too was also rushed to the hospital, but unlike McLean, Bedel did not return to the track. Walthour and Menus's brother John both needed a teammate and paired up. They knew by the rules of the race, a "created" team was forced to concede a lap to the field. With Blanche cheering from a box close to the track, her husband and Bedell made tremendous efforts to gain back the penalized lap. For an hour, they sprinted and relieved one another, but the field would not yield. Even so the Garden spectators were enthralled by the courage and determination of the two riders.[4]

At 2 a.m. on Wednesday, 13 teams were tied at 936 miles and 6 laps, one lap ahead of the Walthour-Bedell combination. From the identical set of box seats where Charles Miller had been married 8 years before, he reported for the *World*:

Just as I took my seat last night, which Pat Powers has so kindly placed at my disposal, there came an earsplitting roar from the mass of humanity. The occasion for the outburst was the appearance of Bobby Walthour, who came out to relieve his partner, John Bedell, just before 6 o'clock. The latter, in anticipation of the relief, shot out of the bunch of grinding riders like a catapult, and almost before the others were aware of it, he had gained a quarter of a lap.

Then Walthour, riding like mad, relieved his partner, and circled the track at a terrific speed. The others panted and humped themselves far over their handlebars. But Walthour, after a hurried glance over his shoulder, redoubled his almost superhuman efforts, and just as it seemed as if he had gained the coveted lap, Bedell again appeared on the track. Whatever gave him the strength and speed, I do not believe even he could tell, but he went like the wind.

Slowly, almost imperceptibly, his wheel crawled nearer and nearer to the rear tire of the last man's wheel. Scarcely an inch separated him from what to himself and his partner would mean partial victory, when Root and Hollister, who were tearing along in a mad endeavor to overcome the flying leader, slipped, came together, and fell on the Twenty-sixth Street side of the track, and under the rules, the lap that meant so much to the tail-enders slipped from their grasp.

Miller, who was sitting a few boxes away from Blanche, was sympathetic: "It's too bad, little woman. Just when he looked to have the lap too."

Blanche choked back tears. "Well I don't care. I can't help thinking they fell on purpose. I knew Bobby could get that lap. And if Root and Hollister had only kept their balance. . . ."[5]

By Wednesday evening, it was estimated that fifty thousand people had paid entrance to the Garden since the doors had opened on Sunday, and firemen were put to work making sure the aisles were clear of fans. Tickets sales were suspended. Many city officials were opposed to the race, and Assistant Corporation Counsel John O'Brien obtained a summons for Patrick Powers, charging an infraction of the Sanitary Code by endangering life and limb in blocking the main entrance.[6]

Once more Walthour found himself mired in the middle of controversy at the Garden. The *New York Times* reported, "On all sides, however, dissatisfaction reigns, and the smoldering embers of discontent are frequently fanned into flames of open demonstrations of actual hostility to the methods by certain riders and the decisions of the officials of the race regarding lap gaining. The chief cause for this discontent yesterday [Thursday] was the failure on the part of the referees to allow Walthour and Bedell the lap they were thought to have earned."[7]

The article reported that Walthour and Bedell had threatened to quit the race, not only because of unfair rulings but because combinations of some of the other teams had been formed against them. Blanche somehow was able to convince her husband and Bedell to keep going. They continued their fight to regain the lost lap, but time ran out on them. At 10 p.m. on Saturday night, they were called off the track to make room for the eight teams left in the race to sprint for the finish.

Bobby and Blanche left New York and reached Atlanta on December 20. Reporters flocked to the train depot. Bobby did not say much, but he was at least happy to know that the public supported him and Bedell. "The New York papers gave us the best of it, and recognized that we were not given anything like a square deal."[8]

❋

Besides Walthour, in 1907 many American riders crossed the Atlantic with contracts to race on European tracks in the spring. They included Major Taylor, Nat Butler, Floyd MacFarland, Menus and John Bedell, Woody Hedspeth, Walter Bardgett, Joe Fogler, and Louis Mettling.

One of Walthour's first motor-paced races of the year for 1907 was on March 10 at the Vélodrome d'Hiver. In the hour-long race, he rode on a Clement bicycle with Continental tires. Frenchman Paul Guignard was in the race, as well as Floyd MacFarland. Guignard got away fast at the start but was quickly overtaken by Walthour. After ten kilometers Walthour had lapped Guignard once and MacFarland twice. As Walthour, paced by Franz Hoffmann, breezed by MacFarland a third time at kilometer twenty, he stuck his tongue out at MacFarland. The tall Californian told Walthour to "go to hell" in a method that would not alert the track stewards.

At the 30-minute mark Walthour was on pace to beat Eugenio Bruni's 1904 track record of 79 kilometers and 200 meters in the hour. He continued at a blistering speed, testing the 333-meter track for all it was worth and was still on record pace after 60 kilometers. But an accident caused Hoffmann to slow down, and Walthour finished just 500 meters short of the record.[9]

On Sunday, March 17, Walthour raced again inside the Vélodrome d'Hiver, in another *course de l'heure* behind the motors, against Guignard, Nat Butler, and Bruni. Walthour got out in the lead and quickly lapped all the other contestants. When he attacked and passed Guignard, he completed a lap in fourteen seconds and kept in Hoffman's slipstream at upward of fifty-two miles per hour. At kilometer forty-six Walthour's thin Continental tire blew. He made an attempt to save his fall and almost did so by skidding on the grass inside the track. But he was upended by a post and sprawled to the ground. He flipped over but managed a nice tuck and roll. Almost instantly he stood up, bloody and dirtied, signaling for another Clement bike. An attendant ran one to him.

As if he had not been involved in the accident at all, Walthour tucked into the rear of Hoffman's motorcycle and quickly resumed his incredible speed, clicking out laps in less than 15 seconds, while the crowd cheered wildly for him. By kilometer 50, Walthour led by 4 laps over Guignard, by 5 over Butler, and 8 over Bruni. But 7 minutes before the end of the hour, the handlebar on his replacement bike broke, and Walthour crashed a second time, this time hard down onto the boards. He rose up gingerly and waited for what seemed a long time to receive his third bicycle. With 4 minutes to go, he was only a half lap, or about 150 meters, in front of Guignard. With grit and determination Walthour poured enough power onto his pedals to hold off a hard-charging Guignard. In spite of the two crashes, Walthour covered 75 kilometers and 320 meters in the hour and won the race. The noise from the crowd was never louder than when Walthour took his lap of honor. He received perhaps his greatest ovation on French soil.[10]

Walthour sent a letter to the *Boston Daily Globe* from Berlin, postmarked April 25. He was in the best condition of his life, he wrote, and he was confident that his successes in the 1907 season would eclipse those of earlier years. Enclosed was a clipping about his 100-kilometer race in

Stieglitz on April 20 in front of 30,000 fans. Racing with Walthour behind the motors at Stieglitz were Frenchman Paul Guignard, and Germans Thaddeus Robl and Anton Huber. Walthour finished 1,220 meters in front of second-place finisher Guignard. The headline asked, "Where was Thaddy?" and reported sarcastically that Robl would have finished last had it not been for Huber. Walthour rode the 100 kilometers in 1 hour 10 minutes 20 seconds, averaging 54 miles per hour.[11]

On May 5, 1907, Walthour raced in Erfurt, Germany. Immediately after he crossed the finish line, winning the race against Arthur Vandersuyft by a close ten meters, his handlebar broke, and Walthour fell, striking his head against a wooden railing and knocking himself unconscious.[12] Newspapers all over the United States carried stories of the incident including Atlanta; New York; Boston; Los Angeles; Washington, D.C.; and Chicago. Some months later Walthour gave an account of his medical treatment in Germany: "They discovered signs of life and again took me to the hospital. There, when I came to, they were going to give me chloroform before sewing up the cuts in my head. I yelled and my wife came in. They did the sewing without chloroforming me. I guess the chloroform would have killed me in that condition."[13] Astonishingly, two days later, Walthour was already training for a May 12 engagement in Leipzig.

In 1915 Walthour was asked which of his crashes he had endured during his long career had been most spectacular and memorable:

> Well, I guess it happened in Leipzig [on May 12, 1907]. A bunch of riders went down in front of me. I was so close to them that I couldn't steer clear. I hit the bunch and down I went. That's the last thing I remember until I came to in America four weeks later. However, the most peculiar part of that spill is that after I hit the boards I got up, climbed on my bike and although I had a broken collar bone, two broken fingers, a nasty gash in my head and a ten inch rip in my leg, I finished and won the race which had only about six laps to go from the place where the spill occurred. I don't remember a thing about getting up. My memory was a blank from the time I capitulated from the saddle until I "came to" nearly a month later in my home in New Jersey.[14]

With Walthour out of commission, German promoters wanted an American motor-pacer in his place. Louis Mettling was a dark-haired twenty-two-year-old from Jamaica Plains, Massachusetts, who had come out of nowhere with a number of impressive motor-pacing victories in the United States. But to take Walthour's place in Europe and to represent the United States was his greatest honor as a bike racer. Mettling first substituted for Walthour in Dresden on June 9 and was allowed to use Franz Hoffmann as a pacer.

In a turn of extraordinary bad luck, Mettling died as a result of injuries in a crash at that same June 9 race in Dresden. On June 23 the accident was reported on the front page of the *Boston Daily Globe.* The day before, Thomas and Caroline Mettling had received a cablegram that no parent should ever receive. It read, "Dresden, June 22, 1907. Mettling, Forest Hills, Boston: Our dear Louis died peacefully while sleeping last night. Cable wishes regarding burial. Give me authority to accept his affects. Schreyer."[15]

Walthour woke up from his month-long coma in New Jersey, which may have been where his mother or brother lived, and eventually received the sad news about Mettling:

> I am pained, but not surprised to hear that Mettling had been killed following the big machines in Germany. In fact, I cannot understand how there are any more men left on the German path, for the game a bicycle rider is up against in the Fatherland is the most strenuous anywhere. In this country and in France the men are following small motors, for both here and in the French capital it was discovered that the game was too hazardous and the public kindly consented to give the racing men half a chance for their life. In Germany, however, the game is entirely different.
>
> The Germans are today passing through the stage of speed madness which is a curse to the game in this country and France a few years ago and which in the United States cost the lives of such great riders as Harry Elkes and Johnny Nelson. Today the game is even worse in Germany than it was three or four years ago in this country, when we were following the big 14-horsepower single cylinder pac-

ing machines; for in Germany they are using two and four cylinder pacing machines, developing 24 and even greater horsepower which means that a man must travel at a mile-a-minute gait if he hopes to get in the money. Darragon's record of a trifle more than 59 miles in one hour shows conclusively what it means, for in that hour some of the miles were ridden in less than one minute.

Let the public stop and realize what this means. Their hair would stand on their heads if they were in a motor car with four strong wheels under them and well balanced if they traveled at that speed. A bicycle rider has nothing but a little bicycle, made as light as possible and fitted with tissue paper tires made of French silk, a little rubber and a little fabric, which are faster than the regular rubber tires in use here. That wheel must be balanced to a nicety, and yet the men are fairly flying. It is practically impossible for a man to see where he is going. The body of his pacemaker is in the front, and the bulk looming up before him is all he has to go by. It is a case of dig, dig, dig, onto the pedals, over on your side most of the time, for the track for this speed must be built almost on a curve, and the stretches as well as the turns must be banked. But enough of the risk: If the tracks were built for the speed it would not be so bad, for a man would be making a continual turn and it would not be so near suicide. The tracks, however, were never built to stand the speed at which the men travel behind the motors, and the result is that, swinging out of the turn, a man is wrenched in his seat and his arms almost torn from the socket[s] in trying to swing his front wheel in line to preserve his equilibrium . . . I am sorry for Louis, for he was a good boy and a fine rider.[16]

✳

In late July Walthour took a rare trip out west. He took a train from New York to Salt Lake City, where his old friend John Chapman was managing a race track. Although he considered the trip a "recuperation," he raced a number of times behind the pace of Gussie Lawson. Walthour had an easy time beating Utah state records. Behind pace, he beat the one-mile, five-mile, and ten-mile state records. He even went back to his old days and did some sprint racing. He beat world class sprinters Floyd MacFarland and also Gussie's brother Iver Lawson. He loved it there but had to hurry home.

In early September, Walthour was home in Atlanta once again. He did not have much time to socialize, but he did have a short interview with a *Constitution* reporter who could not help notice the big red scar he had on his sunburned forehead, as well his missing front tooth. "I'm not afraid to ride fast for I haven't got but one time to die, and I don't believe that it will be on the track," said Walthour. "I've got to hurry to Germany to keep my racing contracts. . . . My contractors in Germany heard about me riding over there and they sent me a cable to quit and come across. They claim I am under contract to ride for them in Germany and nowhere else. Well, I'm well and I go across next week. But you ought to go out to Salt Lake. It's a case of come on in; the water's fine. I'm going to have to move out there, sure. No, I have no other wives out there; just one in Atlanta."[17]

Walthour arrived in Germany on September 17 in time for some good workouts before the race at the Spandau track on September 29, behind the big, powerful motors that he had promised not to race behind anymore. The race was a one-hundred-kilometer affair in which he went up against a crowded field of Paul Guignard, John Bedell, Menus Bedell, Bruno Salzmann, and Arthur Vanderstuyft. At the crack of the pistol, Menus Bedell was in the lead, but was quickly passed by Guignard and Walthour. Bedell eventually caught up to the pair, and the three rode side by side until Bedell took the lead again. A thunderous ovation exploded from the great crowd in appreciation of Bedell's efforts.

After several more laps though, Walthour pulled ahead of Guignard and eventually took the lead from Bedell. By the halfway point, Guignard was rounding the lower turn when his pacing-machine's front tire burst. Guignard's pacer, Stiploschick, went down, and Guignard crashed right behind him. Man and machine rolled over and over and slid along the homestretch of the cement track. Suddenly the tank caught fire, and the motorcycle was soon engulfed in a mass of orange flames and black smoke. Panic reverberated throughout the stadium. Track attendants ran to extricate Guignard and Stiploschick from the wreckage. Both were far enough from the flames not to have been burned, and amazingly Guignard had escaped with just a few abrasions.

An attendant helped Guignard off the track then rushed back to help Stiploschick, who had a broken arm. Without looking, the attendant ran out on the track, right into the path of Franz Hoffmann, who was pacing Walthour at over fifty-five miles per hour. The attendant did not have time to jump aside before the heavy motorcycle struck him head on. Hoffmann and his machine fell to one side and rolled over several times. Walthour executed a somersault, as if he had been hurled from a catapult. He hit his head on the cement, then fell over on his back. An audible groan went up from the immense throng of spectators at the sight of the catastrophe. Walthour lay still, as did the ambulance attendant, and people turned their eyes away from the spectacle.

Walthour was rushed to the hospital, where the doctors found he had only a slight brain concussion and that he had not broken his back, as had been feared. The ambulance attendant was killed instantly. His head was crushed in, and one hand was completely severed. Hoffmann escaped with a badly wrenched leg and bruises, but his motor was smashed to pieces.[18]

❇

Walthour was back in the States by December. Dressed in a long gray overcoat with a red vest, he dropped into the office of the New York newspaper the *World* and had an interview with a reporter who remarked to Walthour, "You look in pretty good shape."

A chipper Walthour responded:

Pretty good shape for a man who has been pronounced dead twice within a year. Yes, twice in Germany they threw a blanket over me to "cover the corpse." Those German tracks are the most dangerous in the world. I will never ride on them again. They are all of cement. Two men were killed outright and several more badly injured in the five races I rode in Germany. I fell in four races out of five. Once I was sent to the hospital for five days; and a queer thing about that fall is that I can't remember anything about it or about being in a hospital or about the people who visited me there. Another fall put me in the hospital for three weeks. In one race I protested against one of the pacers riding for Verbist, the Belgian. The pacemaker rode too close and crowded the other riders. The officials wouldn't pay any attention to the protest and the foreign riders didn't seem to care. They are absolutely careless about the danger of being killed anyway.

In the next race the pacemaker rode too close to somebody and threw him. Five men went down and a timer named Wolff, standing at the edge of the track, was killed. At Spandau, Berlin, a pacemaker [Hoffmann] hit a man crossing the track and killed him. When I fell I was laid out cold. The doctors looked me over and ordered the attendants to throw a blanket over me to hide the "corpse" from the spectators. My wife forced her way in and told them to take the blanket off so I could breathe. The doctor said, "Oh, he doesn't need to breathe. He's all through with that. You go home and we'll attend to burying him." But she insisted and they pulled the blanket away from my face. I guess that saved my life.[19]

{22}

Nine Lives

I n November 1907 the leading weekly French sports magazine *La Vie Au Grand Air* featured an article by Louis Darragon called "Les Pistes Sanglantes" ("The Bloody Tracks"). The piece had an accompanying drawing of a skeleton riding a pacing motorcycle followed by the superimposed photos of many of the professional motor-pacing men who had been killed, including Louis Mettling, Johnny Nelson, Paul Dangla, Albert Brécy, George Leander, and Harry Elkes.[1]

Darragon wrote that he and Walthour and men like them needed to make a living somehow. To have chosen another occupation seemed unthinkable. Put quite simply, competitive cycling was what they did. The rider who possessed the nerve, skill, speed, and endurance to follow the motor for so many years and not to fall victim to a fatal accident was one of a rare and lucky breed. Darragon reasoned that the reward-to-risk factor was such that each race was worth the possibility of a crash.

In the light of the trauma Walthour had suffered in 1907, he was extremely fortunate to have avoided inclusion in that appalling photo gallery of dead cyclists. The accidents that put him out of commission in May and September might well have been fatal for a less experienced rider. Walthour had told the press that the Germans were going through a phase of speed madness, but he must have been the maddest of them all since he himself continued at full force on the German tracks. How the injuries affected him and his family is difficult to know, but the repercussions of his accidents must have been significant—both physically and mentally— as the brain and body cannot endure that level of abuse without some degree of permanent damage.

During the six weeks in Atlanta that winter, Walthour was able to rest and enjoy the Christmas holiday. The 1908 New Year also marked his thirtieth birthday, which he celebrated with his family. After the Garden six-day in December, he had become a physical wreck and looked gaunt. But once home, he ate like a bear out of hibernation and gained back his normal weight of about 160 pounds, although he appeared a little huskier on his 5-foot-10 frame than he had been.[2] During his rest he had daily massage and electricity treatments applied to his torn shoulder ligaments.[3]

In late January Walthour was scheduled to leave his home so that he could be in Europe for a February 2 race at the Vélodrome d'Hiver against Paul Guignard. Before he left, however, he signed a contract to race in Boston at the Park Square Garden. On January 6 Walthour traveled with Gussie Lawson by train from Atlanta, arriving the next day in Boston. For his appearance at the Garden he would earn $500. If he beat Nat Butler he would receive a $250 bonus.[4]

Walthour and Lawson practiced on the wooden boards, which were similar in size and shape to the track at Madison Square Garden. He loved the short indoor track and followed Lawson for a mile in one minute thirty-seven seconds, the best time ever recorded on the oval. A few days later Walthour and Butler lined up for a best of three five-mile heats. Walthour had not raced in Boston since July and was given a huge welcome by the sellout crowd, which he happily acknowledged by bowing and waving.

In the first heat both riders flew around the saucer, following their motorcycles, going up and down the steep banking at breakneck speeds. With less than a mile left Walthour lost his pace, and Butler won the first heat. In the second heat Walthour hung onto a quarter-lap advantage. Butler closed the gap and came within five yards, but time ran out and Walthour won, averaging more than forty miles per hour. For the third and deciding heat Lawson gunned his pacing machine from the start, and somehow Walthour was able to cling within its draft. Butler and his motorman, Charles Turville, made a valiant and desperate chase, but the motorcycle's rear wheel slid around the corners and Butler was forced off his pace. Thus, Walthour won his first race of the year and earned $750 ($18,000) before leaving the country for Europe.[5]

Walthour and Lawson boarded the ship *Kronprinz Wilhelm* and crossed the Atlantic on yet another journey. They arrived in Europe in late January and set out at once to prepare for the race against Guignard—the hour world record holder behind pace—by practicing on the three-hundred-meter wooden track at the Vélodrome d'Hiver.

The race covered three heats: twenty, forty, and fifty kilometers. In the first heat Walthour and Guignard battled for the lead, but the American eventually took control. Guignard stayed fifty meters behind until the halfway point, when Walthour's tire went flat. By the time he and Lawson returned to the track, the first heat was lost. In the second heat Walthour gained a lap on Guignard by peddling at nearly fifty miles per hour. Then Guignard crashed. The crowd voiced their disappointment when, as a result, Walthour slowed his pace to conserve his energy for the last heat. In the final Walthour experienced an easy victory when the injured Guignard was unable to match his speed.[6]

Strangely, in his second race at the Vélodrome d'Hiver a week later, Walthour was clearly not himself. He took a drubbing from Louis Darragon and second-place finisher Henri Contenet. Consequently Walthour went to the hospital for X-rays of the shoulder, which showed that it had not healed properly and was still separated by several centimeters.[7]

Months later on July 26, he raced at the Buffalo track in Paris against Charles Parent (French), Louis Darragon (French), and Albert Edward Wills (English) in a fifteen-kilometer race. *Les Sports* called it "Le Reveil de Walthour" ("The Wakeup of Walthour").[8] The victory was his first in nearly six months, ending the longest losing streak in his professional career. He continued to win in July and August with four more races—one in Lyon[9] and three in Paris.[10]

Some in the French press speculated that Walthour was finally performing well because of his supposed financial desperation and that he was eager to maintain his commercial value.[11] He had guaranteed appearance fees and contracts for his races, for racing with certain bicycle makes and using particular brands of tires, so he was making money, although not as much as he had before. Perhaps if he had chosen to stay at home in Atlanta and rest his shoulder rather than risk further injury, his ability to win would have improved. Walthour spent September and October racing in Europe but achieved only lukewarm results. Many race commentators predicted that Walthour had reached the end of the line for his career.[12]

※

Back in the United States word had spread of Walthour's poor European showing. He had no recourse but to prove his doubters wrong. He was not going to quit; racing was what he did in life. His reputation was on the line. In late October Walthour and Lawson steamed from Cherbourg aboard the *Kaiserin Augusta Victoria* and arrived in New York City on November 7.

Almost immediately he went to work and trained at the Paterson armory in New Jersey. On November 18 he raced George Wiley, a young motor-follower from Syracuse, New York, in a best of three five-mile races. Wiley was paced by his motorman, Bob Schulz. Walthour was expected to walk away with an easy victory, but in the first heat he was shaken from his pace. Wiley passed Walthour and won by twenty yards. The second heat was not much better for Walthour, and his first race in the United States since January was another loss.[13]

Walthour, however, remained popular and was considered the best behind the motors in America. Promoter Patrick Powers matched him up against Albert Wills, the current holder of the world hour record behind pace at 61 miles and 976 yards.[14] His race against Wills was the most anticipated of the preliminary races before the main event.

Ten thousand spectators at Madison Square Garden stood as Walthour and Wills lined up on the yellow "soup bowl" ten-lap-to-the-mile track for the ten-mile race. Loyal Lawson was pacing for Walthour, and Charles Turville paced Wills. By the time the engines warmed up, the revving and exhaust stirred the crowd into a pitch of excitement. The gun cracked, and the two riders caught their pace, racing at a dizzying speed. The first five miles were close until Walthour yelled at Lawson that his tire had punctured, and he rode down the embankment. When the race was restarted, Wills held a fifteen-yard lead, and he proceeded to lap Walthour, who was forced to come down off the track again with another flat tire.[15]

The next night at precisely one minute past midnight, Italian marathoner Pietro Dorando fired the gun that launched the sixteenth edition of the Garden six-day race, which New York fans looked forward to every year as if it were Christmas. Sixteen two-man teams got underway for 144 hours of continuous riding. The teams represented counties including Australia, France, Russia, Italy, Luxembourg, Holland, Germany, and the United States. Francois Faber from Luxembourg had won four stages and took second overall in the 1908 Tour de France. He was partnered with Frenchman Henri Lafourcade. Victor Dupre, the one-eyed French sprinter, was paired with his countryman Leon Georget. The great German sprinter Walter Rutt was partnered with Johan Stol. Americans Floyd MacFarland and Jimmy Moran were paired up, and Walthour teamed with Eddie Root, who was on the winning team in the New York six-day grind on three different occasions, in 1904, 1905, and 1906.[16]

Longtime friend and fellow Georgian John Chapman managed Walthour and Root from the side of the track. Chapman brought the necessities of a six-day race: clothing, surgical supplies, a bed, wheels, and tires. He also had enough food to stock a good-sized restaurant: potatoes, corn, rice, bacon, peas, sugar, salt, pepper, eggs, steak, pork chops, coffee, bread, apples, celery, oranges, grapefruit, chicken, vinegar, brandy, soda, beer, wine, champagne, and calf's foot jelly.[17]

The *World* captured life in the stands during the Garden six-day: "The regular rooters have reduced the sleeping thing to a science. They close one eye at a time. In this way they manage to watch the racers and at the same time watch those who are waiting to decorate them at the first sign of slumber. . . . The regular lives on cigarettes, sandwiches, frankfurters, chewing gum, chewing tobacco and anything in the liquid line that gets within hailing distance."[18]

The pace of the six-day started slowly, but there were occasional outbursts of speed. At 2:35 p.m. on Monday afternoon Jimmy Moran unleashed a powerful breakaway from the group. Moran's partner, MacFarland, was there to relieve him in the well-timed attack on the field. The fans shouted, and trainers ran around to prepare their riders to go out onto the track. Walthour was unable to keep up the killing pace, but when

Root relieved him, Root almost succeeded in gaining a lap back. According to *Bicycling World and Motorcycle Review,* Root was not happy with Walthour's lackluster performance.[19]

The unprecedented 28-minute sustained effort by Moran and MacFarland at the front resulted in 8 teams remaining tied for the lead, while 4 other teams—including Walthour-Root—were a lap down. At the twenty-sixth hour of the race, the leading teams had ridden 552 miles and 4 laps.[20]

As it turned out only three teams were tied for first place at the end, and MacFarland outsprinted both Rutt and DeMara in the final mile. Walthour and Root split the $500 fourth place winnings. Thus, the six-day did not go well for Walthour, and he ended the year with another poor finish. He returned home to Atlanta thankful that the 1908 season was over.

❋

In January 1909 Gussie Lawson supervised the construction of Atlanta's newest track, a tiny twelve-lap-to-the-mile track in the St. Nicholas stadium, at Ponce de Leon Park, that could hold three thousand attendees plus several hundred on the inside of the circle. The track was a joint capital project between Bobby Walthour and Walter Taylor, a well-known sporting man in Atlanta. Walthour was to be the star attraction, and many professionals signed contracts to ride at the new facility. Lawson wrote about it to English rider Albert Wills, who was pleased with the description of the track and was confident that records would fall once he arrived in Atlanta with his English motors.[21]

When Wills arrived in Atlanta, the Londoner practiced at St. Nicholas stadium with numerous quick training laps behind his pacemaker, Charles Turville. Walthour prepared too, riding behind Lawson for a best of three five-mile heats, which he hoped would not be a repeat of the race at Madison Square Garden. Wills was nursing a cut over his left eye that had been stitched up in Boston from a crash on the Revere track.

In his unmistakably English accent Wills told a reporter, "Do you know that I thought Atlanta was but a small village? Once I started not to come, but the chance of getting another race with Walthour spurred me on. You see, I am after Bobby, and while we are good friends off the track, I want to beat him fair and square in his home town if I can. That will be something to add to my record."[22]

On February 2, 1909, three thousand people crammed into the building, including Mayor Robert Foster Maddox and Governor Hoke Smith. Five hundred more shoved their way to the overflow area. Half an hour before the main event the excited crowd shouted for the race to begin, anxious to see if Walthour could make up for his loss to Wills in New York.

The fans cheered as the riders appeared with their noisy machines the track, which was lit by thousands of electric lights. Spectators lined the track, the pistol was shot, and the cyclists tore out after their motorcycles. Wills won the first heat by only twelve yards, and Walthour tied him with a close win in the second. The final heat was close until Walthour found an extra burst of speed, which propelled him to win. The home crowd enthusiasm shook the small venue.[23]

Walthour loved his new little track and trained on it continuously. One day Lawson became tired of pacing him. "I will not ride another mile for you until afternoon. You simply get too anxious and are liable to overdo the whole thing." Walthour ignored his good friend's warning and proceeded to ride ten more miles without pace. He came down off the track dripping with sweat before he sat down to towel off. He then told a reporter from the *Atlanta Journal,* "You see it is this way—I get the feeling on me to ride, and when it comes I am worse off if I stop than if I go on. This is what has kept me up all these years."[24]

Walthour had several more successful motor-paced races in Atlanta and beat some of the best riders in the United States. At last he seemed to have gained the luster he had lost in 1908.

❋

In late April 1909, Walthour crossed the Atlantic aboard the *Lusitania* (the ship that would be sunk by a German torpedo on May 7, 1915), accompanied by Gussie Lawson and also by Hugh McLean.[25] Though McLean won the U.S. motor-pacing title in 1908, he had no bicycle racing ambitions on this trip. Instead, he was managing a professional boxer named John H. "Sandy" Ferguson. McLeans's brother, Alec, was well known in boxing circles, but Hugh was more familiar with France, where the 6-foot-3, 220-pound Ferguson had two scheduled fights.

Ferguson ducked nobody—black or white—including a young man from Texas named Jack Johnson, who would go on to become world champion. Johnson beat Ferguson five times from 1903 to 1905.[26] For McLean, it must have been a nice break away from the dangerous sport of motor-pacing. Earlier in the year, McLean had threatened to permanently retire from the cycling game.[27]

By all accounts, Walthour had a horrible season in 1908, and he wanted to come back to France to erase the bad impression he had left. Rejuvenated by his recent success and rehabilitation in Atlanta, he was ready to come back to Europe and prove that he could continue to be a great champion.

At the Buffalo Velodrome, on May 30, in an hour contest against Charles Parent (the French national champion) and Louis Darragon, Walthour won by more than a lap, going 72 kilometers and 450 meters.[28] He won again at Buffalo on June 10.[29]

Bicycle World and Motorcycle Review reported (perhaps not accurately) that Walthour was "happy" when Lawson's motorcycle caught fire at Parc des Princes on the big cement track because Walthour got "tired."[30]

At one time, Walthour may have rubbed someone at that magazine the wrong way, because it seemed to have a grudge against him. "Robert J. Walthour [For years the magazine incorrectly used J. as his middle initial when in fact it should have been H. for Howe.], the American pace follower, now riding in Europe, is a keen business man as well as a crack rider. He never lets slip a chance to turn his name to financial profit. Witness the following testimonial which appeared in the last issue of *La Vie au Grand Air*, set off by a picture of Walthour mounted on a bicycle, and holding a fountain pen in his hand: 'After using your pen Blank I find it the most perfect pen I have ever used. (Signed) Robt. Walthour.'"[31]

In addition to the pens, the bicycles, and the tires that he endorsed for money, Walthour also was in a Coca-Cola advertisement in a local Atlanta newspaper in 1909. Quite possibly, he was the first ever sports figure to endorse the soft drink bottled in his home city.[32] In the advertisement, Walthour said he first used Coca-Cola at the 1901 six-day race.

In early July, Walthour and Gussie packed up their bicycles, motor-pacing machines, and equipment and went to Brussels, where Walthour put together another impressive victory, winning three straight heats of twenty, thirty, and fifty kilometers, beating Charles Parent, Julian Samson, and Leon Vanderstuyft.[33]

On August 15 in Copenhagen at the Velodrome d'Ordrup, Walthour rode in the fifteenth annual world championships. Three days before he had competed in Paris at Buffalo and won in straight heats over Paul Guignard. Why he chose to race so near the world championships—the most important race of the year—is hard to understand. Although Walthour did not come close to winning in Copenhagen, fellow American Nat Butler was in first place with less than three miles to go. However, he was passed by Frenchmen Louis Darragon and the eventual winner, Charles Parent.[34]

A scant four days later Walthour and Lawson were back in Paris at the Buffalo track in a race that was promoted as a rerun of the one-hundred-kilometer Copenhagen world championships. The results were a complete flip-flop, and Walthour won, beating second place finisher Darragon by six laps. Butler and Parent finished third and fourth respectively.[35] Walthour was in great form. Had he been better prepared and left more time before the races in Copenhagen, he may have come away with his third world championship.

✺

While Walthour was having success throughout Europe, cyclist and current boxing manager Hugh McLean was preparing his fighter, John Ferguson. On May 8 in Paris, Ferguson succeeded with a first round knockout of opponent Herbert Hall. Less than three weeks later Ferguson battled Joe Jeanette for twenty rounds but lost on a points decision. When McLean and Ferguson returned to the United States, the boxer fought Jeanette once again, this time winning in twelve rounds. Ferguson's third fight with Jeanette took place on August 27 in New York City.[36]

Six days later on September 2, McLean was in Boston, working out at the Revere track. He followed his pacing motorcycle in preparation for a contest against Elmer Collins. As he peddled, McLean's front wheel caught in his pacer's roller mechanism, and he was hurled high into the air. He hit the track, and his body crumpled. McLean bled profusely while being attended to by the track doctor, Dr. Van Magness, and was then moved to his Revere home. Dr. Van Magness found that McLean sustained a fractured skull and was in desperate condition, predicting correctly that McLean's death was inevitable.[37]

On September 5 the *Boston Daily Globe* reported, "An autopsy was performed by Medical Examiner Magrath yesterday on the body of Hugh McLean, the bicyclist who met death at the Revere bicycle track a few days ago. At the time it was believed that McLean had died as a result of a fractured skull. Dr. Magrath stated that while riding McLean burst a small blood vessel in his brain and that caused dizziness which resulted in his losing control of his wheel. When he struck the track the force of the fall tore his liver from its attachments and the attendant hemorrhage caused death. The report further stated that there was no fracture of the skull."[38] A large number of cyclists and friends viewed the body of the twenty-eight-year-old, including Floyd MacFarland, who was nursing a broken arm; Elmer Collins; Jimmy Moran; and Billy Saunders.

Once again death fell upon the motor-pacing world—the most violent and deadly sport in the modern era. That riders of Walthour's and Darragon's caliber had survived and continued to compete regularly—pursuing a path that would most likely lead to their own deaths—seemed inconceivable. Were they driven onward by a sense of duty to their sport? Was it the life in the bright lights, in front of huge crowds of people, that gripped and obsessed them? Was it the lure of the money? Was it the sheer thrill of speed or the pursuit of the seemingly impossible distance that might be accomplished in that magical hour? Or was it—in the end—a kind of death wish? They were aware of the danger and took some precautions but ultimately consigned their lives and futures into the hands of fate for the sake of the thrill of the moment.

{23}

Herr Walthour

by 1910 Walthour had crossed and recrossed the Atlantic ten times for his career. As his family grew (the four children were now between four and twelve), traveling became more difficult, what with gathering up belongings and moving to a temporary location thousands of miles away across an ocean. Steaming to and from Europe was expensive as well. Walthour needed a place centrally located to training and racing, where the money was good and where Blanche and the children would be safe and happy. In January 1910 the Walthours sold their Atlanta home and moved permanently to Dresden, located near the Czech border along the River Elbe. [1]

In addition to having one of the best tracks in Germany, Dresden was surrounded by cities with cycling tracks: Berlin and Bremen to the north, Leipzig, Chemnitz, and Cologne to the west, and Nuremberg to the south. Walthour justified his move: "Bicycle riding is the national sport in Germany, just as baseball is here. It is nothing to see 45,000 persons out for a race. And they even pay us to train. Our contracts call for us to begin training on Thursday, and we must train in public every day until Sunday. On that day we race. They have cement tracks abroad and six or seven motor-paced riders will take part in one race. It is pretty exciting too."[2]

The Walthour family arrived in Dresden in early March and checked into the Palmengarten Hotel, owned by sporting promoter Max Strohbach.[3] Eventually the Walthours settled into a rented mansion on Weix-dorf Avenue, where they lived for four years in a comfortable lifestyle.[4] The children were enrolled in school with German as their new language.

During this time Walthour had great success racing. He never attained the glory of 1904, when he won nearly all his races, but his statistics were impressive. Walthour proved that his 1908 season was merely a low point in his career. He was the top money winner in Germany in both 1911 with 44,550 marks[5] ($10,500 in today's currency) and in 1913 with 30,750 marks ($7,500).[6]

❋

Brussels was the site of the 1910 cycling world championships, and the field of motor-pacers was so large that the race organizers held five fifty-kilometer preliminary heats composed of fifteen riders trying to qualify for the one-hundred-kilometer final. For the qualifier on July 24, Wal-thour had to beat his old nemesis Louis Darragon, the world motor-paced champion in both 1906 and 1907, as well as Bruno Demke, a tough German from Berlin. With Lawson pacing, Walthour scored a great win over Darragon and Demke and went on to the final. Charles Parent (the defending world champion from France), Leon Vanderstuyft from Belgium, Victor Linart from France, fellow American Nat Butler, and Walthour constituted the final lineup.

The next day the five riders began the race with their pacing motor-cycles one hundred meters behind. The Belgian track was an open-air, four-hundred-meter, cement-surfaced oval that was slick and discolored with splotches from the recent rains. At the start each rider stood on his pedals, forcing the cranks around as hard as possible and swaying their bicycles from side to side. Each man's motorcycle came out in front to pace; Vanderstuyft took first position with Walthour in second and Parent in third. Not long thereafter, Lawson gunned his motor, and Walthour followed inches behind, passing Vanderstuyft and his pacer. The Belgian crowd cheered for their countryman, but Walthour steadily increased his lead.

As time and the kilometers clicked away Walthour reached a point where his lead was nearly insurmountable. He was well on his way to his third world championship; the old lion had awakened. But inexplicably

Lawson's gas tank burst, and suddenly Walthour was vulnerable without pace. By the time Lawson obtained another motorcycle, he had lost four laps. More misfortune followed as one of Walthour's tires punctured.[7] He found a new bicycle quickly, but the damage was done; Charles Parent won his second consecutive world championship. Various viewers debated as to whether Walthour had finished second or third to Vanderstuyft. The officials finally gave Walthour third, but the local press stated that he was second.[8]

Walthour compiled dozens of great victories and many second-place efforts during his residency in Germany. He won consecutive European championships in 1911 in Breslau and 1912 in Leipzig. The European championship was second in prestige only to the world championship.

Every week Walthour put his life on the line seeking fame and fortune. Few in the world, if any, were more successful at following the motors than he, and none had ever come back from more high-speed crashes. But the more years he raced, with the sport's death rate as regular as clockwork, the more of his fellow motor-pacers were eliminated.

According to Fredy Budzinski, a contemporary sports writer of the time, Thaddeus Robl was "one of, if not the most popular sportsman in Germany."[9] Robl had written about his life on the cycling tracks of Europe, but Budzinski helped so much with the autobiography that many claimed he should have been its coauthor. The writer and the rider became good friends over the years. On Budzinski's birthday in 1910 Robl invited him to fly in a plane over Stettin, a German town near the Polish border. Budzinski thanked his friend but politely declined, remarking that he wanted to live longer. They shared a good laugh.

Robl learned to fly a Farmen biplane in the days when *all* aircraft were experimental. He loved to fly and rapidly became proficient. On June 18, 1910, winds at Stettin were forceful and unpredictable, and Robl was advised not to go up. A crowd had assembled to see the flight and became unruly when they were told of Robl's possible cancellation. To appease the unreasonable clamor of the gathering, Robl decided to risk it.

Robl attained a height of two hundred feet when treacherous winds caught the wings and capsized the plane. He crashed and was found bloody and buried in the wreckage with a broken neck. Robl became the eleventh person ever to be killed in an aircraft.[10]

Nearly a year after Robl's death, on June 4, 1911, Walthour raced at Zehlendorf, a section of Berlin, against an up-and-coming German motor-pacer named Fritz Theile. Walthour had placed second to Theile at the 1910 European motor-pacing championship in Dresden. Theile was six years younger than Walthour and was a good sprinter. But he, like Walthour, found he could make a better living at motor-pacing. With Theile in the lead in the race, cycling upward of fifty miles per hour, he lost control and crashed to the cement and was killed.[11] A week later Walthour was racing again behind the motors.[12]

✳

In the fall of 1910 Gussie Lawson signed on to pace Frenchman Paul Guignard, the world record holder in the paced hour at an incredible sixty-three miles. Why Lawsonleft Walthour one can only speculate. Perhaps it involved money; maybe Lawson's drinking had become a problem or some other unresolved conflict stood between the two friends. Whatever it was, Lawson left, and Walthour needed to find a new pacer. For the 1911 and 1912 seasons, Walthour was paced by a German named Christian Junggelburth. In 1913 Walthour switched to a Belgian driver named Constant Ceurremans.

The two pacemakers served Walthour well, but they were not as good as Lawson. Guignard certainly benefitted from the switch, even if it did cost him a good amount of money having the best motorman in the business. Not long after Guignard won his world championship in 1913, he and Lawson raced at a one-hundred-kilometer event in Cologne on Sunday, September 8, in front of twelve thousand spectators. The field was composed of three other riders: Gunther, Richard Scheuermann, and Stellbrinck, and their motor men. Guignard led at kilometer sixteen going more than fifty miles per hour until Lawson's back tire began to lose air. He turned his head to let Guignard know he was leaving the track. Guignard was not surprised, because he heard the tire whistle.

Lawson's motorcycle buckled between his legs. He tried to keep his handlebars steady, but the motorcycle zigzaged furiously. With one big yaw, the motorcycle toppled onto its left side, with metal parts twisting,

breaking, and scraping against the cement. Guignard had but one moment to escape safely to the right. He looked to see if Lawson was okay.
To his horror he saw Scheuermann's motor-pacer, Meinhold, go straight
at Lawson at fifty miles per hour. The violent collision made debris fly in
all directions, and a fire ignited at the scene of the wreckage. Guignard
thought that Lawson, who had been thrown to the grass inside the track,
had been killed. Without thinking of the other two victims, Scheuermann
and Meinhold, who were in desperate condition, Guignard threw himself
on Lawson, embraced him, and cried.[13]

The three men were rushed to a hospital but not one survived. Twenty-
eight-year-old Gussie Lawson lingered until 10 a.m. the next morning.
News of the Cologne catastrophe quickly spread throughout Europe and
the United States. All three men were universally well known and appreci-
ated, but Lawson had been especially loved and admired. In Paris Louis
Darragon called for benefit races for Lawson's wife and three young children at Buffalo and also at Vélodrome d'Hiver.

Walthour was affected deeply, first with sympathy in his heart for Robl's death, then with horror to witness firsthand the death of young Theile, and finally with the knowledge of the death of his good friend Gussie
Lawson. Nothing though, could have prepared him for the worst during
his German sojourn.

❀

In the early twentieth century, diphtheria was a deadly and devastat-
ing disease with no cure. By the 1920s a vaccine was produced, and the
incidence of diphtheria declined rapidly. Today in the United States all
children are required to have DPT shots before starting school—protect-
ing against diphtheria, pertussis, and tetanus. Antibiotics also have helped
fight the disease since the 1950s, and it is now rare in the developed world.
Diphtheria cases typically come on gradually, with symptoms such as fatigue, fever, and a mild sore throat. The disease is highly contagious. At
its worst, the throat is covered with a membrane that prevents the victim
from breathing.

In the fall of 1911, the Walthour household was afflicted with diphtheria, and their eleven-year-old daughter, Nona, had the worst of it. Blanche
and the rest of the children gradually recovered, but Nona died that No-

vember. The Walthours received letters of condolence from around the world at their Dresden home. A grieving Bobby told the press that they were appreciative of the many acts of kindness, but that they could not possibly thank everyone individually.[14] Never one to shirk his racing contracts, Walthour took third in a six-day race in Frankfurt, Germany, less than a month later.[15]

Nona's body was placed in a vault until it could be brought over to the United States to be buried.[16] Nearly a full year after her death, Bobby, his oldest daughter Viva, and Nona's coffin arrived in New York harbor aboard the steamer *Kronprinzessin Cecilie* on October 29, 1912. Before he headed south to Atlanta, Walthour went north for a few racing obligations in Boston.[17]

Walthour arrived in Atlanta in time for the funeral on November 26 at Barclay and Brandon chapel; Nona's interment followed at West View cemetery.[18] An *Atlanta Constitution* reporter inquired about the health of his other three children. "Three little Dutchmen," he beamed:

I've got to bring them home soon, or they'll forget they are Americans. When I come home at night they chatter their Dutch at me until I have made it a rule that they shall not speak anything but English when I am around. You see, they go to school with German children and naturally German has come to be the most familiar tongue to them, until I had to put a stop to it. I couldn't have them grow up anything but Atlantans. And then too, the men I ride with speak either French or German and I don't get a chance to hear English unless I insist that my wife and children speak it at home.[19]

Not surprisingly, the family had had enough of Europe and Germany— Walthour had brought them home early fall of 1913 to the United States just before Lawson was killed. They took up residence in Newark, New Jersey. Although Walthour made threats about retirement from the cycling game for years, he continued racing behind the motors—but only in the United States—"on account of his children."[20]

{24}

Russian Roulette Survivor

On June 28, 1914, Archduke Franz Ferdinand of Austria and his wife, Sophie, were murdered in Sarajevo. A month later Walthour was back in the United States, living in Newark, New Jersey—then the very hub of professional American cycling. Two months later Europe was fully engaged in World War I.

During the war Walthour continued to race but with limited success and with significantly less money than he had before. He traveled to France in September 1917 and raced at Parc des Princes, where he was nearly killed. He fractured his skull and lay unconscious in a Paris hospital for seven weeks.[1] French doctors gave up hope, while Blanche sent message after unreturned message from the United States. According to sportswriter Willie Ratner, Walthour's appearance at home in New Jersey in November 1917 "couldn't have been more surprising if a ghost had crossed the threshold."[2]

Writer Ernest Hemingway was well acquainted with motor-pacing and wrote that he had started many stories about cycling, but none were as good as the races themselves. He described Parc des Princes and an accident there: "the wickedest track of all where we saw that great rider [Gustave] Ganay fall and heard his skull crumple under the crash helmet as you crack an hard-boiled egg against a stone to peel it on a picnic."[3]

Even before his latest near-death accident, Walthour had become less well known for his motor-pacing prowess and more for his injuries. In 1915 the *Washington Post* listed them: "broken his right collar bone twenty-seven times; broken left collar bone eighteen times; suffered rib fractures thirty times; had more than forty stitches taken in both legs; has more than 100 body scars as a result of bruises; he has about sixty stitch marks in his face, forehead and head as a result of sewed up wounds; has broken six of his ten fingers, has been pronounced dead twice and fatally injured at least six times." Walthour claimed he had been in more than 250 crashes and credited his longevity to having never broken a leg.[4]

Once he had arrived back in the United States, after his serious head injury in Paris, Walthour signed up to race at Madison Square Garden in the annual six-day, which started on December 2, 1917. His partner from Switzerland, Paul Suter, was not fit, however, and their team was out of contention the first day. Walthour was unable to find another partner, and he was forced to quit. As luck would have it, three days later Walthour slipped on a patch of ice right near his home in Newark and broke his leg in two places.[5]

❀

To help pay for their war effort the German government seized foreign bank accounts. Walthour's German holdings were thus lost forever. Exactly how much he had deposited may never be known, but certainly he lost a fortune.[6] The best revenge for Walthour was to join in the war effort against Germany. He signed up with the Y.M.C.A. as an athletic director for the French Army. In July 1918 he started an intensive training camp at Columbia University, and by September he was back in France in Neufchateau training French soldiers.[7] "I want to coach the *poilus* [French infantrymen] in bike riding," Walthour said, "so we can be the first to chase the Kaiser out of Berlin."[8]

While he was in France Blanche Walthour again was home alone, coping with three young children and the death of Nona only three years previously. Blanche also was living a life she to which she was unaccustomed—one of financial struggle. Over the years she had come to terms with the fact that her husband never intended to quit his extraordinarily dangerous occupation and that he was most likely to die from a crash on the cycling track. On many occasions she had seen her husband in desperate condition. Understandably she might have become numb to the reality of it, but she never did. As late as July 1914 Blanche "became hysterical," according to the *New York Times*, after Walthour had ripped his leg open and was rendered unconscious in a crash at the Brighton Beach Motordrome.[9] He had earned an incredibly good living, though, and their wealth had been some compensation.

But to have seen her eleven-year-old daughter die from diphtheria while her husband continued with his Russian roulette–like chances of survival in motor-pacing was hard for her to tolerate. While Bobby was away, possibly even before he had left, Blanche turned to alcohol to cope with the strain of not knowing her husband's fate and his prolonged absences. In addition she became infatuated with another man. When Bobby returned from the war, these problems became plainly evident to him. Blanche tried to kill him on several occasions while he slept and nearly made good on the threat with a butcher knife. Walthour filed suit for divorce in 1920. Bobby was forty-two years old, and Blanche was thirty-eight.[10]

Unfortunately other than newspaper accounts of the activities leading up to the divorce, not much is known. Apparently Walthour kept no scrapbook or diary, and no correspondence has been found between him, Blanche, or any of the Walthour children before, during, or after these troubled times.

A grandson of Walthour's, James K. Woodley Jr. (the son of baby Blanche, born in 1905), never met his grandfather. But he did meet his grandmother, the elder Blanche, decades after the 1920 divorce. In the late 1940s, Woodley recalls her as being very nice but also being a little different than most people. She wore a bandana wrapped around her head and lived in a small house that was cramped with cats and plants. The garage was also filled with bicycles. She was married to a painter named Jack, whom Jim remembers as an exceptionally gracious person. Jim's mother emphasized to her young son, however, that Jack was not his grandfather.[11]

In 1915 Walthour was not the only veteran cyclist having problems. On April 17 a Brooklyn confectionary salesman, David Lantenberg, was attaching advertising signs along the railings of the Newark Velodrome with a screwdriver. Floyd MacFarland, now the general manager of the track, took issue with the signs, and the two became involved in a heated exchange of words. As 150 or so spectators watched riders training, they heard the two men arguing to a point where it became a physical confrontation. MacFarland grabbed Lantenberg's arm to stop him from putting up the signs, and immediately both lost their tempers. Lantenberg struck at MacFarland with the hand containing the screwdriver. MacFarland attempted to dodge the blow, but the point of the screwdriver went into his ear with sufficient force to enter his brain. As trainers and riders rushed to the scene, MacFarland dropped down dead.[12]

On April 30, 1918, Louis Darragon met his fate crashing on the boards of Vélodrome d'Hiver. The June 1918 edition of *La Vie Au Grand Air* carried the same image that appeared with Darragon's article called "Les Pistes Sanglantes" ("The Bloody Tracks") ten years earlier: a drawing of a skeleton riding a pacing motorcycle, followed by superimposed photos of half a dozen riders killed in the sport. The updated article included a photo of Darragon.[13]

Other friends of Walthour fared better. Jack Prince continued to design and build board race tracks across the country and expanded his production to tracks for motorcycles and cars. Between 1910 and 1928 Prince built seventeen of the twenty-four automobile board speedways in the United States. For many of these tracks, rather than working from well-drawn and engineered plans, Prince marked out the tracks by driving stakes in the ground.[14] When Prince died on October 7, 1927, at the age of sixty-eight, his estate was valued at $200,000 ($2,470,000 in today's dollars).[15]

Albert Champion, who like Walthour started out in life as a bicycle messenger, died vacationing in Paris on October 27, 1927—three weeks after Prince—at the age of forty-nine.[16] In 1908 he had moved to Flint, Michigan; founded the AC Spark Plug Company; and became a self-made millionaire. He was in Paris at the Hotel Meurice, where he was being honored for making the spark plugs that helped Charles Lindbergh cross the Atlantic. He died of a heart attack while escorting his ex-showgirl wife to the hotel's dance floor. [17]

Charles and Genevieve Miller celebrated their fiftieth wedding anniversary on December 10, 1948, at the Edgewater Beach Hotel in Chicago.[18]

✺

Bobby Walthour Jr. picked up where his father left off, starting his amateur cycling career at age seventeen in 1920 in front of twenty thousand fans on March 28 at the Newark Velodrome.[19] The next year he clinched the American amateur sprint championship. His father was not there—he was racing behind the motors in Germany.[20] Both Bobby Jr. and his cousin Jimmy Walthour Jr. (Walthour's twin brother's son) had stellar professional cycling careers with great success in the six-day races that became very popular in the 1920s and 1930s.

Walthour Sr. eventually did retire from racing permanently in 1923 at the age of forty-five. He enjoyed watching his son race, but the joy was bittersweet. According to Walthour's grandson Bob Walthour III, father and son rarely spoke. Walthour disapproved of his son marrying a Roman Catholic.[21]

Bob III met his grandfather only twice, once at the Nutley Velodrome in New Jersey and another time in Madison Square Garden. Bob III was a youngster, however, and only remembers that his grandfather was very quiet. Walthour Sr. liked his privacy and preferred to sit high up in the cheap seats to view the races. Sometimes reporters sought him out and requested that he come down for a better view of the races.

The 1930 census taker found Walthour in Manhattan, managing a bowling alley. In 1932 Walthour was invited to Atlanta for a celebration given in his honor. The mayor ranked Walthour alongside Bobby Jones and Ty Cobb as the three men who had done the most to carry the name and embody the spirit of Georgia.[22]

At sixty-one years of age, Walthour made the news again by riding a bicycle eight-hundred miles from Miami to Atlanta.[23] "I just wanted to see some old friends," said Walthour.[24] Presumably Walthour visited with his very first trainer and friend, Gus Castle, who owned a Harley-Davidson dealership in Miami.

In 1941 Walthour moved to Jamaica Plains, Massachusetts, where, according to Walter Bardgett, the former professional cyclist who made his

European debut at the same time as Walthour, "he worked for a service paper in the automobile field." [25]

By early 1949 Walthour became seriously ill but was cheered up, according to his son, from the many letters he received from friends in the United States and Europe. Bobby Jr. said that his dad's spirit "was remarkable."[26] Walthour Sr. died of pneumonia on September 1, 1949, at the Boston City Hospital. He was seventy-one years old.[27] In addition to his son, he was survived by his two daughters, Viva Q. Stuart and Blanche Woodley;[28] two brothers, Charles Tatnell (C. T.) Walthour and Palmer Walthour; a nephew, William L. Walthour[29]; and several grandchildren. In a twist of irony, Walthour befriended a Catholic priest in Boston and converted to Catholicism shortly before he died.[30]

Bobby Walthour was enshrined in the State of Georgia Hall of Fame in 1964 and inducted into the United States Bicycling Hall of Fame in 1989. Today the average sports fan or even an enthusiastic supporter of cycling is unlikely to know about Walthour's career and probably does not even recognize his name. Moreover, the entire story of professional motor-pacing as a sport, within which Walthour's career was played out, has disappeared in the United States, having never been fully documented.

While Gino Bartali, Fausto Coppi, Jacques Anquetil, and Eddy Merckx—all famous road riders—became legends in Europe, Walthour's sport virtually disappeared in the United States. Many attempts were made by the sport's enthusiasts to revitalize the old six-day races in the 1940s through the 1960s, but they fell flat. Had cycling not lost its popularity in America, Bobby Walthour and other great cyclists of his era might have retained legendary status in American sports history. Today they might stand as equals of sports heroes such as Babe Ruth, Joe DiMaggio, Willie Mays, Jesse Owens, Bobby Jones, Joe Louis, Jack Dempsey, and Arthur Ashe.

Today thanks to Greg Lemond and especially Lance Armstrong's victories in the Tour de France, professional and amateur cycling has blossomed in the United States. Although Armstrong's hold on worldwide superstar status is very strong right now, particularly because of his miraculous battles against cancer, persistent rumors continue to circulate as to whether he has used performance-enhancing drugs. While Armstrong maintains his innocence and has passed more drug tests than any other athlete in the world, he lives under a microscope that cannot be understood or comprehended by anyone but the most famous people in the world. If he is ever proven guilty, the popularity of Armstrong and cycling could be lost again in a few decades.

George Santayana, a Spanish-born American author from Walthour's era, wrote, "Those who cannot remember the past are condemned to repeat it." With hope, one hundred years from now, Lance Armstrong's name will remain synonymous with all things great in cycling, and the legend of Bobby Walthour Sr. will continue.

{notes}

Introduction
1. Lawrence H. Officer and Samuel H. Williamson, "Purchasing Power of Money in the United States from 1774 to 2010," MeasuringWorth, 2009, www.measuringworth.com/ppowerus. This site is used throughout the book for historic-to-current price computations.
2. William A. Harper, *How You Played the Game: The Life of Grantland Rice* (Columbia, MO: University of Missouri Press, 1999), 103.

Chapter 1. Georgia Peach Blossom
1. "Walthour's Cyclone Finish," *Bicycling World*, December 19, 1903, 317–18.
2. Jesse Outlar, "World Famous Georgian," *Atlanta Constitution*, September 3, 1949.
3. Pearl Rahn Gnann, ed., *Georgia Salzburger and Allied Families* (Savannah, SC: Southern Historical Press, 1976), 350.
4. Victoria Logue and Frank Logue, *Touring the Backroads of North and South Georgia* (Winston-Salem, NC: John F. Blair, Publisher, 1997), 374.
5. George A. Rogers and R. Frank Saunders Jr., *Swamp Water and Wiregrass: Historical Sketches of Coastal Georgia* (Macon, GA: Mercer University Press, 1984), 78.
6. David V. Herlihy, *Bicycle: The History* (New Haven, CT: Yale University Press, 2004), 202.
7. Ibid., 163.
8. Stephen B. Goddard, *Colonel Albert Pope and His American Dream Machines* (Jefferson, NC: McFarland and Co., 2000), 84.
9. Herlihy, *Bicycle*, 246.
10. Ibid., 262.
11. Andrew Ritchie, *Flying Yankee: The International Cycling Career of Arthur Augustus Zimmerman* (John Pinkerton Memorial Publishing Fund, 2009), 33.
12. Herlihy, *Bicycle*, 252.
13. "Races at the Fair," *Atlanta Constitution*, December 1, 1895.

Chapter 2. Bobby and Blanche
1. "Romance of a Bicyclist," *Boston Daily Globe*, December 22, 1901.
2. "He Won the Piggott Road Race," *Atlanta Journal*, April 27, 1895.
3. "Romance of a Bicyclist."

4. "Contests of the Wheel," *Atlanta Constitution*, April 29, 1896.
5. "Brilliant Saucer Light is Young Atlanta Rider," *Atlanta Constitution*, May 19, 1907.
6. "Walthour Greedy," *Columbus (GA) Enquirer-Sun*, May 10, 1896.
7. "World's Champion Cycle Rider Tells How He Struggled and Won," *Atlanta Constitution*, June 17, 1906.
8. "Walthour Injured," *Atlanta Constitution*, May 15, 1896.
9. "World's Champion Cycle Rider Tells How He Struggled and Won."
10. "An Atlanta Boy Won Out First," *Atlanta Constitution*, May 9, 1896.
11. "Walthour Wins with All Ease," *Atlanta Constitution*, May 10, 1896.
12. "Went on a Tandem to Their Wedding," *Atlanta Journal*, August 12, 1897.
13. "Rode on a Tandem to His Wedding," *Atlanta Constitution*, August 12, 1897.

Chapter 3. Prince of Atlanta

1. "The Bicycle Races were Witnessed by a Large Crowd," *Atlanta Constitution*, May 10, 1894.
2. "Jack Prince, Promoter; Former World Champion," *Atlanta Constitution*, May 27, 1905.
3. *Bicycle News*, June 1915, 10.
4. "Jack Prince is in Town," *Atlanta Constitution*, March 24, 1897.
5. "Walthour Tells the Story about Forgetting His Speech on Stage," *Atlanta Journal*, February 8, 1904.
6. "Jack Prince is in Town."
7. "Races at the Park," *Atlanta Constitution*, April 6, 1897.
8. "Circuit Racers Wheel Tonight," *Atlanta Constitution*, April 12, 1897.
9. "Crack Riders Make First Run," *Atlanta Journal*, April 13, 1897.
10. "Riders Have Gone," *Atlanta Constitution*, April 15, 1897.
11. "Circuit Not Dead but is Sleeping," *Atlanta Constitution*, July 11, 1897.
12. "Races at Racine," *Milwaukee Journal*, July 2, 1897.
13. "An Atlanta Rider Wins in the West," *Atlanta Journal*, July 6, 1897.
14. "Bert Repine Wins; Is Now Champion," *Atlanta Constitution*, July 14, 1897.
15. "Bobby Walthour Beats Bert Repine," *Atlanta Journal*, July 22, 1897.

Chapter 4. Bipartite Bicycling

1. "Eaton to Run the Coliseum," *Atlanta Constitution*, April 19, 1898.
2. "Harry Silverman Will Volunteer," *Atlanta Journal*, April 27, 1898.
3. "Walthour Won from Kraemer," *Atlanta Constitution*, April 27, 1898.
4. "Gardiner Has Fifty Wins," *Washington Post*, June 29, 1898.
5. "Secede from the L.A.W.," *Chicago Daily Tribune*, September 27, 1898.
6. "Cause of Revolt," *Boston Daily Globe*, September 30, 1898.
7. "The Wheel," *Los Angeles Times*, June 5, 1899.
8. Eddie Bald, "A Glance at the Cycling Outlook," *Decatur Daily Review*, June 4, 1899.
9. "L.A.W. to Control Racing," *New York Times*, February 11, 1899.
10. "Racing at Newark," *Boston Daily Globe*, August 14, 1899.
11. "Notes of the Wheelmen," *New York Times*, June 16, 1900.
12. "Plans of the Cycle Racers," *New York Times*, March 11, 1900.

Chapter 5. In the Slipstream

1. John Howard and Peter Nye, *Pushing the Limits* (Waco, TX: WRS Publishing, 1993), 224–5.
2. Gear inches are taken from the high-wheel days when one pedal rotation made the wheel go around once; 48-inch diameter equaled a 48-inch gear. But a chain-driven bicycle allowed for a much higher gear. If a rider selected a 48-tooth front chain ring and a 12-tooth rear sprocket, a wheel will take four revolutions (taking 48 and dividing by 12) for every full pedal stroke. With a 27-inch diameter wheel and a 48 x 12 gear combination, a bicycle would be said to have 108 inches (27 inches times 4).
3. *Van Wert (OH) Times*, August 28, 1896.
4. "Gossip of the Cyclers," *New York Times*, June 18, 1899.
5. "Great Bicycle Ride," *Davenport (IA) Daily Republic*, July 2, 1899.
6. "Minute and Five Seconds," *Washington Post*, June 22, 1899.
7. "Great Bicycle Ride."
8. "He Rides a Mile in 57 4/5," *Chicago Daily Tribune*, July 1, 1899.
9. "A Whirlwind Ride," *Portsmouth (NH) Herald*, July 1, 1899.
10. "The World of Sport," *New York Times*, July 9, 1899.
11. "He Rides a Mile."
12. "World of Sport," *Sandusky (OH) Star*, July 11, 1899.
13. Ibid.
14. "Racing Gossip and Record Talk," *Atlanta Constitution*, July 21, 1895.
15. "Many Champions to Ride Tonight," *Atlanta Constitution*, October 29, 1897.
16. "Best Race Comes Last," *Atlanta Constitution*, November 2, 1897.
17. "Michael Rides Tomorrow," *Atlanta Constitution*, November 7, 1897.
18. "Michael Loses His Great Race," *Atlanta Constitution*, November 9, 1897.

Chapter 6. Six Daze

1. "Walthour Goes to Win New Fame," *Atlanta Constitution*, December 1, 1897.
2. "Many Cyclists Were Injured," *New York World*, December 5, 1897.
3. "Great Race is Over; Miller the Winner," *New York World*, December 12, 1897.
4. "Winner's Diary for the World," *New York World*, December 12, 1897.
5. "Against Six Day Races," *Chicago Daily Tribune*, December 4, 1898.
6. "Bicycling Carnival Opens," *New York Times*, December 4, 1898.
7. "Will Get $5,000. Miller Makes a New Record and Lots of Money," *Boston Daily Globe*, December 11, 1898.
8. "Limiting Continuous Racing," *Lima (OH) Daily News*, May 23, 1899.
9. "Gimm Fully Recovered," *Daily Iowa Press*, June 17, 1899.
10. "Miller Again the Winner," *Washington Post*, February 19, 1899.
11. "Ready for the Grind," *Bicycling World*, December 4, 1902, 222.
12. "Bobby Walthour is Home Again," *Atlanta Journal*, October 7, 1899.
13. "Six-Day Bicycle Race is On," *New York Times*, December 4, 1899.
14. "Eaton and Walthour Leading the Riders by One Lap," *New York Times*, December 5, 1899.
15. "Eaton Out, but His Partner Tries for Individual Prize," *New York Times*, December 6, 1899.
16. "The Six-Day Bicycle Race," *New York Times*, December 9, 1899.

17. "More Quit the Six-Day Race," *New York Daily Tribune*, December 7, 1899.
18. "Miller and Waller Win," *New York Daily Tribune*, December 10, 1899.
19. "Prizes for Six-Day Riders," *Boston Daily Globe*, December 12, 1899.

Chapter 7. Gentlemen, Start Your Engines
 1. "Bicycling Carnival Opens," *New York Times*, December 4, 1898.
 2. "Miller Expected to Win," *New York Times*, December 10, 1898.
 3. "Notes of the Wheel," *Daily Iowa Press*, May 27, 1899.
 4. "Cooper Champion," *Syracuse Herald*, October 1, 1899.
 5. "Crack Riders to Be Seen at State Fair Next Week," *Atlanta Constitution*, October 14, 1899.
 6. "Local Wheelmen Buy a Motor Cycle," *Atlanta Journal*, October 14, 1899.
 7. Ibid.
 8. "Motorcycle Came to Town Yesterday," *Atlanta Journal*, October 17, 1899.
 9. "Brilliant Bicycle Races Will Begin Today," *Atlanta Constitution*, October 20, 1899.
10. "Bicycle Races Draw Crowds," *Atlanta Constitution*, October 21, 1899.
11. *Atlanta Constitution*, October 22, 1899.
12. "Bicycle Races Today," *Atlanta Constitution*, October 23, 1899.
13. "Bob Walthour Equals Record," *Los Angeles Times*, November 13, 1899.
14. "Bloody End to Kline's Ride," *Atlanta Constitution*, July 19, 1897.
15. Ibid.
16. "His Head Crushed In," *North Adams (MA) Evening Transcript*, May 31, 1900.
17. "Feared a Mishap," *Boston Daily Globe*, June 1, 1900.
18. Title unknown, *Boston Daily Globe*, May 31, 1900.

Chapter 8. Twentieth Century Fox
 1. "Taylor Best Behind Motor," *Chicago Record*, July 5, 1900.
 2. "American Championship," *Boston Daily Globe*, September 2, 1900.
 3. "Start of Six-Day Race," *New York Times*, December 10, 1900.
 4. "Six Day Cycle Race Begins," *New York Daily Tribune*, December 11, 1900.
 5. Andrew Ritchie, *Major Taylor: The Fastest Bicycle Rider in the World* (San Francisco, CA: Van der Plas/Cycle Publishing, 2009), 46.
 6. "Cycling Records Beaten," *New York Times*, December 12, 1900.
 7. "Exciting Finish of Greatest of Six Day Bicycle Races at Madison Square Garden Cheered by 15,000 Spectators," *New York World*, December 16, 1900.
 8. "20th Century World's International Championships Six-Day Bicycle Race," *Boston Daily Globe*, December 30, 1900.
 9. "For Finish," *Boston Daily Globe*, January 5, 1901.
10. "Walthour Wins," *Boston Daily Globe*, January 6, 1901.

Chapter 9. Cold Start, Big Money
 1. "Veteran Coach Dies," *Chicago Daily Tribune*, June 6, 1926.
 2. "Bobby Walthour Suffers from Overmanagement," *Atlanta Constitution*, April 24, 1901.
 3. "News for Wheelmen," *Boston Daily Globe*, March 21, 1901.
 4. "Up from the South," *Boston Daily Globe*, April 15, 1901.

5. "Taylor's Debut," *Boston Daily Globe*, April 7, 1901.
6. "By 100 Yards," *Boston Daily Globe*, June 18, 1901.
7. "Walthour Beats Michael," *New York Times*, June 23, 1901.
8. "Standing of the Cyclists," *New York Times*, July 12, 1901.
9. "Moran Leading," *Boston Daily Globe*, July 3, 1901.

Chapter 10. At the Edge of the Garden
1. "Prizes for Six Day Riders," *New York Daily Tribune*, December 17, 1900.
2. "Racing Cyclist Injured," *New York Times*, June 25, 1901.
3. "Not in Final," *Boston Daily Globe*, July 30, 1901.
4. "Raced Behind Motor Pace," *New York Times*, August 18, 1901.
5. "Walthour's Record Ride," *New York Times*, August 27, 1901.
6. "Racing Cyclist Injured," *New York Times*, September 5, 1901.
7. "Walthour Beats Elkes," *New York Times*, September 6, 1901.
8. "His Leg Broken," *Boston Daily Globe*, September 10, 1901.
9. "Johnny Nelson Dead," *Washington Post*, September 10, 1901.
10. "Only Liberal Purse Can Tempt Walthour to Race," *Atlanta Constitution*, November 4, 1901.
11. "Cycle Experts Discuss Dangers to Pacemakers," *Atlanta Constitution*, November 10, 1901.
12. "Who Will Race Walthour at Opening of Coliseum?" *Atlanta Journal*, November 25, 1901.
13. "Bobby Walthour, Marvel, Surprises New Yorkers," *Atlanta Journal*, December 20, 1901.
14. "Six-Day Cycle Race is On," *New York Times*, December 9, 1901.
15. "Cyclists Gain on the Record," *New York Herald*, December 11, 1901.
16. Ibid.
17. Jimmy Michael, "Americans Lead in Six-Day Race," *New York World*, December 12, 1901.
18. "France is All Out," *Boston Daily Globe*, December 13, 1901.
19. "Broken Collar Bone Puts Swedes Out of Big Race," *New York Herald*, December 14, 1901.
20. "An Ovation for Bobby," *Atlanta Journal*, December 16, 1901.
21. "Walthour Wins Bicycle Race," *New York World*, December 15, 1901.
22. "Joy Unconfined at His Victory," *Atlanta Constitution*, December 15, 1901.
23. "Racers Gained Weight," *New York Times*, December 16, 1901.
24. "Bobby Walthour, Marvel."
25. "Walthour Wins Six Day Race in Desperate Chase," *New York Herald*, December 15, 1901.
26. "A Dinner to Walthour Given by Harry Silverman," *Atlanta Journal*, December 26, 1901.

Chapter 11. Sunday Preacher
1. "Bobby Walthour Begins to Train," *Atlanta Constitution*, March 23, 1902.
2. "Walthour Turns Down Big Offer from Paris," *Atlanta Constitution*, February 14, 1902.
3. Gus Castle, "Bobby Walthour Refuses $3,000 to Ride on Sunday," *Atlanta Journal*, March 6, 1902.

4. Ibid.

5. Ibid.

6. "Walthour Is Asked to Ride in Paris," *Atlanta Journal*, March 22, 1902.

7. "Prince after Walthour, the Champion Rider," *Atlanta Journal*, February 12, 1902.

8. "Walthour Meets Leander in Three Swift Heats Tonight," *Atlanta Constitution*, March 7, 1902.

9. "Six-Day Bicycle Race Ended in a Riot," *Boston Evening Transcript*, January 6, 1902.

10. "Leander Defeats Walthour in Motor Race Last Night," *Atlanta Journal*, March 8, 1902.

11. "Cyclist Walthour Hurt in Race," *New York Times*, March 9, 1902.

12. "Bobby Walthour Injured During First Heat, Loses Race with Leander," *Atlanta Constitution*, March 8, 1902.

13. "Caldwell and Hunter Race at the Coliseum Tonight," *Atlanta Constitution*, March 11, 1902.

14. "Walthour Lacked Pace," *Bicycling World*, July 18, 1903, 487.

15. "John Lawson Dead," *Nebraska State Journal*, March 15, 1902.

16. "Tinhorns Fail to Bribe Bobby," *Atlanta Constitution*, May 26, 1902.

17. "Silverman Fined $10.75," *Atlanta Constitution*, March 8, 1902.

18. "Famous Riders in Their Day—Stevens and Eaton. Once Suspended for Life, to Return to Bicycle Racing," *Boston Daily Globe*, February 6, 1902.

19. "Is Not 'Bobby' Walthour," *Atlanta Constitution*, January 22, 1903.

20. "Bobbie's Brother Will Team with Him during Winter," *Atlanta Journal*, November 27, 1901.

21. "Nerve and Power," advertisement, *Atlanta Journal*, April 24, 1903.

Chapter 12. American Champion

1. F. Ed Spooner, "Midget Michael to Try His Luck as a Jockey," *Atlanta Constitution*, February 9, 1902.

2. Ibid.

3. "Walthour and Billy Rutz Are Training for Race," *Atlanta Journal*, March 22, 1902.

4. "Riders Training Hard for Race Thursday," *Atlanta Journal*, March 25, 1902.

5. "Raced to Death," *Boston Daily Globe*, May 14, 1902. Also, Arnold Devlin, "Canada's First Six-Day Star," 6-Day Racing website, http://www.6day racing.ca/riders/mceachern/mceachern-bio.html.

6. John J. Donovan, "With His Wheel," *Boston Daily Globe*, July 18, 1902.

7. John J. Donovan, "Fast Riding," *Boston Daily Globe*, July 25, 1902.

8. "Kramer's Sprint," *Boston Daily Globe*, May 5, 1902.

9. "Broke Record," *Boston Daily Globe*, September 3, 1902.

10. "Half a Lap," *Boston Daily Globe*, September 7, 1902.

11. "Notes for the Wheelmen," *New York Times*, September 12, 1902.

Chapter 13. Back in Dixie

1. "Elks' Carnival Opens Today," *Atlanta Constitution*, September 22, 1902.

2. "Bobby Walthour Wanted on Charge of Contempt," *Atlanta Journal*, October 4, 1902.

3. "Bobby Walthour Wins Over Five Horses; Crowd Went Wild as He Came in Victor," *Atlanta Constitution*, October 18, 1902.
4. "Munroe Fatally Hurt in Race at Baltimore," *Atlanta Constitution*, September 13, 1902.
5. "Walthour Will Be Kept Off Track All Winter," *Atlanta Constitution*, November 13, 1902.
6. "Atlanta Entry Still in Doubt," *Atlanta Constitution*, December 1, 1902.
7. "Walthour and Caldwell to Run Opening Race," *Atlanta Constitution*, February 18, 1903.
8. "Champion Race On at the Coliseum Tonight," *Atlanta Constitution*, March 11, 1903.
9. "Walthour Won in Both Heats," *Atlanta Constitution*, March 12, 1903.
10. "Walthour and Leander Give Free (?) Race Friday," *Atlanta Constitution*, March 18, 1903.
11. William A. Harper, *How You Played the Game: The Life of Grantland Rice* (Columbia, MO: University of Missouri Press, 1999), 104.

Chapter 14. Baptism of Blood

1. "Elkes Is After Championship," *Atlanta Constitution*, May 9, 1903.
2. "Elkes Training Hard for Race with Walthour," *Atlanta Journal*, May 8, 1903.
3. "Bobby Won in Red Hot Finish," *Atlanta Journal*, May 12, 1903.
4. "Walthour Wins in Whirlwind Finish," *Atlanta Constitution*, May 14, 1903.
5. "Elkes Rode Swift Mile," *Boston Daily Globe*, May 28, 1903.
6. "Hoffman Discusses Tragic End of Harry Elkes and Jimmy Michael," *Atlanta Journal*, April 10, 1904.
7. "Harry Elkes Killed in Fearful Bicycle Mixup," *Boston Daily Globe*, May 31, 1903.
8. "To His Home," *Boston Daily Globe*, June 1, 1903.
9. "Walthour Quit Race," *Boston Daily Globe*, June 2, 1903.
10. "Pluck and Luck," *Boston Daily Globe*, June 3, 1903.
11. "Walthour Breaks Record," *Atlanta Constitution*, June 10, 1903.
12. "News of the Wheelmen," *Boston Daily Globe*, June 13, 1903.
13. "Champion Rides a Mile in 58 4-5s," *Boston Daily Globe*, July 12, 1903.
14. "Walthour's Close Shave," *Bicycling World* (July 18, 1903), 498.
15. "Walthour Sets New Mile Mark," *Boston Daily Globe*, July 8, 1903.
16. "Blaze on Track," *Boston Daily Globe*, August 23, 1903.
17. "Walthour Not Dead Much," *Atlanta Constitution*, August 27, 1903.

Chapter 15. Dixie Flyers

1. "Why Walthour Can't Retire," *Bicycling World* October 24, 1903, 87.
2. "Bobby Returns from the North," *Atlanta Constitution*, September 10, 1903.
3. Baseball Almanac, April 10, 2010, www.baseball-almanac.com.
4. "Why Walthour Can't."
5. "Puttering Motors Will Be Heard when Bobby Meets Bennie Tonight," *Atlanta Constitution*, September 14, 1903.
6. "Walthour and Champion Will Meet in Two Races," *Atlanta Constitution*, September 16, 1903.

7. "Frenchman Beaten Two Straight Heats," *Atlanta Constitution*, September 18, 1903.
8. "New York Men Send Contract," *Atlanta Constitution*, November 3, 1903.
9. "Heady Riding Won Race for Walthour," *Atlanta Journal*, December 23, 1903.
10. "Cyclists Are Off on the Long Race," *New York World*, December 7, 1903.
11. "Cycle Team Drops Out," *New York Times*, December 8, 1903.
12. "Champion Kramer Says Fisher Should Be First," *New York World*, December 9, 1903.
13. "Riders Crippled in Six Day Race," *New York World*, December 10, 1903.
14. "Bicyclists Many Miles Behind Record at the Garden," *New York Daily Tribune*, December 9, 1903.
15. "Root and Dorlon Out," *New York Daily Tribune*, December 11, 1903.
16. "Seven Teams Yet Tied," *New York Daily Tribune*, December 12, 1903.
17. Andrew Homan, "The Six-Day Grind," *Cycle Sport Magazine*, December 2006, 126–31.
18. "Walthour Wins Six-Day Race; Beats Leander by Ten Lengths," *Atlanta Journal*, December 13, 1903.
19. "Money Won by Riders in Race," *Atlanta Journal*, December 14, 1903.
20. "Walthour and Leander to Meet Xmas," *Atlanta Journal*, December 17, 1903.
21. "Walthour Here; Tells of Race," *Atlanta Constitution*, December 22, 1903.

Chapter16. L'Imbattable Walthour

1. Weidenfeld and Nicolson, *The Official Tour de France Centennial 1903–2003* (London: L'Equipe, 2003), 16–17.
2. "Paris Paper Interviews Walthour," *Atlanta Journal*, March 4, 1904.
3. "Walthour's Physical Development During His Past Racing Season," *Atlanta Journal*, February 5, 1904.
4. "Cup Presented to Walthour," *Atlanta Constitution*, February 10, 1904.
5. "Walthour a Paris," *Le Vélo*, February 23, 1904.
6. "A Letter Received from Walthour," *Atlanta Journal*, March 15, 1904.
7. "Walthour to Meet Dangla Thursday," *Atlanta Journal*, March 9, 1904.
8. "In Easy Style Walthour Wins," *Atlanta Journal*, March 18, 1904.
9. "Walthour Writes of Hard Luck in Race," *Atlanta Journal*, April 1, 1904.
10. "Une Belle Réunion," *Le Vélo*, March 21, 1904.
11. William A. Harper, *How You Played the Game, The Life of Grantland Rice* (Columbia, MO: University of Missouri Press, 1999), 96.
12. "Bobbie Walthour Carries All Before Him in Berlin," *Cycling*, April 13, 1904.
13. Ibid.
14. "Latest Cycle News and Gossip," *Atlanta Journal*, April 20, 1904.
15. "Victoires de Rutt et de Walthour," *Le Vélo*, April 11, 1904.
16. "Walthour Imbattable," *Le Vélo*, April 18, 1904.
17. "La Pénalité de Walthour," *Le Vélo*, April 29, 1904.
18. "Walthour Encore Vainqueur," *L'Auto*, April 25, 1904.
19. "Prix de France," *L'Auto*, May 9, 1904.
20. "Le Vrai Match," *L'Auto*, May 13, 1904.

21. "Foreign Press Says Walthour is the Greatest Living Cyclist," *Atlanta Journal*, May 27, 1904.
22. "Bobby Walthour Writes Back Telling of His First Defeat," *Atlanta Journal*, May 13, 1904.
23. "Inclinons-Nous," *L'Auto*, May 16, 1904.

Chapter 17. On Top of the World
1. "Sues for Death of Cycle Rider," *Atlanta Constitution*, February 16, 1904.
2. "Walthour to Remain in Paris," *Atlanta Journal*, March 28, 1904.
3. "La Vraie Première de Buffalo," *La Vie au Grand Air*, April 24, 1904.
4. "Mr. Eli Winesett," *Ellis Island*, accessed January 10, 2011, http://www
.ellisisland.org/search/passRecord.asp?MID=03477240760175132640&
LNM=WINESETT&PLNM=WINESETT&last_kind=0&TOWN=null&SH
IP=null&RF=1&pID=102530160244.
5. "Funeral of Mrs. Kah Today," *Atlanta Constitution*, October 23, 1904.
6. "Walthour Balks," *Boston Daily Globe*, May 26, 1904.
7. "Walthour Has Speed to Burn," *Boston Daily Globe*, May 29, 1904.
8. "Walthour Gets 26 New Records," *Boston Daily Globe*, June 1, 1904.
9. "Champion Bob Walthour Given a Dixie Welcome," *Atlanta Constitution*, June 3, 1904.
10. "Bob Walthour Comes Home Again," *Atlanta Journal*, June 3, 1904.
11. "La Mort de Dangla," *La Vie Au Grand Air*, June 30, 1904.
12. "Champion Hurt in Fast Race," *Atlanta Constitution*, June 16, 1904.
13. "Walthour Gets Nasty Fall," *Bicycling World*, July 2, 1904, 428.
14. "Rider Crashes Through Rails in Awful Fall," *Atlanta Constitution*, July 1, 1904.
15. "Plucky Bob Walthour Will Not Stop Riding," *Atlanta Constitution*, July 2, 1904.
16. "Leander Killed on Track," *Bicycling World*, August 27, 1904, 632.
17. "La Revanche de Bruni," *L'Auto*, August 22, 1904.
18. "George Leander," *La Vie Au Grand Air*, September 1, 1904.
19. "George Leander Killed on Paris Cycle Track," *Atlanta News*, August 23, 1904.
20. "Cycling the World's Championship," *London Times*, September 5, 1904.
21. "Giovanni Gerbi," Aver Associazione Velocipedisti Eroici Romagnoli, last modified May 12, 2009, http://aver.myblog.it/archive/2008/11/13
/giovanni-gerbi-il-diavolo-rosso.html.
22. "Walthour Home Again," *Bicycling World*, October 22, 1904.
23. "Velocipedie," *Le Figaro*, August 1904.
24. "Après la Réunion," *L'Auto*, September 5, 1904.
25. "The Grand Prize of Europe," *Cycling*, September 21, 1904, 252.
26. "Walthour Home Again," *Bicycling World*, October 22, 1904, 81.
27. "How Walthour Lost," *Atlanta Journal*, October 13, 1904.
28. Weidenfeld and Nicolson, *Official Tour de France Centennial*, 12.

Chapter 18. Sputtering Skyrocket
1. "Walthour Home Again," *Bicycling World*, October 22, 1904, 81.
2. "Funeral Notice," *Atlanta Constitution*, October 23, 1904.

3. "Walthour's Way," *Cycling*, November 23, 1904, 434.
4. "Munroe is Selected," *Bicycling World*, November 26, 1904, 210.
5. "Hoffman Discusses Tragic End of Harry Elks and Jimmie Michael," *Atlanta Journal*, April 10, 1904.
6. "Jimmy Michael Dies on Ocean," *Chicago Daily Tribune*, November 26, 1904.
7. Stella Bloch, "Jimmy Michael: An Appreciation," *Cycling*, December 13, 1905, 537–388.
8. "McLean Victor," *Boston Daily Globe*, December 4, 1904.
9. "Race Starts in the Garden," *New York World*, December 5, 1904.
10. Ibid.
11. "Thirteen Teams Tied in the Six-Day Race," *New York Times*, December 6, 1904.
12. Title unknown, *New York World*, December 7, 1904.
13. "Cyclists Revolt in the Six-Day Race," *New York Times*, December 8, 1904.
14. "Five Teams Quit the Race," *New York Daily Tribune*, December 8, 1904.
15. Ibid.
16. "The Most Sensational of Six-Day Races," *Bicycling World*, December 10, 1904, 252–533.
17. "Walthour Says Six-Day Race Is Not a Fake," *New York World*, December 9, 1904.
18. "Root and Dorlon First in Cycle Race," *New York World*, December 11, 1904.
19. "Blow Falls on Bicycle Riders," *Boston Daily Globe*, December 15, 1904.
20. "Bob Walthour Opposes N.C.A.," *Atlanta Constitution*, December 16, 1904.
21. "Racing Cyclists Accept Penalties," *New York Times*, December 26, 1904.
22. "Walthour Asks for Mercy," *Bicycling World*, February 11, 1905, 427.
23. "Will Inflict Fine on Bobby," *Atlanta Constitution*, February 2, 1905.
24. "Bobby Aspires to Handle Auto," *Atlanta Constitution*, February 17, 1905.
25. "Bobby Walthour Will Take a Rest," *Atlanta Constitution*, March 3, 1905.
26. "Kramer's Trip Abroad," *New York Times*, March 19, 1905.
27. "Prince to Hold Big Six-Day Race," *Atlanta Journal*, March 8, 1905.
28. "Butler to Meet Walthour," *Atlanta Constitution*, March 31, 1905.
29. "Bobby Walthour May Soon Ride," *Atlanta Constitution*, April 5, 1905.
30. "Fine of $100," *Boston Daily Globe*, April 11, 1905.

Chapter 19. Déjà Vu

1. "Walthour Unfolds Plans," *Bicycling World*, April 22, 1905, 85.
2. "To Ride a Mile in One Minute Behind Motor is Greatest Ambition of My Life," *Atlanta Constitution*, April 16, 1905.
3. "Walthour Rides in Great Form," *Atlanta Constitution*, April 28, 1905.
4. Louis Darragon, "Mon Voyage chez les Yankees," *Les Sports*, January 7, 1908.
5. "Saved by His Safety Riggin'," *Bicycling World*, May 13, 1905, 181.
6. Title unknown, *Atlanta Constitution*, May 6, 1905.
7. "To Ride a Mile."
8. "Ty Cobb," *Baseball Almanac*, accessed January 10, 2011, http://www.baseball-almanac.com/players/player.php?p=cobbty01.
9. "Walthour Quits at Boston," *Bicycling World*, July 8, 1905, 379.
10. "Le Champion des Champions," *L'Auto*, July 16, 1905.

11. "Victoire Réelle et Morale de Butler," *Les Sports*, July 21, 1905.
12. "World's Championship," *Cycling*, August 2, 1905, 114.
13. "Zuschrift von Tommy Hall: (Betr. Weltmeisterschaft in Antwepen)," *Radwelt*, August 4, 1905.
14. "Bob Walthour Still Winning," *Atlanta Constitution*, August 17, 1905.

Chapter 20. An American Superstar in Paris
1. "Bobby Riding in Great Form," *Atlanta Constitution*, November 12, 1905.
2. Bobby Walthour, "World's Champion Cycle Rider Tells How He Struggled and Won," *Atlanta Constitution*, June 17, 1906.
3. "Bobby Walthour 'For Ever,'" *L'Auto*, November 13, 1905.
4. "Au Vélodrome D'Hiver," *Les Sports*, November 13, 1905.
5. "Bobby Walthour Now in Gotham," *Atlanta Constitution*, November 26, 1905.
6. "No More Big Motors for Walthour," *Atlanta Constitution*, November 16, 1905.
7. "Walthour Home Next Tuesday," *Atlanta Constitution*, December 5, 1905.
8. Weidenfeld and Nicolson, *Official Tour de France Centennial*, 31.
9. Paul Ciniraj, "U.S. Statistics in the Year 1905," *Free Republic*, June 17, 2005, http://www.freerepublic.com/focus/f-chat/1425436/posts.
10. "Sent Them Off at 12:05," *New York World*, December 5, 1905.
11. "Walthour Had Rough Trip," *Atlanta Constitution*, February 27, 1906.
12. "Walthour Was Not Mobbed," *Bicycling World*, March 31, 1906, 13.
13. "Friol Transformé Triomphe," *Les Sports*, February 26, 1906.
14. "Bicycle Stars Working Hard," *Boston Daily Globe*, May 21, 1906.
15. "Walthour's Long Stern Chase," *Bicycling World*, June 9, 1906, 311.
16. Walthour, "World's Champion."
17. "Bobby der Fleissige," *Radwelt*, July 19, 1906.
18. "Americans Not in It," *Bicycling World*, August 18, 1906, 53.
19. "Le Vélodrome Buffalo Mis a Sac," *Les Sports*, August 16, 1906.
20. "83 Kilomètres 140 Mètres sans Coupe-Vent," *L'Auto*, August 20, 1906.

Chapter 21. Crash and Burn
1. "Cycling Records May Go," *New York Times*, December 8, 1906.
2. "Walthour Wins Race," *New York Daily Tribune*, December 9, 1906.
3. "Teams That Begin Struggle of a Week in Madison Square Garden," *New York World*, December 10, 1906.
4. "Two Riders Injured in the Bicycle Race," *New York Times*, December 11, 1906.
5. Title unknown, *New York World*, December 12, 1906.
6. "May Stop Bicycle Race on the Garden Track," *New York Times*, December 13, 1906.
7. "Twelve Teams Remain in the Six-Day Race," *New York Times*, December 14, 1906.
8. "Walthour Home from New York," *Atlanta Constitution*, December 21, 1906.
9. "Paris Races Drawing Well," *Bicycling World*, March 23, 1907, 735.
10. "La Triomphe de Walthour," *Les Sports*, March 18, 1907.

11. "Letter from Walthour," *Boston Daily Globe*, May 7, 1907.
12. "Cyclist Walthour Hurt," *New York Times*, May 7, 1907.
13. "Were Ready with Shroud Twice for Bob Walthour," *Atlanta Constitution*, December 3, 1907.
14. Frank G. Manke, "Bike Racer Breaks Collar Bone 27 Times in 18 Years," *Lima (OH) News*, July 27, 1915.
15. "Race Mishap Costs Mettling His Life," *Boston Daily Globe*, June 23, 1907.
16. Ibid.
17. "Walthour Whizzes Through the City," *Atlanta Constitution*, September 9, 1907.
18. "How Disaster Came to Walthour," *Bicycling World and Motorcycle Review*, October 12, 1907, 76.
19. "Were Ready with Shroud."

Chapter 22. Nine Lives
1. Louis Darragon, "Les Pistes Sanglantes," *La Vie Au Grand Air*, November 6, 1907, 374–75.
2. "Walthour Does Some Big Riding," *Boston Daily Globe*, January 11, 1908.
3. "Walthour to Race Here," *Boston Daily Globe*, January 9, 1908.
4. Ibid.
5. "Walthour Takes Two," *Boston Daily Globe*, January 12, 1908.
6. "Walthour Triomphe!" *Les Sports*, February 3, 1908.
7. "Walthour et les Rayons X," *Les Sports*, February 11, 1908.
8. "La Réveil de Walthour," *Les Sports*, July 27, 1908.
9. "Will Follow Pace," *Boston Daily Globe*, August 26, 1908.
10. "Walthour Triomphe de Darragon," *Les Sports*, August 1, 1908.
11. Title unknown, *Les Sports*, July 31, 1908.
12. "Les Adieux de Walthour," *Les Sports*, October 24, 1908.
13. "Wiley Gets Walthour's Measure," *Bicycling World and Motorcycle Review*, November 21, 1908, 297.
14. "Better Than a Mile a Minute," *Boston Daily Globe*, December 2, 1908.
15. "Grueling Sprints in the Garden Grind," *Bicycling World and Motorcycle Review*, December 12, 1908, 399–403.
16. "Cyclists Start on Week's Grind," *New York Times*, December 7, 1908.
17. "Riders All Ready for Six Days Struggle," *Bicycling World and Motorcycle Review*, December 5, 1908, 359–66.
18. "Spills and Thrills in Great Bike Race," *New York World*, December 8, 1908.
19. "Grueling Spints."
20. "Cyclists Injured in Six-Day Race," *New York Times*, December 8, 1908.
21. "Bobby Walthour to Race Albert Wills of England," *Atlanta Constitution*, January 25, 1909.
22. "Wills-Walthour Race at Velodrome Tuesday," *Atlanta Constitution*, January 31, 1909.
23. "Walthour Evens Up with Wills," *Bicycling World and Motorcycle Review*, February 6, 1909, 781.
24. "Bobby Walthour Will Race with Albert Wills Once More," *Atlanta Journal*, February 6, 1909.
25. Title unknown, *Radwelt*, May 8, 1909.

26. "John H. 'Sandy' Ferguson," *Cyber Boxing Zone*, accessed January 10, 2011, http://www.cyberboxingzone.com/boxing/sferg.html.
27. "That's What They All Say," *Bicycling World and Motorcycle Review*, April 3, 1909, 58.
28. "Walthour Vainqueur," *Les Sports*, May 31, 1909.
29. "Doings of Americans Abroad," *Bicycling World and Motorcycle Review*, July 3, 1909, 59.
30. Ibid.
31. "Walthour and a Fountain Pen," *Bicycling World and Motorcycle Review* (July 31, 1909), 702.
32. "Bobby Walthour Ad," *Coca-Cola Conversations*, last modified November 13, 2009, http://www.coca-colaconversations.com/my_weblog/2009/11/spotlight-on-the-world-of-cocacolabobby-walthour-ad.html.
33. "Walthour Rides Well at Brussels," *Bicycling World and Motorcycle Review*, July 24, 1909, 675.
34. "Butler Fails in Big Contest," *Bicycling World and Motorcycle Review*, August 28, 1909, 839.
35. "Walthour Defeats the Champion," *Bicycling World and Motorcycle Review*, September 4, 1909, 393.
36. "John H. 'Sandy' Ferguson."
37. "Hugh McLean Dead," *Boston Daily Globe*, September 3, 1909.
38. "Burst a Blood Vessel," *Boston Daily Globe*, September 5, 1909.

Chapter 23. Herr Walthour

1. "Bobby Walthour Will Move Family to Europe," *Atlanta Constitution*, January 27, 1910.
2. Title unknown, *Washington Post*, February 6, 1910.
3. Title unknown, *Radwelt*, March 8, 1910.
4. Title unknown, *Radwelt*, May 23, 1911.
5. *Radwelt*, date unknown.
6. "Bob Walthour Tops Prize Winners List," *Bicycling World and Motorcycle Review*, January 27, 1914, 20.
7. "Brussel–Karreveld," *Radwelt*, July 28, 1910.
8. "Row at World's Championship," *Bicycling World and Motorcycle Review*, August 3, 1910, 826.
9. Thaddeus Robl, *Der Radennsport* (Leipzig, Germany: Grethlein and Co., 1905).
10. "Herr Robl Killed," *Flight*, June 25, 1910, 489.
11. Title unknown, *Radwelt*, June 6, 1911.
12. Title unknown, *Radwelt*, June 12, 1911.
13. "Après la Tragédie de Cologne," *L'Auto*, September 10, 1913.
14. Title unknown, *Radwelt*, November 21, 1911.
15. "Rutt and Stol Win German Six-Day," *Bicycling World and Motorcycle Review*, December 23, 1911, 624.
16. "Funeral Notice," *Atlanta Constitution*, November 26, 1912.
17. John J. Donovan, "One Team Out of It Already," *Boston Daily Globe*, November 5, 1912.
18. "Nona Walthour," *Atlanta Journal*, November 27, 1912.

19. "Funeral Notices," *Atlanta Constitution*, November 27, 1912.
20. "Walthour Will Race Only in United States," *Atlanta Constitution*, December 3, 1913.

Chapter 24. Russian Roulette Survivor

1. "Goullet and Magin Win Six-Day Grind," *New York Times*, December 9, 1917.
2. Willie Ratner, "Bobby Walthour Sr., Colorful Cyclist, Dies in Boston at 71," *Newark Evening News*, September 3, 1949.
3. Ernest Hemingway, *A Moveable Feast* (New York: Scribner Classics, 1996), 64–65. First published
4. "Bike Racer Memento of 18 Years in Game," *Washington Post*, August 22, 1915.
5. "Goullet and Magin."
6. "Bobby Walthour Held Triple Crown as Champion Cyclist," *Boston Daily Globe*, September 2, 1949.
7. N.E. Brown, "Bobby Walthour," *Tucson Daily Citizen*, December 18, 1919.
8. "Bobby Walthour in Army Y.M.C.A. Work," *Salt Lake Telegram*, July 20, 1918.
9. "Bobby Walthour and Ralph Ginder Carried to Hospital, the Latter with Fractured Spine," *New York Times*, July 13, 1914.
10. "Walthour Asked for Divorce," *New York Times*, February 20, 1920.
11. Andrew Homan, interview with James K. Woodley, April 2010.
12. "Floyd MacFarland Stabbed to Death," *New York Times*, April 18, 1915.
13. "La Mort de Darragon," *La Vie Au Grand Air* (June 1918), 22.
14. Larry L. Ball Jr., "John Shillington 'Jack' Prince," National Sprint Car Hall of Fame and Museum, 2003.
15. "Contest Over Will Ends in Settlement," *Los Angeles Times*, November 21, 1933.
16. "Champion, Spark Plug Maker, Dies," *Los Angeles Times*, October 28, 1927.
17. "Albert Champion," *Wikipedia*, last modified November 19, 2010, wikipedia.org/wiki/Albert_Champion.
18. Walter Bardgett, "On the Bell Lap," *American Bicyclist and Motorcyclist* (December 1948), 38.
19. "Kramer is Winner in Newark Opening," *New York Times*, March 29, 1920.
20. "Walthour King of Amateur Cyclists," *New York Times*, August 22, 1921.
21. Andrew Homan, interviews with Robert Howe Walthour III, 2005–2007.
22. "Bobby Walthour Held."
23. "Veteran Bicyclist Pedals 800 Miles," *Los Angeles Times*, June 15, 1933.
24. Jesse Outlar, "Bobby Walthour Dies in Boston Hospital," *Atlanta Constitution*, September 3, 1949.
25. Bardgett, "On the Bell Lap."
26. Ibid, 68.
27. Outlar, "Bobby Walthour Dies."
28. "Mrs. John A. Stuart," *Asbury Park (NJ) Evening Press*, February 6, 1971.
29. "Bobby Walthour Dies; Former King of Cyclers," *Atlanta Journal*, September 2, 1949.
30. Homan interviews.

{index}

{about the author}

Andrew Homan was raised in the San Francisco Bay Area and received a degree in economics from California State University, Hayward (now East Bay), in 1988. In high school and college, he ran track and cross-country but switched to competitive cycling in 1989. Homan began researching and writing about historical cycling in 2003. His work has been published in three competitive cycling journals in the United States. *Life in the Slipstream: The Legend of Bobby Walthour Sr.* is his first book. Homan currently works with disadvantaged youth and helps coach their cycling and cross-country teams. He lives in South Lake Tahoe, California, with his wife, Shelli. Homan's website is www.bobbywalthour.com.